Freedom of Speech

Aperçus: Histories Texts Cultures

a Bucknell series

Series Editor: Greg Clingham

Aperçu (apersü). 1882. [Fr.] A summary exposition, a conspectus.

Relations among historiography, culture and textual representation are presently complex and rich in possibilities. Aperçus is a series of books exploring the connections between these crucial terms. Revisionist in intention, Apercus seeks to open up new possibilities for humanistic knowledge and study, and thus deepen and extend our understanding of what history, culture, and texts have been and are, as these terms are made to bear on each other by new thinking and writing.

Titles in the Series

Critical Pasts: Writing Criticism, Writing History
ed. Philip Smallwood

History and Nation
ed. Julia Rudolph

Europe Observed: Multiple Gazes in Early Modern Encounters
ed. Kumkum Chatterjee and Clement Hawes

Beyond Douglass: New Perspectives on Early African American Literature
ed. Michael J. Drexel and Ed White

The Patient
ed.. Kimberly Myers and Harold Schweizer

Masculinity, Senses, Spirit
ed. Katherine M. Faull

Freedom of Speech: The History of an Idea
ed. Elizabeth Powers

Scotland As Science Fiction
ed. Caroline McCracken-Flesher

Freedom of Speech

The History of an Idea

Edited by
Elizabeth Powers

Lewisburg: Bucknell University Press

Published by Bucknell University Press
Co-published with The Rowman & Littlefield Publishing Group, Inc.
4501 Forbes Boulevard, Suite 200, Lanham, Maryland 20706
www.rowmanlittlefield.com

Estover Road, Plymouth PL6 7PY, United Kingdom

British Library Cataloguing in Publication Information Available

Library of Congress Cataloging-in-Publication Data

Freedom of speech : the history of an idea / Edited by Elizabeth Powers.
     p. cm.
   Includes bibliographical references and index.
   ISBN 978-1-61148-366-6 (cloth : alk. paper) — ISBN 978-1-61148-385-7 (pbk. : alk. paper)—
ISBN 978-1-61148-367-3 (ebook)
   1. Freedom of speech—History. I. Powers, Elizabeth, 1944– II. Title.

K3254.F75 2011
342.08'53—dc23

                                                                        2011028338

∞™ The paper used in this publication meets the minimum requirements of American National
Standard for Information Sciences—Permanence of Paper for Printed Library Materials, ANSI/
NISO Z39.48-1992.

Printed in the United States of America

Contents

vii Acknowledgments

ix Introduction: Freedom of Speech:
Contemporary Issues and a History
ELIZABETH POWERS,

1 *Libertas Philosphandi* in the Eighteenth Century: Radical
Enlightenment versus Moderate Enlightenment (1750–1776)
JONATHAN I. ISRAEL

19 In Praise of Moderate Enlightenment: A Taxonomy of Early
Modern Arguments in Favor of Freedom of Expression
JORIS VAN EIJNATTEN

45 Cynicism as an Ideology behind Freedom of Expression in
Denmark-Norway
JOHN CHRISTIAN LAURSEN

61 Alexander Radishchev's *Journey from St. Petersburg to Moscow*
and the Limits of Freedom of Speech in the Reign of
Catherine the Great
DOUGLAS SMITH

81 Print versus Speech: Censoring the Stage in Eighteenth-
Century Vienna
PAULA SUTTER FICHTNER

103 The Crisis of the Hispanic World: Tolerance and the Limits of
Freedom of Expression in a Catholic Society
JAVIER FERNÁNDEZ SEBASTIÁN

133 Rousseau, Constant, and the Emergence of the Modern Notion
of Freedom of Speech
HELENA ROSENBLATT

165 Toward an Archaeology of the First Amendment's
Free Speech Protections
LEE MORRISSEY

191 Conclusion: A Way Forward?
     ELIZABETH POWERS

199 Appendices: Milestones in the History of Freedom of Speech

     —The Netherlands and Britain

     —Northern Europe, Habsburg Lands, and Russian Empire

     —Spain

215 Bibliography

221 Notes on Contributors

223 Index

Acknowledgments

THIS VOLUME HAD ITS ORIGINS IN A SERIES OF TALKS HELD IN 2007–2008 at the Columbia University Seminar on Eighteenth-Century European Culture. Robert Belknap, director of the Columbia University Faculty Seminars, provided much initial enthusiasm for this series on the eighteenth-century intellectual background of modern free speech legislation, and I am deeply appreciative of the institutional and financial assistance the Columbia University Seminars was able to offer. The staff of the Seminars office—Alice Newton, Pamela Guardia, Gessy Alvarez, and Jonathan Bourdett—likewise offered tremendous assistance to me and to the contributors, several of whom traveled to New York from far afield.

Along with Bob Belknap, other individuals have been unstinting sources of advice and support in preparing the essays in this volume for publication. First and foremost among them is John Christian Laursen, who has been unsparing with inspiration and sage criticsm. I am grateful to my wonderful colleagues at the Eighteenth-Century Seminar, in particular to Randolph Trumbach. Daniel Carey brought Bucknell University Press and Greg Clingham to my attention, for which I am most grateful. Richard Sussman is well aware of how indebted I am to him.

I would also like to express my thanks to the New York Public Library, where I was fortunate to enjoy a yearlong residence in the Wertheim Room devoted to research for my own contributions to this volume. I could not have prepared this volume for publication were it not for the resources of the Information Technology division of the Graduate Center and University Center of the City University of New York.

Finally, my deepest thanks are due to the contributors, all of whom cheerfully suffered my persistent editorial badgering.

Introduction: Freedom of Speech: Contemporary Issues and a History

BY THE BEGINNING OF THE TWENTY-FIRST CENTURY FREEDOM of speech seemed a settled issue in the United States, so much so that a major scholar of constitutional law, Ronald Dworkin, has maintained that it is a basic principle that admits of no division.[1] Certainly free speech law in the United States has for the past several decades been hostile to regulating "public discourse" on the basis of the content expressed—whether it be citizens petitioning the government, outrageous theatrical or artistic works, or the provocative language and behavior of protesters of any stripe—and has instead favored content-neutral regulation.[2] Thus, the objections by Catholics to paintings of the Virgin Mary by Chris Ofili, at an exhibition at the Brooklyn Museum of Art in 1999,[3] only bore out the non-exempt status of even the most revered religious figures.

Freedom of speech is not unique to the United States, as all the European democracies have either included that freedom in their constitutions or subscribe to relevant European Union conventions.[4] These countries, however, do not have America's robust and nearly century-long body of free speech jurisprudence, and their different social histories have led to restrictions now unthinkable in the United States.[5] It is inconceivable that *Skokie*, a suit brought by the ACLU to allow the National Socialist Party of America to march in a largely Jew-ish town in 1977,[6] would ever have been litigated in Europe, where Jewish suffering in World War II constitutes part of modern Europe's self-understanding. Holocaust denial is even forbidden by law in sev-eral countries. Nevertheless, "European" history—as distinct from the individual national histories—might be said to be founded on the right of individuals to criticize authority: religious, political, even artistic.[7]

Thus, Europe was radically unsettled in 2005, when the legiti-macy of one of its most ancient privileges—the right of artists to carica-ture an object of religious reverence—was suddenly under attack. This was the so-called Mohammed cartoons controversy, following on the appearance of twelve cartoons, on September 30, 2005, in the Danish newspaper *Jyllands-Posten*. The cartoons had been solicited after another Danish newspaper, *Politiken*, had carried an article entitled "Profound Anxiety About Criticism of Islam" (on September 14, 2005) on the difficulties an author encountered in finding an illustrator for a chil-dren's book on the life of the Prophet. Shortly after the publication of the cartoons, Muslim organizations in Denmark filed with police a complaint against *Jyllands-Posten* for offenses committed under sections of the Danish criminal code concerning blasphemy or degradation with malice toward persons based on, among other things, race, color of skin, national or ethnic roots, or faith and sexual orientation.[8] Europe's restrictions on free speech—as in the case of Holocaust denial—were now being invoked against ridicule by cartoonists of the Islamic holy figure. The matter did not rest with legal objections: within six months of the publication of the cartoons, protesters burned European embas-sies, consulates, and churches in the Middle East, and indeed an entire country was boycotted.

Europe had experienced a similar tempest in 1989, after the publi-cation of *The Satanic Verses*, but that case offered a problematic precedent.[9] Although the novel, depicting the Prophet engaged in disreputable behavior, was felt by many Muslims to be an insult to their religion, Salman Rushdie was himself a Muslim by background. The book was also published for an English-speaking market in the U.K., where Rush-die had lived for decades and where unflattering portrayals of Christian religious figures by artists and writers were not uncommon. With some exceptions,[10] the Western media and public intellectuals were generally supportive of Rushdie, as was the British government in its defense of the author after the death sentence (fatwa) imposed by Iran's Ayatollah Khomeini.

The cartoons controversy, however, found the West more cautious and brought to the fore a divide within the West itself concerning freedom of speech.[11] Despite the extensive legal protection afforded speech in the U.S., encompassing, as in the Danish case, freedom of artistic expression, there has been a continuous debate about the aims of politics in the same 100-year period, during which a growing body of scholarly and legal dissent has been directed against an expansive interpretation of the First Amendment.[12] Meanwhile, in the past forty years, postmodernists have cast considerable doubt on the neutral or universal nature of Western rights,[13] thereby challenging what only a decade or so ago seemed bedrock legal policy in the United States.

During the height of the cartoons controversy, in the spring of 2006, one could not but be struck by the irresolvable nature of this division concerning freedom of speech. John Stuart Mill's respectable if instrumental view, that tolerance even of repugnant views may lead to truth, competed with the postmodernist insistence on cultural relativism.[14] To express a belief in universal rights, much less to speak of "basic moral laws" engraved, as Voltaire would have it, on the minds of men, invited the charge of being an "Enlightenment fundamentalist."[15] Clearly, for its defenders freedom of speech had become such a part of their self-understanding, regarded as inalienable, along with other democratic rights, that they were at a loss when confronted with the contention that Islam had an equal right not to be discussed, much less insulted, even in the heart of Europe itself.

It was this inability to articulate a defense of freedom of speech that led me, as chair of the Columbia University Seminar on Eighteenth-Century European Culture, to initiate a series of talks in 2007–2008. What seemed required—since even legal scholars were neglecting it—was a renewed understanding of the historical background that preceded the institutionalization of the right of freedom of speech. While it is true that some people—namely, thinkers like the radical *philosophes* who will be discussed below—spoke of the universal nature of rights, these assertions of universality had much to do with the spread of intellectual commerce, including the dissemination of their own ideas, from one intellectual coterie of Europe to another, to towns small and large, in the course of the eighteenth century. Beyond Europe, it was less the power of such intellectual commerce than something more tangible, namely the control of world trade that helped to spread the notion of universal norms.

As Kumkum Chatterjee and Clement Hawes have written, there has been a "profound *unevenness*—as one ponders Asia and Africa on the one hand and the Americas on the other—of European dominance in the early modern era."[16] Within Europe itself and its offshoots, it was not at all foreordained, indeed not foreseeable, that the right of freedom of speech would become a foundational element of modern liberal societies. Free speech legislation as it came to exist did not grow in a vacuum but, instead, emerged from soil that had been well prepared and cultivated by several generations of thinkers and writers. The essays in this volume show how men (and a few women) articulated the issue, preparing the intellectual groundwork for the eventual institutionalization of this right. There was no particular uniformity in this process, and at times it was retarded violently. Freedom of speech, like other liberal rights, has been historically achieved and is part of the West's cultural patrimony.

Thus, this volume takes no position on the rightness or wrongness of freedom of speech as it currently exists in the West, nor does it plead for expansive or limited readings of this right, whether in the interest of truth or of social comity. Instead, the postmodernist view is readily acknowledged: modern Western civil society, in which both freedom of speech and equal protection under the law are constituent parts, is anything but a natural state of affairs.[17] In a multiculturalist world, our current liberal rights are products of a distinctive culture, one that arose in "Europe," an admittedly ambiguous designation, and that now broadly encompasses "the West."[18] While these rights have been incorporated in law and in international declarations, in truth, even if the matter were not complicated by the different institutional and intellectual histories of the nations of Europe, one cannot speak of "universal" rights.

The fall of the Berlin Wall in 1989 precipitated two events that have proven that there is no such thing as an ideology-free, universal political order. One event took place in a spirit of triumph, namely, the attempt to expand the European Union to eastern Europe, to the nations cut off from Europe's material progress for half a century by the Soviet Union. This extension has not proceeded like a corporate buyout. The differences between Holland and Bulgaria were not to be overcome simply by a transformation of banking systems and the adoption of constitutions. Thus, freedom arrived, not so much with the spirit of re-generation, but with the release of ancient antagonisms. These returned with a vengeance, slipping in initially through Europe's back door, its southeastern border, in Yugoslavia. Western liberal democracies, confronted with forms of behavior and thinking that they imagined dis-credited with the end of the U.S.S.R., were unprepared, indeed hapless in the face of genocide.[19]

The second consequence of the fall of the Wall was that large numbers of "non-Europeans," also without experience of limited gov-ernment or of the rights of citizens under the law, began to pass through the formerly impenetrable borders and arrived in the heart of western Europe. The assimilation of these immigrants has not always preceded smoothly, as the Mohammed cartoons controversy demonstrated, fur-ther challenging the West's confidence in universal standards.

The seeming victory of the Western liberal political model in 1989, one premised on limited government and a free market economy, had more to do, as Biancamaria Fontana has written, with the failure of other "competitors for modern political legitimacy."[20] Following the fall of the Old Regime at the end of the eighteenth century, however, there were certainly other visions of society and of the rights of citizens. The present division over the extent of allowable speech within the West reflects these competing visions, involving struggles for political legiti-macy that have intensified since the fall of the Berlin Wall but that are also foreshadowed in eighteenth-century debates.

The Western liberal order would seem to have become a victim of its own success, so long without competition that it has forgotten the source of the freedoms it enjoys. The macro-picture of the centuries-long struggle for rights in the West has been well described by scholars.[21] Suffice it to say here that it was an uneven, centuries-long process that was facilitated, at first incrementally and then increasingly, by the free flow of wealth and of information across borders, which led in some places to localized improvements in the rights of citizens.[22] Ironically, it was precisely the relative backwardness of the West vis-à-vis the Islamic world that allowed capitalism to flourish in northwestern Europe.[23] The Reformation and the spread of scientific, technological, and artistic exchange following on the maritime exploration (and, indeed, exploitation) of the Earth knitted the lands of western Europe together, both culturally and economically, and contributed to an outlook that was skeptical of authority, whether secular or religious. While some nations rushed ahead (England) and others languished (Portugal), a common intellectual habitus took shape among elites. By the end of the seventeenth century competition and interchange had begun to produce a consumer market that increasingly connected and improved the daily life of "Europeans."[24] Thus, the notion of progress became absorbed into the mentality of "the West." Still, as R. W. Davis has written, without the survival of English Parliament—"entirely a matter of good luck"—in the late seventeenth century and of the States General during Holland's period of greatness, "the history of Western freedom would be very different."[25]

It was in these two dynamic commercial nations that the arguments for freedom of speech received their first consistent articulation. Nevertheless, as will be seen in the essays that follow, eighteenth-century thinkers did not generally distinguish between print and speech, even if salons and coffeehouses provided forums for voicing ideas. (The rulers were a different matter and seemed to have understood quite early and sought to monitor as well as manipulate "opinion.")[26] In particular, the radical thinkers described by Jonathan Israel had their intellectual roots not only in Spinoza but also in older traditions devoted to the pursuit of philosophic truth and to which they were connected through centuries of writing, including print. While self-interest certainly played a role in their demand for freedom from censorship, the debate concerned print and was also primarily carried out in that medium.

Thus, not even the most radical thinkers of the eighteenth century seem to have grasped the emergence of a dynamic commercial republic like the United States in which political life would be driven by the power of competing, changing interests and in which individuals, in a variety of associations, would pursue their own visions of the good

life—and be voluble about their interests. Embedded in earlier traditions (despite their claim that they acknowledged none), the *philosophes*
believed in the power of their own ideas to lead or mold their fellow
citizens toward truth or virtue. Their legacy is still strong in Europe,
where governments are more active in promoting social equity and other
overriding social goods. The political institutions that the United States
has created seem more modest, based on the notion that, in a world of
goods, the Good cannot be established with finality. These differences
are reflected in the legal approach to freedom of speech in the European
nations and the United States.[27]

The subjects of the first two essays in this volume, namely, the
advocates of a "radical" and a "moderate" Enlightenment, foreshadow
contrary positions of twenty-first-century theorists concerning freedom
of speech. The so-called radicals, for instance, would seem to be First
Amendment radicals, espousing universal rights, including that of
freedom of opinion and expression, applicable to all men and women, in
all places and at all times. The moderates, in contrast, sought to ground
rights in distinctive national, religious, and traditional sources. So,
already in the eighteenth century there were competing visions within
the individual western European lands, perhaps indeed skepticism toward the concept of universal rights.

The distinction between "radicals" and "moderates" owes much to
three studies by Jonathan Israel[28] that have shifted the focus of Enlightenment scholarship from Britain and France to the Dutch Golden Age
and the figure of Benedict Spinoza. From 1670, when Spinoza's *Tractatus*
appeared, there was, according to Israel, "a continuous, unbroken dispute
within the European Enlightenment as to whether the publication and
general discussion of the fundamental philosophical, religious, moral, and
political issues was in fact beneficial or actually harmful to the general
good." In his contribution to this volume Israel portrays differences among
the educated classes in France during the High Enlightenment, the years
from 1750 to 1776. Carried out mostly in print, these concerned whether
the "freedom to philosophize"—and the subsequent voicing of the fruits
of that freedom—was a limited or an unlimited right.

For moderates like Voltaire or Dutch Cartesians (and for "enlightened monarchs" like Frederick the Great), the stability of Old Regime

institutions depended on a "two-tiered" approach to the publication of unsettling scientific or philosophical materials: one for specialists, another for the general public for whom it was important to maintain superstition and credulity. For radicals like Baron d'Holbach, Condorcet, Diderot, and Helvétius, on the other hand, absolute freedom of expression was necessary in order to arrive at "truth." With their sights set on the future perfection of society, these thinkers believed that open, public debate would remove prejudice and error from men's minds and advance society politically, morally, and scientifically. Ultimately these debates were not merely theoretical or rhetorical since, in 1770, the kingdom of Denmark-Norway, as Israel writes, became the "first state in the history of the world to proclaim full freedom of the press and to declare it to be a public benefit." After his overthrow, arrest, and imprisonment, the Danish chief minister Johann Friedrich Struensee revealed his familiarity with the chief ideas of both the moderate and the radical Enlightenment.

Despite the influence of philosophical Spinozism, it is the contention of Joris van Eijnatten that lesser-known, "moderate" figures probably played a greater role in advancing freedom of speech in England and Holland. These were men who, while rationalists, stopped short of denying a providential deity or the benefits of traditional beliefs and institutions. Eijnatten's "taxonomy" of their arguments for freedom of expression includes familiar radical Enlightenment tropes—for instance, the contribution of open debate to technological and scientific progress—but these men also drew on national traditions of liberty; on long-established oratorical and ethical authorities as found in ancient Greek and Roman texts; and on Christian teaching. Looking forward (if not explicitly) to modern liberal societies and certainly not to utopia, they also argued that transparency would prevent politicians from acting treacherously and enhance national security. Utilitarian arguments (the impracticality of forbidding the circulation of offensive materials and the disadvantages of state monopolies on printing) are evidence of the interaction between the spread of commerce and of emancipatory ideas in the modern period.

As stated above, this emancipatory idea traveled to towns small and large throughout the eighteenth century. The following essays demonstrate the challenges the idea presented to traditional political, religious, and social structures, and they also further underline the absence of consensus, not to mention a unified development concerning the allowable extent of speech.

As far as practice goes, Johann Friedrich Struensee (1737–1772) is certainly the most radical Enlightener represented here. As prime minister of the kingdom of Denmark-Norway, he instituted top-down reforms that were the first imposition of a radical political program for social change. But John Christian Laursen's essay on Struensee also shows the continuing relevance of earlier elite intellectual paradigms in eighteenth-century debates, in this case the residue of the Cynic philosophy of Diogenes of Sinope in both the writings and the behavior of Struensee. Struensee's cosmopolitan leanings and elitism, for instance, were as characteristic of the Cynic tradition as of the attitudes of eighteenth-century *philosophes*. His failures, especially in his offenses to local pieties and to his Danish subjects (a German, he did not even bother to learn Danish), might seem to offer a lesson in the dangers of abolishing established authority, including restrictions on publication, at one stroke. It was, after all, his abolition of press censorship that precipitated a flood of pamphlets against Struensee and led to his downfall.

Indeed, Struensee's case suggests that political reform is most successful when it builds on specific historical circumstances and is accompanied by healthy moderation. More importantly, his reforms remind us of the fate of rights when these have not been fought for by citizens themselves. As Douglas Smith's essay shows, what is granted to subjects by a "benevolent" ruler, in Russia by Catherine the Great (1729–1796), can also be taken away by a ruler. Catherine is justly known for introducing a spirit of openness in Russia, which included sponsoring a translation of the *Encyclopédie* when it was still banned in France. In 1767, in her *Great Instruction*, she argued that freedom of expression is a natural right of all citizens, which it was the duty of the state to protect. Though endorsing this liberal policy, she did not go so far as to institute it in law. Perhaps the execution of Struensee in 1772 suggested moderate reform might be more successful. Thus, in 1783 she allowed the establishment of private presses. Like the *philosophes* with whom she was acquainted, Catherine cited the positive value of publication to society, in particular its contribution to the spread of knowledge.

Catherine's rhetoric, however, turned out to be shallow when a work appeared that tested the limits of criticism of a sovereign. This was Alexander Radishchev's *Journey to St. Petersburg*, a work that has been compared to *Uncle Tom's Cabin* and that would be mined in the twentieth century for its portrayal of the evils of tsarist Russia, particularly serfdom. Radishchev's work shows the "European," if not yet "international," nature of the movement of ideas. In the chapter of *Journey* exploring freedom of expression and censorship, Radishchev appropriated a work by Herder, which he then edited to make even more radical. Though no printer would touch the manuscript, even after he received publication approval from the St. Petersburg police, Radishchev took advantage of the edict of 1783 to set up a press in his own house. The timing of this explosive publication could not have been worse for its author, appearing in 1790, and it was only the distraction of the war with Sweden that saved him from execution.

Lèse majeste divine and lèse majeste were terms frequently invoked in the eighteenth century in connection with print and public opinion. Their connectedness, especially in relation to freedom of speech, is underlined by a character in Radishchev's *Journey*: "[T]imid governments are not afraid of blasphemy, but of criticism of themselves. He who in moments of madness does not spare God, will not in moments of lucidity and reason spare unjust power. He who does not fear the thunders of the Almighty laughs at the gallows." It was precisely the power of laughter that made the rulers of another empire nervous, the Habsburgs. For several centuries already, European governments had developed mechanisms for controlling the written word, especially of articulate critics, and the Habsburgs had done so in order to enforce confessional orthodoxy in its central European empire. Ruling over a nation of theater lovers, especially in Vienna, the Habsburgs also had to contend with theatricals that gave voice, in local dialect, to political, social, and economic resentments.

Paula Sutter Fichtner surveys the attempts of Habsburg emperors and their censors to monitor and channel the power of the stage to influence public opinion. By midcentury the raucous, often obscene language of theater became the victim of language purification. The desire for progress advocated by so many thinkers in the eighteenth century was not restricted to material improvements but also encompassed the moral life. Thus, Habsburg rulers and censors, in the spirit of the Enlightenment, opportunistically sought to improve the morals of their subjects by elevating the standards of theater. Censors discovered, however, that, even with texts of plays in hand, they could not control the improvisations for which the popular stage was renowned. Thus, from the 1770s low-level bureaucrats and police officials regularly attended theatrical performances in order to confirm that propriety was observed and that nothing departed from scripts previously approved by censors. After the French Revolution it was impermissible for words like liberty, freedom, or enlightenment to be spoken on stage, and actors were likewise forbidden to refer to tyranny or despotism.

The imposition by the Habsburg rulers of morals from on high, for the "improvement" of the populace, indicates that even benevolent rulers could not distinguish between their own interests and those of their subjects. "Citizen," as a concept and a category, would not be widespread until the French and American revolutions. This lack of separation was a feature of the pre-liberal order and even more so in Spain, where, moreover, Catholicism was the dominant marker of identity from time immemorial. According to Javier Fernández Sebastián, Catholicism united all classes and formed "the very center of the system over which the Spanish monarchy reigned." Thus the ecclesiastics who largely forged Hispanic liberal culture could not conceive of a totally secular society. Freedom of speech was correspondingly affected, and such other long-debated English subjects—freedom of conscience and worship—were not part of the political vocabulary of Hispanic liberals.

Still, the relationship between religious tolerance and economic progress did not escape the educated class, sensitive as it was to Spain's backwardness, due to the slow acceptance in that country of the seventeenth-century scientific revolution. Many of the arguments enunciated by Spanish enlighteners for freedom of speech recapitulated arguments put forward by the moderate enlighteners discussed by Joris van Eijantten: tolerance of new ideas would lead to commercial and technical progress; rulers would be aware of their subjects' opinions and rule more wisely. The beginnings of a constitutional order, with freedom of press and public opinion occupying a prominent place, began only after the Napoleonic invasion of the peninsula and the succeeding long patriotic war. Nevertheless, even the Constitution of Cádiz of 1812 and the constitutions of the newly independent Hispanic republics in the Americas (Mexico, Peru, Chile, Colombia, Venezuela, etc.), proclaimed the confessional nature of the state and, thus, official religious intolerance. What seems incoherent to us moderns—Catholic confessionalism in a constitution—was not perceived as such at the time. Nevertheless, these new constitutions replaced the Church of Rome with civil law, thus setting in motion a new phase.

The slowness with which Spain came to absorb liberal ideas shows anew that "Europe" has been an uneven, evolving process. While anathemas against works by *philosophes* only increased interest in those works in eighteenth-century Spain, the controversial Habermasian notion of the public square in the spread of Enlightenment cannot be mechanically applied.[29] Despite what Fernández Sebastián calls "extraordinary historical acceleration" after the first decade of the nineteenth century,

it was only late in the twentieth century that Spain finally joined "Europe." Meanwhile in Russia, the Radishchev affair led Catherine to establish a system of censorship in order "to put an end to various inconveniences resulting from the unrestricted publication of books," while the nineteenth century, according to Douglas Smith, was even more hostile to freedom of expression. Freedom of speech was legalized only in 1905, before falling victim to Soviet repression.

The French and American revolutions are regarded as signaling the transition to modern political liberalism and the institution of civil rights for citizens. Among the French revolutionaries, however, there remained elements of the "enlightened absolutism" of the Old Regime monarchs, especially in regard to public morality and virtue. As Helena Rosenblatt writes, after initially promulgating freedom of speech and of the press, by 1793 they had imposed a system of censorship even more restrictive than that of the Old Regime.[30] By 1795, individuals who departed from patriotic unity, whether they voiced royalist or clerical sentiments or uttered pessimism about the war, were sentenced to death. The French Revolutionary period brought the power and the fear of *speech* to the fore; denunciations of nay-sayers, as in twentieth-century totalitarian regimes, became the rule. Like the monarchs before them, the

Revolution's rulers could not separate the interests of the state—which they identified with their own interests—from those of the ruled.

Rosenblatt subjects to analysis the views of three philosophic radicals, intellectual forefathers of the revolutionaries—Holbach, Mercier, and Rousseau—and shows them to be distinctly pre-liberal in their views. Again, we see that, for most eighteenth-century thinkers, freedom of expression was grounded in a "republic of letters," with its traditional allegiance to the written word. Moreover, believing that only people like themselves wrote meaningful books, books that moreover were intended to educate the public both morally and intellectually, the radicals were not opposed to government interference with other people's right to express themselves. Indeed, Mercier's utopian novel, *Year 2440* (publ. 1771), described Red Guard–like punishments for bad books: authors would be forced to wear masks and submit to interrogations by virtuous citizens until they abjured their errors. Rosenblatt ascribes these views to a deep discomfort with dissent and free debate, epitomized by Rousseau, who went so far, in *Julie* and *Emile*, as to declare that true communication was the avoidance of words. Thus, the General Will was to emerge from "the voice of duty," not from the opinions of individuals.

According to Rosenblatt, it was Benjamin Constant, stressing that a "part of human existence" must remain individual and independent of political direction, who rethought the nature of sovereignty. Power, he argued repeatedly, is inevitably corrupting, no matter who wields it. While he largely advanced the usual Enlightenment arguments for the benefits of freedom of expression—instruction, progress, transparency of government—his distinctive liberal contribution lay in the connection he posited between freedom of press and opinion and the protection of individuals from the overreach of government. His crucial innovation was to argue that it was not the role of government to regulate morals or to mold public opinion through education or to "direct, improve, or enlighten" citizens. Nor was it the role of government to decide what was slander; that decision was to be left to juries. If Rousseau wished for the reign of virtue, to be established by a unanimous will, Constant extolled the "collision of opinions."

It was to protect citizens from the power of government (or from "the tyranny of the majority") that the Bill of Rights to the U.S. Constitution was written. And it is the First Amendment of that document in which we seem to find a straightforward enunciation of a right, without qualification (unlike in European and international texts), of freedom of speech, press, assembly, and petition. If, however, as Lee Morrissey writes, we view the Enlightenment as the triumph of secularism, we must find problematic the conjunction of those rights with the right to the free exercise of religion. What happens, for instance, when the rights enumerated in the First Amendment come into conflict with one another? Denmark is not the United States, but it is this conflict between religion and speech that is at the heart of current free speech controversies.

Thus, Morrissey questions the strict separation of rights as currently understood and, indeed, of the triumphalist Enlightenment narrative of continuous progress toward universal tolerance. He examines the views of three prominent writers on religion and the state—Milton, Locke, and Rousseau—and shows the underlying historical tensions in the First Amendment. While both Milton and Locke held that each man had the care of his own salvation, for which the individual use of reason was paramount, the former envisioned England perfecting what the Reformation began. Locke may have called for toleration of all faiths and for the state to be neutral as to particular faiths, but he did not hold that it be neutral as to its citizens' spiritual welfare. For Rousseau, the separation of religion and politics is itself Christian in origin ("Render unto Caesar . . ."). Separation, however, according to Rousseau, does not result in the political stability Locke envisioned, but instead pits citizens, with their claims to a higher moral authority, against the state. Seen in this light, the drafters of the first Hispanic constitutions, as described by Fernández Sebastián, might be said to have avoided what Morrissey refers to as the "historical entanglements" of the First Amendment. Interestingly, as Morrissey mentions, Rousseau approved of Mohammed's combination of mosque and government, which returns us to the present-day conflict over freedom of speech with which I began. The conclusion will address the relationship between eighteenth-century concerns and this present conflict over speech.

Notes

1. Foreword to *Extreme Speech and Democracy*, ed. Ivan Hare and James Weinstein (New York: Oxford University Press, 2009), v–ix.

2. "[T]he key question is now not whether the speech is likely to cause harm but whether the expression in question amounts to mere advocacy of law violation, in which case it retains First Amendment protection, or whether it crossed the line to actual incitement of lawlessness, in which case it is eligible for suppression. The 'clear and present danger' test is relegated to supplying prophylactic protection to the harmless inciter by requiring the government to show that even speech that is directed towards inciting imminent lawless conduct, and thus theoretically eligible for suppression, is in fact likely to produce such conduct. In the following years [after *Brandenburg v. Ohio*, in 1969], the Court more generally 'bright lined' free speech doctrine by subjecting all content-based restriction of public discourse to 'strict scrutiny,' a test that almost always leads to the invalidation of the regulation." James Weinstein, "Extreme Speech, Public Order, and Democracy: Lessons from *The Masses*," in ibid., 42 (note numbers omitted).

3. On the controversy, see http://en.wikipedia.org/wiki/Chris_Ofili.

4. For a list of the conventions and international instruments, see *Extreme Speech*, xlvii–li. Even countries without explicit constitutional provision, such as Australia, recognize freedom of speech based on an implied right in a democracy. See Dieter Grimm, "Freedom of Speech in a Globalized World," in ibid., 11–12.

5. According to Dieter Grimm (ibid., 13), the German Constitutional Court "transformed [proportionality] to a constitutional principle"—thereby striking a balance between freedom of speech and "other protected values, rights, and interests"—that has spread to many jurisdictions, including Israel. Instead of proportionality, U.S. courts apply instead "various degrees of 'scrutiny' depending on the type of speech and the nature of the regulation at issue."

6. 432 U.S. 43 (1977) was a U.S. Supreme Court case dealing with freedom of assembly. The plaintiffs, a neo-Nazi organization, sued for the right to march in the town of Skokie in Illinois, in which many Holocaust survivors lived.

7. The challenge to artistic authority was foreshadowed in the late-seventeenth-century "Quarrel of Ancients and Moderns." On the "Querelle," see Joan DeJean, *Ancients Against Moderns: Culture Wars and the Making of a Fin de Siecle* (Chicago: University of Chicago Press, 1997). Jonathan Swift's satire *The Battle of the Books* (1704) depicted a literal battle, fought in a library, in which various books come to life and attempt to settle arguments between modern and ancient writers.

8. Since this introduction was written, Yale University Press published in 2009 (somewhat controversially; see note 11 below) *The Cartoons That Shook the World* by Jytte Klausen. There is otherwise no impartial book-length study in English of the cartoon controversy. Wikipedia provides a considerable amount of material, including a useful time line of events and many links to media coverage: http://en.wikipedia.org/wiki/Jyllands-Posten_Muhammad_cartoons.

9. Again, Wikipedia offers a convenient time line of this controversy: http://en.wikipedia.org/wiki/The_Satanic_Verses_controversy. The first major book-length treatment in English appears to be that by Daniel Pipes, *The Rushdie Affair: The Novel, the Ayatollah, and the West* (New York: Carol Publishing Corp., 1990; rev. Piscataway, NJ: Transaction Publishers, 2003). More recently, see Kenan Malik, *From Fatwa to Jihad: The Rushdie Affair and Its Aftermath* (Brooklyn, NY: Melville House, 2010).

10. Thierry Chervel, publisher of *Perlentaucher*, writing in the German newspaper *Tagesspiegel* (February 7, 2009) on the twentieth anniversary of the fatwa, reported on the Western response at the time of publication of the novel. This article can be found at http://print.signandsight.com/features/1827.html.

11. The *New York Times*, for instance, covered the controversy, but without reprinting the cartoons, which instead circulated widely on the Internet. (Interestingly, an article on February 8, 2006,

was accompanied by a photograph of Chris Ofili's offending painting of the Virgin covered with cow dung. See note 3 above.) PEN, the organization of writers that "works to defend freedom of expression and resist censorship worldwide" (as per its website), restricted itself to holding forums in New York in the spring of 2006 to explore the question whether there should be limits on the right of speech and artistic expression. The circumspection of Western publishers continues. Most recently, Yale University Press decided to omit the cartoons from its publication on the cartoons controversy.

12. In recent years the concept of "hate speech" has figured prominently in such critiques. Thus, according to legal scholar Steven J. Heyman, speech that injures "fundamental rights ... entitled to protection under the law [i.e., the equal protection section of the 14th Amendment] ... may be regulated by narrowly drawn laws, except in situations where the value of the speech is sufficient to justify the injuries it causes" (http://papers.ssrn.com/sol3/papers.cfm?abstract_id=1186262). See also by Heyman, "Hate Speech, Public Discourse, and the First Amendment, in *Extreme Speech*, 158–81.

13. E.g., such literary scholars as Stanley Fish (*There's No Such Thing as Free Speech: And It's a Good Thing, Too* [1994]) and Judith Butler (*Excitable Speech: A Politics of the Performative* [1997]) have made similar arguments.

14. Citing Thierry Chervel (see note 10): "The West's long-due process of self-relativization at the end of the colonial era, which was promoted by postmodernist and structuralist ideas, has led to cultural relativism and the loss of criteria."

15. The term "Enlightenment fundamentalist" was applied to Ayaan Hirsi Ali by Timothy Garton Ash in a review in *The New York Review of Books* (October 5, 2006) of Hirsi Ali's book *The Caged Virgin: An Emancipation Proclamation for Women and Islam*. The epithet set off a firestorm of polemics and other responses in Europe between liberals and postmodernists. There has not yet appeared a study in English of this controversy, but for the debate online, see http://www.signandsight .com/features/1167.html. "Signandsight.com" continues to add articles to the debate.

16. In *Europe Observed: Multiple Gazes in Early Modern Encounters* (Lewisberg: Bucknell University Press, 2008), 6.

17. Paul W. Schroeder (*The Transformation of European Politics, 1763–1848* [Oxford: Clarendon Press, 1994]) writes (paraphrasing Michael Oakeshott) that the Western "way of life" is a system of "understandings, assumptions, learned skills and responses, rules, norms, procedures, etc." developed over time, without any particular uniformity, but "within the framework of a shared practice." Thus, one tends to forget how the system came to be, how "collective understandings were in turn challenged and altered, sometimes violently, by violations or different versions of the rules" (xii).

18. On Europe's ambiguous geography, see Anthony Pagden, "Europe: Conceptualizing a Continent," in *The Idea of Europe from Antiquity to the European Union*, ed. Anthony Pagden (New York: Cambridge University Press, 2002), 45; Biancamaria Fontana, "The Napoleonic Empire and the Europe of Nations," in ibid., 118. On Europe as a shared cultural space, see Fontana, ibid., 118-19. On the problematic concepts of "Europe" and "the West" generally, see J.G.A. Pocock, "Some Europes in Their History," in ibid., 55–71. According to Pocock (56), "Europe" is a word used "to denote, and to bring together, a great many things that are important in human experience."

19. I am paraphrasing Imre Kertesz, who spoke at the Academy of the Arts in Berlin at a conference entitled "Perspective Europe." His speech appeared in the *Süddeutsche Zeitung* on June 2, 2007. See also Pocock ("Some Europes in Their History," 61): "The expansion of 'Europe' into the Slavic heartlands [at the time of the Crusades] altered the historical map by creating what we think of as the problem of 'Central Europe.'"

20. "The formula ['the bourgeois liberal republic'] was devised by its enemies rather than by its supporters at a time (mid-nineteenth century) when its achievements seemed paltry when set against the high hopes of many for universal fraternity and justice; but it captures . . . the specific character of this political form: the combination of 'limited' government . . . based upon popular representation and constitutional guarantees—and of a free-market economy—a society geared to the promotion of private property and individual interest," in Biancamaria Fontana, ed., *The Invention of the Modern Republic* (New York: Cambridge University Press, 1994), 2.

21. See, e.g., R.W. Davis, ed., *The Origins of Modern Freedom in the West* (Stanford: Stanford University Press, 1995).

22. The historical record shows that in places where rulers encouraged and protected wealth production, so, too, were civil liberties granted and protected, as in Holland. In countries like Spain, economic stagnation and lack of civil liberties went hand in hand. Though there continued to be an uneven history of applying checks on power and authorities in the name of greater freedoms for individuals, the "ubiquitous competition" among the evolving European nations was not only "a deep underlying source of change" but also "a constraint on the options available to rulers" (Douglass C. North, "The Paradox of the West," in ibid., 30).

23. Samir Amin, in *Eurocentrism* (New York: Monthly Review Press, 1989), 8 (quoted in Chatterjee and Hawes, *Europe Observed*, 7 (see note 16 above).

24. An example is the art market, which in the seventeenth century was already "international." Science, too, was "a public phenomenon, conspicuous consumption of new intellectual fashions in competing courts." Jonathan Clark, reviewing Lisa Jardine's *Going Dutch: How England Plundered Holland's Glory*, in the *Times Literary Supplement*, June 13, 2008.

25. R.W. Davis, *The Origins of Modern Freedom in the West*, 314.

26. See Charles Walton, *Policing Public Opinion in the French Revolution: The Culture of Calumny and the Problem of Free Speech* (New York: Oxford University Press, 2009), esp. 25–32.

27. Various chapters in *Extreme Speech* portray the attempts at regulation in western Europe today.

28. *Radical Enlightenment: Philosophy and the Making of Modernity, 1650–1750* (New York: Oxford University Press, 2001); *Enlightenment Contested: Philosophy, Modernity and the Emancipation of Man, 1650-1752* (New York: Oxford University Press, 2006); and A *Revolution of the Mind: Radical Enlightenment and the Intellectual Origins of Modern Democracy* (New York: Oxford University Press, 2009).

29. Lee Morrissey, in *The Constitution of Literature: Literacy, Democracy, and Early English Literary Criticism* (Stanford: Stanford University Press, 2008), critiques the Habermasian notion as it applies to Habermas's exemplary case, namely, England.

30. Charles Walton's recent study, *Policing Public Opinion in the French Revolution* (see note 26 above), provides details of this severe system.

Freedom of
Speech

$\mathcal{L}$ibertas Philosophandi in the Eighteenth Century: Radical Enlightenment versus Moderate Enlightenment (1750–1776)

IT IS NO EASY MATTER TO PROVIDE A GENERAL ACCOUNT OF EUropean debates on censorship and freedom of the press or speech during the High Enlightenment of the late eighteenth century. The indispensable starting point for any reasonably coherent and balanced general perspective, it seems to me, is to accept that the way to grasp and classify the overall play of forces in this controversy (as with most other key themes of the Enlightenment) is to begin with the dichotomy "Radical Enlightenment versus Moderate Enlightenment."

Only one part of the Enlightenment, the radical Enlightenment, held that all men in society should be enlightened and that the entire truth of what is known to men should be expressed so as to be accessible and available to all. Hence, only the radical Enlightenment was inherently committed to the principle of full freedom of expression and liberty of the press. Against this, the moderate "mainstream" Enlightenment, especially as expressed by court officials and such figures as Voltaire and Frederick the Great, held that the vast majority of humanity (in one place Voltaire suggests nine-tenths of mankind) could not and indeed should not be enlightened and that the censorship policy of states thus required an essentially restrictive, two-tiered character. This distinction is important because many general surveys of the Enlightenment either misleadingly suggest that the Enlightenment as a whole was committed to full freedom of thought and expression or else, even more misleadingly, imply that the Enlightenment failed to argue for these freedoms. Both views are not just errors of interpretation in themselves but are also misconceptions that have inevitably given rise to much confusion and fundamentally distort our picture of what was one of the most crucial Enlightenment controversies.

It might be well to begin with an illustration of the working of two-tiered censorship in the field of Enlightenment science in order to provide an idea of how moderate Enlightenment conceptions of censorship worked in practice. In 1762, there was an interesting exchange of letters on the question of censorship between Charles Bonnet (1720–1793), the Genevan Swiss biologist and philosophe, and Malesherbes (1721–1794), the royal minister and director of the librairie in Paris.

Bonnet had achieved a considerable success that year with his book *Considérations sur les corps organisés* (1762), an elegant work of biology designed, first, to summarize the evidence that research with microscopes had thus far presented concerning the reproduction and development of living creatures; second, to attack epigenesis, the theory that the whole embryo is generated and its development fully determined by the embryo's material context, a notion championed in particular by his opponent, Buffon; and third, to put forward Bonnet's own theory of generation, palingenesis, a partly Leibnizian conception, according to which souls and bodies exist in pre-existent germs before generation, pass through many lives, and grow slowly more perfect while sharing a kind of immortality.

Bonnet's work enjoyed the enthusiastic support of Albrecht von Haller (1708–1777), a Swiss teaching at Göttingen who was the most prestigious naturalist at the time in Germany, as well as the approval of the Prussian royal academy of sciences in Berlin. Despite such support the French *Académie royale des sciences*, after examining the text with great care, thought it best to ban the book in France. On their advice, Malesherbes ruled that the book's sale should not be officially allowed, although, as he explained in one of his letters to Bonnet, no obstacle would be placed in the path of French scholars and naturalists obtaining a small number of copies from abroad for their own scientific purposes.

In his reply Bonnet did not at all dispute that works of biology, any more than a whole range of other books, needed to be censored or that censorship was entirely necessary. He expressed amazement, however, that his own book should be banned: "comment est-il possible qu'un livre où il n'y a pas un seul mot qui choque le moins du monde la religion, le gouvernement, les moeurs soit interdit par des juges aussi éclairés qu'équitables!" (How is it possible for a book where not a single word occurs to shock in the least religion, government, and customs, to be banned by judges as enlightened as fair-minded!)[1]

In a further letter, of October 1762, Malesherbes willingly granted that Bonnet's book was far too useful and important to be denied "aux physiciens et aux naturalistes"; but as he explained, even though Bonnet's book contained no statements detrimental to religion or government, and though it was clearly essential reading matter for naturalists, the delicacy of the subject of generation and embryos in a work touching on metaphysics, as his book did, "peut en rendre la lecture dangereuse pour le public" (may render reading it dangerous to the public).[2] What was fitting for specialists was simply not something that should be absorbed by the general population.

Dissatisfied, Bonnet wrote again to Malesherbes. Why does he label his book "un ouvrage de métaphysique" when it is solely concerned to argue that all living creatures are subject to the law of development and that what we call generation is only the evolution of a preformed tiny embryo, or germ? His main intention was to demonstrate the ever-present hand of the Supreme Being in all those wonderful productions of life the formation of which some writers had attributed to purely mechanistic cause and effect "as if an animal had the same origin as a piece of cheese" (comme si un animal avait la même origine qu'un fromage). Bonnet suggested that someone was trying to pull the wool over Malesherbes' eyes in characterizing his work as one containing "des pensées métaphysiques et dangereuses" for the public, hinting that his rival Buffon might have had something to do with the decision to ban his work in France. In fact, Buffon was innocent and the ban was soon lifted, after a few weeks, but the principle that had motivated the ban and the two-tiered thinking it prompted in both Malesherbes' and Bonnet's minds nevertheless remained intact.

3

That the official Enlightenment of courts and churches could not dispense with a two-tiered conception, that is, one rule for specialists and an entirely different one for the general public, was made doubly clear in the wake of the single most unsettling clandestine publication event of the later Enlightenment, the appearance in rapid succession in 1770 of two of the most sweepingly radical books of the baron d'Holbach: the *Essai sur les préjugés* and the *Système de la nature*. The anonymous publication of these two books was of great historical as well as intellectual and philosophical importance because they almost immediately achieved an unprecedented degree of penetration and notoriety for works of an author generally unknown, stirring perhaps the biggest and widest public controversy of any radical works since the appearance of Spinoza's *Tractatus Theologico-Politicus* exactly a century before, in 1670.

The Paris police pursued the *Système de la nature, ou Des Loix du monde physique et du monde moral* in particular with unprecedented energy. The Prussian *roi philosophe* Frederick the Great, for his part, was notably angry and disturbed, albeit less by d'Holbach's atheistic materialism than by the social and political conclusions the author drew from them. D'Holbach's principle, that the consent of the governed is the only source of legitimacy in politics, thought Frederick, threatened the entire edifice of Europe's Old Regime institutions. Concerning the *Système de la nature*, Frederick was especially indignant about the author's imagining "to himself treaties made between monarchs and ecclesiastics, by which the former promise to honor and support the priesthood, provided the priests will preach submission to the people."[3] In the case of the *Essai sur les préjugés, ou De l'influence des opinions sur les mœurs et sur le bonheur des hommes* ("Londres," 1770), it is striking and particularly relevant in the present context that Frederick especially opposed d'Holbach's claim that the truth should be told to all men. Examining d'Holbach's text, in his palace at Potsdam, barely a month after its clandestine publication, the irate monarch at once took up his pen to compose a sharply critical and extremely negative reply, denouncing the unnamed d'Holbach as an "ennemi des rois" who had set out to make all monarchical government "odious," a rabid hater of aristocracy, and a pillar of "philosophic pride" who with his overly optimistic hopes for the future had embarked on an absurdly naive quest bound needlessly to agitate the people and to end in disaster.

Frederick argued that the anonymous author was wrong to try to enlighten the common people and extend to them the freedoms and opportunities that can come only with education.[4] "The author" evidently believed, like Diderot and Helvétius, that the gradual advance of reason, dissipating the errors and credulity of the people, is the veritable engine of human progress.[5] Such a perspective is profoundly mistaken, contended Frederick, because not just religion and tradition but also "superstition" and credulity remain wholly essential to ordinary folk and hence also to the maintenance of the moral and social order. Without the power of popular credulity and church to hold sway over the lower orders, men's fears and ignorant prejudices would have no firm anchorage. Without popular belief, prejudices, and simple faith in authority, royalty and aristocracy could not be secure; and, without royalty and nobility, there could be no order, only chaos.

Frederick's contention that it was better not to teach the truth to most men was, in turn, scathingly rejected by Diderot in a batch of private notes that he penned at this time on Frederick's intervention. Quite the contrary, observed Diderot, vigorously siding with his friend and ally d'Holbach, albeit he was as much concerned with defending his own stance as that of his ally. There can be no doubt that man's happiness and best interest "est fondé sur la verité."[6] If the Prussian monarch disagreed, why was he bothering to write at all or to complain that the *Essai sur les préjugés* was full of errors? What could be more incoherent than to claim that truth is not made for men and then to take up one's pen to correct the errors of others? If the truth is valueless to humanity, held Diderot, "pourquoi les efforts successifs de l'esprit humain ont-ils eu quelques succès?" (Why did succeeding efforts of the human spirit achieve some successes?).[7] Moreover, what could be more preposterous than to champion in print the arrogant pride of those with age-old coats of arms or to speak of the indispensability of ignorance, credulity, and superstition, which kings, aristocrats, and priests then went on systematically to exploit?[8] From 1770, Diderot regularly condemned Frederick as a "tyrant" and "un monarque detestable" and, in 1774, vigorously reprimanded Helvétius for being an uncritical, or at

5

least insufficiently critical, admirer of enlightened despotism.[9] Unsurprisingly, Raynal's *Histoire philosophique* included a fierce denunciation of Frederick, inspired doubtless by Diderot and d'Holbach, to which the king again took great offence and indirectly replied via a riposte published under the name of one of his academicians, the Berlin Huguenot pastor, Moulines.[10]

Another radical text penned in 1770 and vigorously assailing the *Système*'s adversaries, the "*Discours préliminaire*," probably by Naigeon, entirely agreed with Diderot's and d'Holbach's great principle, so utterly rejected by Voltaire and Frederick, that the truth alone is capable "de procurer aux mortels un bonheur solide et permanent" (to give mortals a solid and enduring happiness).[11] And if the common people were to learn the truth, this could happen only through the advancement of reason, held Naigeon, since reason alone enables man to distinguish between true and false, real and illusory, and the useful and damaging. Furthermore, if reason is to provide this service, society's entire system of education has to be taken out of the hands of theologians and "religious fanatics" who, instead of forming children into "citoyens humains, magnanimes, vertueux," turns them instead into fanatical and useless *dévots*, credulous and superstitious men, blind believers and opinionated ignoramuses, perfectly lacking in true morality.[12]

Another outspoken opponent of Frederick's and Voltaire's notion that the truth is only for a few was Condorcet.[13] Even during the Middle Ages and the Renaissance, periods the eighteenth-century radical *philosophes* regarded as highly oppressive, the triumph of superstition and theology had forced philosophers like Ibn Rushd, and later the Italian naturalists, to form hidden networks that were guided by reason alone and that rejected all credulity, cultivating "philosophy" and the "truth" in secret, and thus concealing the truth from the majority. But this exclusion occurred in circumstances in which clandestinity offered the only means of undertaking "le prosélytisme philosophique" and even then, argued Condorcet, such tactics had inevitably incurred undesirable moral and political consequences. Since what he called "the natural equality of men" is the chief basis of men's rights, as well as "le fondement de toute vraie morale," the concealment practiced by the secret adherents of Ibn Rushd and the Italian naturalists, even if more excusable than the attitude of eighteenth-century defenders of censorship, was bound to foment a hypocritcal politics and a secret morality.[14]

Moderate enlighteners, however, regarded Frederick the Great's attitude, and the strategy of concealing the truth from most men, in a very different light. Praising the Prussian king for his vigorous refutation of the *Système*, a work that he too regarded as dangerous and undesirable, Voltaire took a grim view of the overall situation in which the *philosophes* now found themselves. (His standpoint was to a degree self-contradictory since he was on record as supporting liberty of the press but nevertheless thought most men would and should not be enlightened.) For decades, there had been a split between the materialists and the conservative deists like Voltaire, but this split had now become an open, public fact: "voilà une guerre civile entre les incrédules" (there you see, a civil war between unbelievers), he commented in a letter of July 27, 1770, to d'Alembert, noting that the king was growing restive and indignant because more than a few *philosophes* "ne soient pas royalistes" (are not royalists).[15] What chiefly troubled Voltaire was not the philosophy of the radical *philosophes* as such (from which he was no longer as estranged as he had once been—his letters revealing that his old veneration for Locke and Newton had receded somewhat), but the fact that his radical critics were proposing to attack God, the devil, rulers, and priests, as he put it, all at the same time. Their strategy rendered a "civil war" among the *philosophes* unavoidable, one bound to be not just long and bitter but also irresolvable. Voltaire hastened to assure Frederick that he was firmly on his side, and indeed he emerged as one of the most outspoken opponents of radical thought in the 1770s anywhere in Europe.

But while Voltaire agreed with Frederick that Enlightenment was not for the majority and that firm censorship policies were indispensable, he was also more than a little troubled by the king's dogmatic insistence on excluding the great majority of men from access to the truth. Indeed, the question of how precisely to draw the line worried him more than a little. In his short text *Jusqu'à quel point on doit tromper le peuple* (1771), he calls it as "une très grande question" (a very great question) but one as yet little discussed, to ascertain precisely "jusqu'à quel degré le peuple, c'est à dire neuf parts du genre humain sur dix, doit être traité comme des singes" (up to what degree the people, that is, nine tenths of the human race, must be treated as monkeys).[16] Whatever his reservations, however, he never departed from his view that the comprehensive, sweeping strategy of such works as the *Système de la nature*, attacking kings as well as priests, was neither desirable nor feasible and must have disastrous consequences, not least for the *philosophes* themselves.

By seeking to enlighten the majority and to politicize their struggle, Voltaire complained, Diderot and d'Holbach were bound to antagonize not just churchmen but also kings and aristocracy. That Louis XV and his ministers were now actively opposing *la philosophie* was, in his view, entirely the fault of the radical *philosophes* and their disciples. It filled him with deep pessimism and dismay. "Ce maudit Système de la nature" (This damned System of nature), he assured his ally d'Alembert, on January 18, 1771, has ruined us, "et nous voilà perdus pour un livre que tous les gens sensés méprisent" (and here we are lost on account of a book that all sensible people despise).[17] Had the book been as good as it is actually bad, the "author" should still not have published it, but thrown it on the fire: we shall never recover, he predicted gloomily, from "cette blessure mortelle" (this mortal wound). The ideas of the *Système*, he wrote in January 1771 to the Prussian crown prince, Friedrich Wilhelm, had no basis in sound philosophy or science: "Spinosa lui-même admettait une intelligence universelle" (Spinoza himself admitted [the existence of] a universal intelligence). The great question bequeathed by Spinoza's system to the *philosophes* was whether or not this "intelligence universelle" had a will and adhered to the path of justice. Yet it seems impertinent, to say the least, Voltaire added, to postulate "un Dieu injuste" (an injust God).[18]

Voltaire, like many others at the time, no doubt correctly regarded Spinoza's philosophy as the philosophical backbone of the materialism of Diderot and d'Holbach. Spinoza had scarcely imagined that the majority of men were capable of absorbing correct ideas from philosophy, but he had nevertheless argued for a more comprehensive freedom of expression and of the press than any other great thinker of the late seventeenth century. From the moment Spinoza published his *Tractatus Theologico-Politicus* in 1670 there was a continuous, unbroken dispute within the European Enlightenment as to whether the publication and general discussion of the fundamental philosophical, religious, moral, and political issues was in fact beneficial or actually harmful to the general good.

Thus, the single most important of the Dutch Cartesian refutations of the *Tractatus Theologico-Politicus* of the early 1670s, by the relatively liberal-minded Utrecht professor Regnerus van Mansvelt, not only insisted on the anonymous author's (i.e., Spinoza's) "utterly absurd confusion of God with his creation, and body with spirit," but fiercely attacked his conception of "libertas philosophandi." Despite the similarity of the wording, his adversary's conception of freedom of thought, he pointed out, was completely different from that advocated by the Cartesians, including himself. What the Dutch Cartesians meant by "libertas philosophandi" was broadly a freedom such as that legitimated by the States of Holland's decree on philosophy of 1656, namely, the freedom to philosophize about everything that does not impinge directly on the interpretation of Scripture and central issues of theology. What his adversary meant by the term, however, was scandalously different and broader: for he meant the right freely to overstep those limits and favor "errors of every kind, to defend and propagate a profane license." Indeed, in van Mansvelt's opinion, Spinoza expounds "principles such that no sooner would they be admitted than all peace of the republic would necessarily be overthrown."[19] Everywhere in the *Tractatus Theologico-Politicus* he detected signs of deliberate subversion: "[A]nd seeing, how greatly the much sounder theses of recent philosophers daily discovered, by a legitimate method, from the principles most happily discovered by the most noble René Descartes, were approved by the wisest, he [i.e., Spinoza] substituted [for these] his most inept and most absurd chimaera which are completely alien to all truth and piety."[20]

Similarly the best known, and longest remembered, among the early German refutations of the *Tractatus Theologico-Politicus* was that published at Jena, with a preface dated April 1674, by Johann Musaeus, a ninety-six page tract, dedicated to Duke Johann Friedrich of Braunschweig-Lunenburg, entitled *Tractatus Theologico-Politicus ... Ad veritatis lancem examinatus.* It was an academic dissertation directing much of its attack precisely against Spinoza's freedom of thought and expression. Musaeus' tract stands out indeed for the vivid way in which it alerts readers to the sweeping cultural, social, and intellectual implications of Spinoza's "freedom to philosophize." A declared defender of ecclesiastical authority and the princely court system of the time in Germany, Musaeus, citing numerous lengthy quotations from Spinoza's text, held that the *Tractatus* sought to replace Christianity with a comprehensive *Naturalismus* that denied the possibility of miracles and everything supernatural,[21] while at the same time being "second to none" in advocating a wide-ranging, pernicious toleration, like that, Musaeus added, to be found in Amsterdam. Spinoza's freedom of thought, he complained, is one that would legitimize all strands of opinion and, therefore, one that removes all barriers presently enforced in the German states against wholly unacceptable theological positions, such as those of Socinianism and other forms of anti-Trinitarianism.

The *Tractatus*, in effect, by making the public the arbiter of everything, would lead to the complete destruction of ecclesiastical authority. What the author really means by "*libertas philosophandi*," contended Musaeus, is the right of every individual to investigate every aspect of truth and to have his own opinion about the state, religion, and morality, making the laws of nature the sole and exclusive criterion of what is true.[22] Natural law in the hands of Spinoza, he warned, was reduced to mere appetite and the striving for power and self-expression of each individual. Scripture, Musaeus held, does not grant liberty of thought; nor, quite rightly, does the princely state.[23] The real role of the Christian state, insisted Musaeus, was by no means "freedom" as maintained by Spinoza, a "homo fanaticus" and someone alien to all religion, but rather to shepherd men either by fear of penalties or by exhortation and admonitions and other suitable means "ad agnitionem religionis verae, et ad virtutem inducere" (to acknowledge the true religion and to show the path to virtue). Nothing could be more apt to disrupt the peace of the state and tranquility of society, Musaeus contended, than the freedom of religion and of thought and opinion advocated by Spinoza.

Spinoza argued for freedom of expression, and especially of the press, as a principle beneficial to society because he thought it would minimize the restrictions on the power of reason to work on opinion and sway men's minds. The removal of such restrictions was also the goal in the early 1770s of Diderot and d'Holbach and of such writers as

Naigeon, Raynal, Deleyre, and others of their circle whom they enlisted to collaborate in the production of the stream of clandestine books that appeared in the wake of d'Holbach's *Système de la nature* in 1770 and that had such a traumatic effect in Europe in the years shortly before the outbreak of the American Revolution. These are works that we know had a considerable impact right across Europe. Indeed, it was the goal, as can be seen from the text of his decree, behind the free press policy of the notorious Danish chief minister Johann Friedrich Struensee (1737–1772), who was overthrown in 1771 and executed after hideous mutilation in 1772.

The kingdom of Denmark-Norway was the first state in the history of the world to proclaim full freedom of the press and to declare it to be a public benefit. The German text of Struensee's decree, issued in Copenhagen via a "cabinet order" dated September 4, 1770, makes it quite clear that the purpose of the removal of all censorship in Denmark-Norway was to further the enlightenment of the people and help remove all prejudices and errors from the people's minds.

11

Wir sind des völligen Dafürhaltens, dass es der unparteiischen Untersuchung der Wahrheiten ebenso nachtheilig, als der Entdeckung verjährter Irrthümer und Vorurtheile hinderlich ist, wenn redlich gesinnte, um allgemeine Wohl und wahre Beste ihrer Mitbürger besorgte Patrioten, durch Befehle und vorgefasste Meinungen abgeschreckt und behindert werden, nach Einsicht, Gewissen und Überzeugung frey zu schreiben, Missbräuche anzugreifen und Vorurtheile aufzudecken. So haben Wir nach reiflicher Überlegung beschlossen, in Unsern Reichen und Landen eine uneingeschränkte Freyheit der Presse solchergestalt zu gestatten, dass von nun an Niemand schuldig und verbunden seyn soll, seiner Bücher und Schriften, die er dem Drucke übergeben will, der bishero verordnet gewesenen Censur zu unterwerfen.[24]

This decree, needless to say, caused quite a sensation, and by no means only in Denmark-Norway. As the news of this unprecedented development spread across Europe, Voltaire was among those who responded enthusiastically, penning an *Épitre à sa majesté le Roi de Danemarc, sur la Liberté de la Presse accordée dans ses États*, which was immediately printed in both French and Danish versions in Copenhagen.[25] Unaware that it was not the king himself but rather a hitherto unknown doctor from Altona who had rapidly risen to supreme power in Denmark (while facing fierce opposition from much of the court) who was the true author of the decree, Voltaire praised the mentally unstable monarch to the skies even including the line: "je me jette à tes pieds, au nom du genre humain" (I throw myself at your feet, in the name of the human race), which also appeared in the published Danish version of Voltaire's text.[26]

Within the kingdom of Denmark-Norway, the immediate consequence of Struensee's decree instituting freedom of the press was an avalanche of publications of a sort that had not been allowed before. Struensee and his colleagues had intended the appearance of tracts advocating new approaches to government and taxation, as well as pleas for more religious toleration and expression of a variety of religious points of views, but there was also a torrent of complaint about the state of Denmark and, especially, a wave of vehement press attacks on Struensee himself and his actions and ideas.

Yet we should not be surprised by the angry reaction. Struensee's press law and the stated principles behind it were bound to transform Danish and Norwegian society fundamentally. Hence the majority of the tracts published in response to the new law, inspired by piety, tradition, and conservative values, were scathing about Struensee, press freedom, and the spread of radical intellectual influence in Danish society more generally. There was talk that the Danes were lost in a madhouse garden of ideas "from which no one could find the exit."[27] One contribution colorfully protested against the vast number of publications proliferating since the introduction of "freedom of the press," conjuring up the nightmarish vision of an immense square crammed with a vast and stinking heap of writings on every imaginable topic, financial writings, "project writings" and also "Machiavellian, Spinozistic writings" of which there were a great many and from which the stink was allegedly "so dreadful" that the author could not bear it.[28] *Ole Smedesvends Begraedelse over Rissengrød* (Ole Smedesvends Complaint over Rice Porridge) protested about the "Dutch Jew who was supposed to be learned but wanted people to believe that the world had made itself," which was as much a lie as if the tract's author had tried to make people believe that his doors could lock themselves: "This fellow was called Spinach or Spinos."[29] The tract also vehemently complained about the "French fool" called La Mettrie.

It turned out that connecting Struensee with Spinozistic influence amounted to something more than mere calumny. The fact that he had lived for many years in Altona and been a close friend of the Sephardic Jewish doctor Hartog Gerson, a known admirer of Spinoza, was not of itself proof of "Spinozism." Though very little survives from Struensee's own pen, there is some rather more solid evidence. A German preacher, Balthasar Münter, was assigned in 1772 the care of Struensee's soul after his arrest and imprisonment by conspirators among the court aristocracy instigated by the queen-mother. After their first interview Münter recorded that Struensee confided to him that he was "no Christian" during the time (1770–1771) that he held supreme power in Denmark-Norway (though he had become one since) and that he had never been able to convince himself that "man consists of two substances" or that there is immortality of the soul. Rather, Struensee had told him that he had "considered himself and all men to be pure machines" and that after death nothing survives. "He had not taken this hypothesis from La Mettrie," his confessor was assured, "whom he had never read," but rather had worked it out for himself.[30] He had totally rejected the possibility of miracles, but was specifically a Spinozist, and not a follower of La Mettrie: he also fervently believed in the reality of morality, albeit this was something existing solely in relations between people, that is, as something that exists "nur insofern sie für die Gesellschaft Folgen hätten" (solely insofar as it has consequences for society).[31]

Struensee, according to Münter, made no mention of Spinoza while in prison; nor did his confessor. But it emerged not only that he was well acquainted with Voltaire, Bonnet, Rousseau, and Reimarus but also that a text which had particularly impressed him and helped shape his radical opinions was Boulanger's *Antiquité dévoilée*.[32] Struensee also confided to Münter, an "enlightened" Lutheran (in Münter's own words) who highly valued Newton's views on religion and miracles as well as the learning of Boerhaave, Stahl, Haller, and Hoffmann, that during his visit to Paris, in the entourage of the king, Struensee had met and conversed with d'Alembert and discussed his views about religion with him. Struensee's

13

admission concerning Boulanger's *Antiquité dévoilée* is interesting, for it was one of the very first radical works to politicize the radical project and broaden the radical Enlightenment's attack into a general campaign for the reform of society and institutions.

Struensee was thoroughly decried by the very Danish press that he himself had liberated, but not all the Danish tracts that followed on the decree of 1770 rejected radical opinions. One that noted the impact of "philosophy" on the Danish capital in a somewhat more positive fashion was *En Grønlaendes Beskrivelse over Kiøbenhavn* (A Greenlander's Description of Copenhagen), which stands out for the remarkable mildness of its condemnation of those persons in Copenhagen who had "torn themselves from and denied all religion" and believed the world has existed as it is since all eternity. These people, the tract states, "take as their model a Dutch Jew by the name of Spinoza who in a thick, tedious book of metaphysical Latin tried to prove that all of nature is only one substance and that all Nature's parts are only just so many modifications of it, so that all that one sees in the whole of nature, was equally as divine, as royal, as grand, so that the writer and his pen were equally important, both alike modifications of nature's whole."[33] Yet while seemingly deriding this strange doctrine, this pamphlet also noted, with remarkable honesty, that while these Danish disciples of Spinoza recognized no sin or any punishment for sin, they nevertheless sometimes "live more virtuously and show more charity than the rest [of society] who pretend to follow and be loyal to their heaven-sent book [the Bible], which is something [i.e., their good morality] which these followers have in common with their originator [i.e., Spinoza]."

Liberty of the press, as Claude-Adrien Helvétius repeated his view of the matter and that of his allies in his posthumously published *De l'homme* of 1772, needed to be viewed as a tool with which society could discover moral and political as well as scientific truth by testing propositions in the proving ground of public discussion and debate. It may often not be in the interest of individuals or of particular interest groups that the truth be openly told in this way; but, according to Helvétius, it is always in the interest of society.[34] Doubtless freedom of the press will stimulate the circulation of all kinds of bizarre and ridiculous notions, but what does that matter, argued Helvétius, rather optimistically?

Block-headed notions, no sooner uttered, will be destroyed by reason and will not harm society. In short, for Helvétius, "la verité n'a pour ennemis que les ennemis même du bien public" (truth's only enemies are the very enemies of the general good).[35]

In the social, moral, and political revolution envisaged by the radical philosophes,[36] it was necessary to proclaim and promote freedom of expression and publication, what d'Holbach called "la liberté dans les écrits" (freedom in writings). In the manner of Helvétius, Struensee, and Spinoza earlier, he argued that the truth always gains from being publicly discussed, and it is truth, as he saw it, that would change the world. Only lies and impostures suffer, he was certain, from the risk of being publicly exposed. D'Holbach agreed that it could be extremely distressing for particular individuals wherever an unlimited right of publication enables the malicious to damage those they detest with calumnies motivated by hatred and envy. But an unlimited right to publish is nevertheless, he insisted, the best and most constructive thing for society as a whole, adding (rather too optimistically) that "tout auteur d'un ouvrage injuste ne tarde pas à être châtié" (any author of an unjust work is punished before long).[37] The indignation of the public, he expected, would revenge all unjustified insult and, if it failed to do so, then it was still better to suffer that inconvenience than to limit in any way the freedom of the citizenry to write about and discuss "des objets importans à leur felicité" (items important to its happiness).[38]

15

Notes

1. Charles Bonnet, *Mémoires autobiographiques*, ed. Raymond Savioz (Paris: J. Vrin, 1948), 213.

2. Ibid., 214.

3. Frederick the Great, "A Critical Examination of the *System of Nature*," in the *Posthumous Works of Frederic II, King of Prussia*, trans. Thomas Holcroft (London, 1789), vol. 5, 147–75, here 165; Ch. Louis Richard, *La défense de la religion, de la morale* [...] *et de la société* (Paris, 1775), 211, 213–14, 222–23, 231; Roland Mortier, *Les combats des Lumières: Recueil d'études sur le dix-huitième siècle* (Ferney-Voltaire: Centre international du XIIIe siècle, 2000), 199.

4. Frederick the Great, *Examen de l'Essai sur les préjugés* ("Londres" [Berlin], 1770).

5. Robert Mauzi, *L'idée du Bonheur dans la littérature et la pensée françaises au XVIIIe siècle* (Paris : Librairie Armand Colin, 1960), 572.

6. Denis Diderot, *Pages inédites contre un tyran*, ed. Franco Venturi (n.p., 1937), 2.

7. Ibid., 8; Anthony Strugnell, *Diderot's Politics: A Study of the Evolution of Diderot's Political Thought after the Encyclopédie* (The Hague: M. Nijhof, 1973), 130–34.

8. Diderot, *Pages inédites*, 23.

9. Ibid.; Denis Diderot, *Réfutation du livre 'De l'homme' d'Helvétius*, 381, 394, 412, and *Lettre apologétique de l'Abbé Raynal à Monsieur Grimm*, 150–51, in *Textes politiques*, ed. Yves Benot (Paris: Editions Sociales, 1960).

10. Carlantonio Pilati, *Lettere di un viaggiatore filosofo: Germania, Austria, Svizzera, 1774* (Bergamo: Pierluigi Lubrina editore, 1990), 70–71.

11. [Jacques-André Naigeon?], *Discours préliminaire* (1770), appendix to Jeroom Vercruysse, *Bicentenaire du Système de la nature, textes holbachiens peu connus* (Paris: Lettres modernes, 1970), 39–56, here 51.

12. Ibid., 47, 51.

13. Jean-Antoine-Nicolas de Caritat, marquis de Condorcet, *Esquisse d'un tableau historique des progrès de l'esprit humain* (Paris, Year III [1795]), 268–69.

14. Ibid., 203–205.

15. Voltaire, *Correspondence and Related Documents*, ed. Theodore Besterman (Geneva: Institut et Musée Voltaire, 1968–77), vol. 36, 354; Mortier, *Les combats des Lumières*, 199.

16. Roland Mortier, *Le coeur et la raison: Recueil d'études sur le dix-huitième siècle* (Oxford: Voltaire Foundation, 1990), 98.

17. Voltaire, *Correspondence*, vol. 37, 216; Mortier, *Les combats des Lumières*, 202–203.

18. Voltaire, *Correspondence*, vol. 37, 208.

19. Regnerus van Mansvelt, *Adversus anonymum Theologico-Politicum* (Amsterdam, 1674), 4.

20. Ibid.

21. Johann Musaeus, *Tractatus Theologico-Politicus* [...] *Ad veritatis lancem examinatus* (Jena, 1674).

22. Ibid., 5.

23. Ibid., 27.

24. "We are entirely of the opinion that it is as detrimental to the impartial investigation of truths, as it is obstructive to the disclosure of entrenched errors and prejudices, if upright patriots, concerned for the common good and the true best interest of their fellow citizens, are deterred and hindered by ordinances and preconceived opinions from freely writing in accordance with their insight, conscience and conviction, and from attacking abuse and unmasking prejudice. We have therefore decided, after careful consideration, to permit unlimited freedom of the press in Our realms and territories in such a way that, from now on, no one shall be obligated or required to submit books and writings that he wishes to send to press to the hitherto decreed censorship." Stefan Winkle, *Struensee und die Publizistik* (Hamburg: Christians, 1982), 81–82.

25. Edvard Holm, *Nogle Hovedtræk af Trykkefrihedstidens historie, 1770–1773* (Copenhagen: J.H. Schultz, 1885), 27.

26. Winkle, *Struensee und die Publizistik*, 82.

27. See the collection of ephemera in the Royal Library, Copenhagen, entitled *Luxdorphs Samling af Trykke-frihedens Skrifter*, vols. 14–15: *Anekdoten eines reisenden Russsen*, A3v.

28. Ibid., vol. 15, no. 6, 14.

29. Ibid., vol. 15, no. 9, 7; John Christian Laursen, "Spinoza in Denmark and the Fall of Struensee, 1770–1772," *Journal of the History of Ideas* 61 (2000): 189–202, here 198. See also the essay in this volume by John Christian Laursen.

30. Balthasar Münter, *Bekehrungsgeschichte des vormaligen Grafen und Königlichen Dänischen Geheimen Cabinetsministers Johann Friedrich Struensee* (Copenhagen, 1772), 10.

31. Ibid.

32. Ibid., 132–33.

33. *Luxdorphs Samling af Trykke-frihedens Skrifter*, vol. 15: *En Grønlaendes Beskrivelse over Kiøbenhavn*, 5.

34. Claude-Adrien Helvétius, *De l'homme : De ses facultés intellectuelles et de son éducation* (1773; repr. Paris: Fayard, 1989), vol. 2, 797–99, 807.

35. Ibid., 799.

36. Paul Henri Thiry, baron d'Holbach, *La politique naturelle, ou discours sur les vrais principes du gouvernement* (1773; repr. Paris, 1998), 288–89.

37. Ibid., 291.

38. Ibid.

In Praise of Moderate Enlightenment: A Taxonomy of Early Modern Arguments in Favor of Freedom of Expression

TO PROCLAIM THAT FREEDOM OF SPEECH, FREEDOM OF THE press, or freedom of expression were self-evident fruits of the Enlightenment would add little to our understanding of the genesis of liberal values or the nature of the eighteenth-century "debate" about them. It would be even less helpful to ascribe freedom of expression to any single manifestation of the Enlightenment, whether Lockean, Kantian, Christian, moderate, radical, cosmopolitan, national (English, French, Dutch, Danish, German, or Spanish), Christian (Catholic or Protestant), or any other variety. Rather than discuss the freedom of expression in relation to the "Enlightenment," I will outline the range of arguments, extant in the eighteenth century, which supported that freedom. Hence my title, "A taxonomy of early modern arguments in favor of freedom of expression." The classification is based on a re-examination of seventeenth- and eighteenth-century treatises on freedom of expression published in Britain (mostly in England) and the Dutch Republic, countries where ample reflection on the issue was allowed to take place. In order to categorize the various arguments I have focused on similarities between these two national contexts rather than on their differences. I have given preference to the less well-known philosophers, writers, journalists, and publishers—those socially active individuals who popularized abstract ideas by adapting them to local situations and traditions. They were important agents of change, and as such they probably exerted greater influence in spreading ideas about freedom of expression than the more well-known philosophers who figure in overviews of the subject.

Most of the treatises discussed in the following, and most of the arguments found in them, concern both speech and the press. Writers did not usually discuss freedom of speech as a separate topic, and in any case the kinds of arguments they used in a defense of print were similar to those made in favor of freedom of speech. For example, William Bollan's *The freedom of speech and writing upon public affairs, considered* (1766) took it for granted that the one referred to the other. Likewise, commentators seldom distinguished between defamatory statements that were spoken (slander) and those that were published (libel). Eighteenth-century writers often discussed freedom of the stage, or the freedom of theatrical performance, as well as the freedom to publish plays—which is another way of saying that they found freedom of speech important. Freedom of expression covers both speech and writing and is therefore in many cases the more appropriate term to use in the context of seventeenth- and eighteenth-century debates.

The debates on freedom of expression, as reflected in the essays, pamphlets, and books, went through three phases. The first phase began in the sixteenth century and ended around the time of the Glorious Revolution (1688) in England. It encompasses such thinkers as the Dutch humanist playwright, engraver, and pedagogue Dirk Volckertsz Coornhert (1522–1590) and the English poet John Milton (1608–1674). During this phase, freedom of expression was treated primarily as an aspect of a wider issue, that of *religious toleration*. The second stage involved reflection on the idea of *preventive censorship* or "prior restraint," the policy of preventing books from being published, as opposed to repressive censorship, which proscribed books only after publication. The debate on such issues obviously has a bearing on freedom of speech, which is particularly difficult to curb beforehand. Discussions on prior restraint took place in both countries, although in England the system of preventive censorship had been abolished at the end of the seventeenth century, while the Dutch Republic had never had such a system. The third phase was mostly concerned with affirming the *rights of man*. No less important in this later period were discussions of proper social codes—in particular polite conduct that emphasized moderation and sincerity—and therefore promoted a careful balance between self-censorship and forthrightness, over fanaticism and hypocrisy, the latter leading to such extremes as the freedom to insult on the one hand and dissimulation in speech and writing on the other. In the following, I shall refer to this chronology in passing.

The Dutch and British source material I have examined suggests at least sixteen categories of arguments in favor of freedom of expression:[1] (1) normative texts; (2) religion; (3) culture; (4) education; (5) nationhood; (6) eschatology; (7) human nature or anthropology; (8) utility; (9) trade and commerce; (10) politics; (11) natural law or human rights; (12) security; (13) history; (14) society; (15) criminal law; (16) constitutional law. The following account is structured according to these categories. To keep the number of references to source material at a manageable level, I have selected a very limited number of seventeenth- and eighteenth-century treatises, which I believe are representative.[2]   21

1. Normative texts

> *Argument:* To speak candidly is an oratorical and ethical requirement adduced in the classical texts of Greek and Roman antiquity. Authoritative sacred texts, such as the Bible, command or justify the pursuit of truth.

John Milton's *Areopagitica* (1644), for all its reputation, is limited in scope. It develops an argument against preventive censorship, rather than making a plea for freedom of the press, and it is concerned mainly with religious liberties, which it restricts to Protestant believers. But it does adduce some of the arguments that continued to be put forward in the eighteenth century. One of these is the "argument from normative texts." Milton was well versed in the classical rhetorical tradition. The title of his tract refers to the Areopagus, the legislative body in ancient Athens, and he would have been familiar with what in Greek oratory appears as "fearless speaking." Cicero, Quintilian, and Tacitus referred to the concept, which duly cropped up in sixteenth-century rhetorical theory as a figure of speech.[3] To speak candidly (the rhetorical figure of permission or *parrhesia*) was regarded as both an oratorical and an ethical requirement. Interestingly, the concept was taken up by continental Protestant theologians such as Zacharias Ursinus (1534–1583), whose preface to the Heidelberg Catechism of 1563 (first English translation, 1587) referred to liberty of speech as a virtue. One of the Catechism's comments on the ninth commandment urged believers to "love the truth, speak it uprightly and confess it."[4] Such texts were still read by large numbers of people in the eighteenth century; in the Dutch Republic, sermons on the Catechism were mandatory on Sunday afternoons.

It is doubtful that many sixteenth-century people saw the Calvinist catechism as an excuse to speak freely. This hesitation was partly due to the traditional Pauline definition of "freedom": The human conscience is liberated only when it has been freed by the grace of God and secured by his Word. Speaking truth is thus speaking Christian truth or, in this case, the Reformed rather than the Catholic or Lutheran truth. Only those truths may be reproduced in public that have the power to liberate spiritually. Not surprisingly, in the Dutch Republic the argument from Christian freedom justified calls for censorship until at least 1750.[5] On the other hand, we should not underestimate the importance of such normative texts to eighteenth-century minds. At the very least, use of this argument shows a recognition that the idea of freedom of expression has origins that are in part classical and/or Christian. One insightful eighteenth-century account of freedom of expression in the English-speaking world is the cluttered and inelegant piece of writing already mentioned above, *The freedom of speech and writing upon public affairs, considered.*[6] The author of this 160-page essay, published anonymously in 1766, was William Bollan (1710?–1776), an English lawyer who acted as agent for the Massachusetts colony in London.[7] In what amounts to a well-informed legal history, based on a vast array of British and continental legal historians and jurists, Bollan elaborated on such topics as Roman imperial law, the use of torture, the history of the Star Chamber, the common law, and trial by jury. Truth figures prominently in Bollan's arguments in favor of a free press. To be able to ascertain the truth is "the honour and happiness of man," he states. Truth is "the mother of justice"; truth comes from God, regardless of who utters it. It is in this context that Bollan appeals to the Bible, including Proverbs 16:6, "By mercy and truth iniquity is purged."[8]

2. Religion

Argument: The sixteenth-century Reformation has demonstrated that the free circulation of ideas leads to the finding of (Protestant) truth and the refutation of (Roman Catholic) error.

D.V. Coornhert defended this argument in his *Synod, or on the freedom of conscience* (1582), a hypothetical account of a discussion in Ciceronian vein held at the fictional town of Vryburch ("Freeburg") among representatives of various religious groups; a certain "Gamaliel" speaks for Coornhert himself. The fifteenth session of the synod debated "the making, publishing, printing, selling, having, and reading of writings and books." People—whether they be learned or unlearned, clergymen or citizens—should be free to contribute whatever will support the "conversion of the church" and thus bring about a Reformation.[9] The point was also made by John Milton, who provided a brief historical outline of censorship, the main thrust of which is that licensing has no classical or ancestral precedent but rather is a Roman Catholic invention, the fruit of the "the most Antichristian Council, and the most tyrannous Inquisition that ever inquir'd."[10] The claim that freedom of expression was something particularly Protestant was immensely popular in the eighteenth century. The Scottish poet James Thomson (1700–1748), who several years earlier had published a vast poem on "Liberty," responded to the Stage or Theatrical Licensing Act of 1737 in an anonymous preface to a cheap edition of *Areopagitica*. A "free Protestant country, without the liberty of the Press, is a contradiction in terms," he said; "it is free slavery, or inchained [sic] liberty."[11]

3. Culture

Argument: Censorship induces cultural stagnation. Therefore, freedom of expression is a means of combating ignorance and increasing knowledge and learning; freedom of inquiry is essential to the progress of the human race.

Milton, again, had already claimed that the reading of books is necessary to man. His principal contention was that the free circulation of ideas leads to the finding of truth and the refutation of error. We need continual debate, i.e., speaking and writing ("much arguing, much writing, many opinions") since "our faith and knowledge thrives by exercise."[12] Later in the seventeenth century, two pamphlets by the radical Whig deist Charles Blount (1654–1693) elaborated at length on this argument. Blount's *A just vindication of learning, and of the liberty of the press* (1679), written against the licensing act of 1662, was largely an adaptation of the main argument in Milton's *Areopagitica*.[13] Blount similarly emphasized the importance of the press as a means of combating ignorance. The argument often crops up in the second phase of the debates on freedom of expression, in the context of early eighteenth-century party politics. A pamphlet, much steeped in irony, called *The thoughts of a Tory author, concerning the press* (1712), has been attributed to the Whig writer Joseph Addison (1672–1719). Addison was concerned to defend the anonymity of political writers—precisely the principle that made possible the patronage of party pamphleteers. Apart from ruining the publishing business, outlawing anonymity would prevent good authors from publishing books, since for various reasons many would be unwilling to have their names mentioned.[14]

24

A cultured or civilized people is an "enlightened" people. Right at the end of the eighteenth century, the Baptist minister and social reformer Robert Hall (1764–1831) mentioned several issues relating to freedom of expression, including public debate, in *An apology for the freedom of the press, and for general liberty* (1793).[15] His main point was that "the most capital advantage an enlightened people can enjoy is the liberty of discussing every subject which can fall within the compass of the human mind; while this remains, freedom will flourish." The "right of unlimited enquiry" guarantees general human progress; restraints have never contributed to the improvement of the arts and sciences. "Unlimited enquiry" applies especially to religion. One need think only of Luther, who unleashed a reformation, or writers such as Locke, Butler, and Clarke, who far surpass the ancient apologists in "precision" and "method of reasoning." They reflect the "superior spirit of enquiry by which modern times are distinguished."[16] Identifying culture with

Protestant culture as well as with "enlightened" culture was common in both Britain and the Netherlands.

4. Education

> *Argument:* People who read freely will be disciplined in such a way that in due course they will begin to subscribe to rationality and freedom as a matter of course.

This argument is often found in juxtaposition with the previous one, the argument from culture. In the Dutch Republic, an interesting account surfaced in the early 1780s in a private association or society at Haarlem called "Diligence, the Mother of Sciences." This was apparently the only association in the Netherlands to successfully organize an essay competition on press freedom.[17] Established in December 1779, the Haarlem society was a rather minor Mennonite affair; and it awarded the first prize to a certain Jan Brouwer (dates unknown), a Mennonite theology student. The question posed by the society ran as follows: "Is freedom of the press a necessary requirement for maintaining the freedom and independence of a commonwealth? And if so, which are the advantages ensuing therefrom?" Brouwer argued that the practical disadvantages of press freedom are not outweighed by the principle on which it is based, which is the freedom of citizens. If a publication oversteps the mark, it should be taken to court. Brouwer also made the point that "civilization" will act as a safety net. Libelous writings will not influence the people, since the common crowd can hardly read, and educated persons will never let themselves be influenced by despicable books. The advantages of press freedom are, on the other hand, perfectly evident. It allows both religious and political truth to prevail in the face of irreligious skeptics, on the one hand, and cowardly flatterers, hired hacks, hypocritical scoundrels and bribed traitors, on the other. The education of citizens, then, was called for.

The gist of Brouwer's apology for press freedom is comparable to that of the so-called Leiden Draft (*Leids Ontwerp*), a political blueprint drawn up in October 1785 at a provincial gathering of the armed corps of Holland—that is, at the height of the Dutch revolution. The draft ended with a number of articles, two of which concerned the "Right of

the People in Respect of Petitions."[18] These articles stated that the right
to submit petitions to the government was constitutional—the Republic
itself owed its existence to the violation by Spain of the right to submit
petitions.[19] Since the people could only make proper use of this right if
they were "enlightened and educated," and since enlightenment (in the
sense of progress in knowledge) and education depended on the liberty
to speak and write, and vice versa, it stood to reason that freedom of the
press must be "inviolably maintained."

5. Nationhood

> *Argument*: The habit of searching out the truth is particularly suited
> to England and the English (or the Netherlands and the Dutch).
> Freedom of the press is a Protestant, British liberty (or a Protestant,
> Dutch one).

Once again, Milton takes pride of place. He claimed that the habit of
searching out truth is particularly suited to England and the English,
"a Nation not slow and dull, but of a quick, ingenious, and piercing
spirit." England's learning is as ancient as it is eminent; after all, Py-
thagorean and Persian wisdom originated here.[20] This Renaissance
myth of an English *prisca scientia* lost its appeal, of course, but nationalist
sentiment ran high in the eighteenth century. Addison later pointed out
that censorship merely favored the dominant party, which smacked of
"*French* Politicks"; in France nothing was printed "but what the Court
pleases." Moreover, freedom of the press is a British liberty, one that the
"*British* Nation," "a Rich, Wise, and Great People," ought to preserve.
The printing trade also contributes to "Publick Welfare," by spreading
knowledge of "Learning, Arts, Religion, & good Manners."[21]

  In the Dutch Republic, patriotic emotions often ran high in the
second half of the eighteenth century. In the 1780s a poetry society
in Leiden organized a competition for the best poem on press freedom.
One participant, known only from his name, Jacob van Dijk, suggested,
in verse, that, above all other peoples, the Dutch should be the ones to
favor press freedom. Had not Laurens Janszoon Coster of Haarlem (ca.
1370–ca. 1440) invented the printing press, long before the German,
Johann Gutenberg of Mainz?[22]

6. Eschatology

Argument: Religious truth will inevitably become public under the guiding hand of God. The dynamics of public debate will through persuasion lead to the public affirmation of truth.

Milton's view of press freedom is in part an eschatological vision. He intimates that the time is now ripe for truth to be revealed. God chose England as the means through which the reformation of the church would be proclaimed to the whole of Europe. He has now decreed "some new and great period in his Church," and the signs of the times suggest that it will begin in England. As Milton phrased it in a famous passage, "What does he then but reveal Himself to his servants, and as his manner is, first to his English-men"?[23] In the eighteenth century the argument from eschatology was often implicit in the so-called postmillennial perspective on the story of mankind, one that was quite widespread at the time, namely, that Christ would return after a Golden Age of peace and prosperity, characterized by a culture of civilized or "enlightened" freedom.

27

7. Human nature (anthropology)

Argument: Man is accountable only to God for making use of his rational faculties, and consequently he must be free to do so. God created man in such a way as to put his mind beyond the reach of others, so that restraint cannot serve any moral good; evidence compels assent to truth, which means that evidence must be publicly accessible.

We also find this argument, which stems from a deep religious conviction, in Milton's *Areopagitica*. Man is meant to learn, to gather knowledge, because God created him with the ability to reason. Admittedly, books can be dangerous, but, on the other hand, "hee who destroyes a good Booke, kills reason it selfe, kills the image of God." Man has been endowed with a free will, of which he should make good use. The ideas that come into his mind cause no damage by themselves; the potential harm lies in what man does with the knowledge he gains.[24] The freedom to learn, to eat liberally from the tree of knowledge, is a theme on which

Milton elaborated at greater length in *Paradise Lost*, the epic poem he began writing a decade after the publication of *Areopagitica*.[25]

In 1710 the deist Matthew Tindal (1655–1733) experienced the effects of repressive censorship when his *Defence of the rights of the Christian Church* was burnt by order of the House of Commons. He had earlier written *Reasons against restraining the press* (1704) in response to attempts to revive the licensing law.[26] Like Milton, Tindal pointed out that men should be allowed to make use of their rational faculty, since they are accountable to God for doing so.

The anonymous *Independant Briton* (1742) addressed a whole range of political issues, including freedoms of the press and the stage. The writer pleaded for freedom of both speech and press; unlike liberties attending property, moreover, he believed this freedom to apply to all men without exception. The Briton's premise was a negative one: "no *good Government* can be in Danger from any *Writings* whatsoever." He adds to this the notion that God created man in such a way as to put his thoughts beyond the reach of others, and that restraints on any expression of those thoughts cannot serve a moral good.[27]

28

8. Utility

Argument: Censorship will not prevent the circulation of scandalous books. In fact, it may even be counterproductive because it will only urge people to read what they are apparently not supposed to read. Also, it is impossible to adequately define the terms of preventive censorship.

That censorship will not prevent scandalous, seditious, or libelous books from being published is an argument that may be found already in both Coornhert and Milton. Samuel Johnson was one eighteenth-century thinker who firmly disagreed with this position:

> [I]f every murmerer at government may diffuse discontent, there can be no peace; and if every sceptick in theology may teach his follies, there can be no religion. The remedy against these evils is to punish the authors; for it is yet allowed that every society may punish, though not prevent, the publication of opinions, which that society shall think pernicious: but

this punishment, though it may crush the author, promotes the book; and it seems not more reasonable to leave the right of printing unrestrained, because writers may be afterwards censured, than it would be to sleep with doors unbolted, because by our laws we can hang a thief.[28]

Similar arguments could be heard in the Dutch Republic. Johann Friedrich Reitz (1695–1778), a German-born professor of rhetoric, held an academic address in 1751, at the end of his term as rector of Utrecht University.[29] *On the censors of books* suggested that official *censores librorum*, a commission of men from different orders in society and experienced in different kinds of disciplines, be appointed to approve or disapprove of works for publication.

The idea of preventive censorship had become popular in some government quarters in the Dutch Republic, so much so that a "plan" or draft concerning the issue was submitted by the Court of Holland to the States of Holland in 1769.[30] The plan was instigated by several orthodox Calvinist preachers involved in a controversy called the "Socratic War," a major pamphlet war sparked off by a Dutch translation of the novel *Bélisaire* by the French philosopher and Encyclopedist Jean François Marmontel (1723–1799). The main issue was the question whether heathens like Socrates could earn entrance to Paradise by living virtuously. In response to this intense public debate that touched on the authority of the Christian tradition, the plan envisaged the appointment of official censors and the imposition of severe penalties on transgressors (ranging from fines and enforced closure of bookshops to banishment).

Several Leiden booksellers chartered their colleague Élie Luzac (1721–1796), in his capacity as lawyer, to write a celebrated rebuttal of the plan on their behalf.[31] Apart from being a well-known publisher, this third-generation Huguenot was a prolific and well-known writer on Dutch political issues. Luzac's *Memorandum* listed six objections to the plan, the sixth of which was that the law would not be effective because people simply cannot be prevented from reading.

9. Trade and commerce

Argument: A monopoly on print controlled by church or government leads to exorbitant prices and bad products.

The argument from utility was closely connected with arguments based on commerce. Luzac had pointed out, in his list of objections, that censorship would ruin the book trade. In Britain, John Locke had drawn up a similar list of the disadvantages of preventive censorship. His observations probably stem from 1694 or 1695, when the licensing act of 1662 was under reconsideration in Parliament.[32] Article 2 of the act outlawed all books "which may tend to the scandal of religion, or the church, or the government, or governors of the church, state, or of any corporation, or particular person." Locke pointed out, with due common sense, that the terms of the law were simply too general and too comprehensive. He also offered practical arguments. For instance, giving the stationers a monopoly would lead to exorbitant book prices, while hardly improving the quality of the product sold.

10. Politics

Argument: A free press guarantees that the pros and cons of an issue will be debated, thereby preventing arbitrary government and corruption. The actions of those who govern can thus be monitored by the governed, who must be able to express grievances or submit petitions to the government. Matters of public concern should, therefore, be freely discussed in public, not in the confines of a council of ministers.

Most of these notions are characteristic of classical republicanism, though formal defenses of press freedom are conspicuously absent from seventeenth-century Dutch republican writings. Spinoza is the exception.[33] This absence is not surprising, perhaps, since many republican authors were also members of the magistracy, and thus governors themselves.[34] Similarly, academic apologies for *libertas philosophandi* (the contemporary term for freedom of expression in word and writing) conspicuously failed explicitly to consider freedom of expression as a principle that also applied to politics.[35] In Britain, Daniel Defoe (1660–1731), a political propagandist for both Whigs and Tories, noted in his brief *Essay on the regulation of the press* (1704, written in prison after he was sentenced for writing a satire on High Church ecclesiastics) that a system of licensing or prior restraint, binding the press to one particular party, would thus bring about arbitrary government as well as foster corruption.[36] Defoe rejected licensing as a means of repressing licentiousness, but suggested that all religious and political issues on which people are not permitted to reflect must be mentioned explicitly in an act of law. Thus "all Men will know when they Transgress," and all who do so may duly be punished.

The political argument was most famously put forward in *Cato's letters*, a series of political commentaries published in the *London Journal* from 1720 to 1723. Written by two experienced political opinion-makers, Thomas Gordon (?–1750) and John Trenchard (1662–1723), the letters rapidly became an authoritative statement of classical republicanism, both in Great Britain and the American colonies (and to some extent also on the European continent).[37] The entire collection was published in four volumes in 1724, and had gone through at least six editions by 1755. Several of Cato's letters are devoted to freedom of expression.[38] They offered a "bold, systematic theory of intellectual and political liberty," providing free speech to everyone.[39] A letter dated February 4, 31 | 1720, for example, opens with the following unambiguous statement

> Without freedom of thought, there can be no such thing as wisdom; and no such thing as publick liberty, without freedom of speech: Which is the right of every man, as far as by it he does not hurt and control the right of another; and this is the only check which it ought to suffer, the only bounds which it ought to know.[40]

During the hectic 1780s the United Provinces experienced a de facto unlimited freedom of political expression, to the satisfaction of a handful of proto-revolutionary Frenchmen and to the general dismay of German commentators. Those who called for far-reaching political reforms during these years—the so-called Patriots, hence the term *Patriottentijd* or "the Time of the Patriots" in reference to this period—celebrated their freedom in a noisy cacophony of debates on the highly complicated and often parochial constitutional arrangements of the Dutch Republic. Discussions were initiated with a pamphlet of seventy-six pages addressed *To the people of the Netherlands*. This sensational indictment of the stadholder's power and influence began to circulate anonymously on September 26, 1781. It was considered so subversive that the

States of Holland immediately forbade both its sale and its possession, and promised a substantial amount of money to anyone who could reveal the writer's identity. More than a century later, the pamphlet was shown to have been written by Joan Derk van der Capellen tot den Pol (1741–1784), a baron from one of the eastern provinces who corresponded with some of the North American revolutionaries and held distinct ideas about representation in government. *To the people of the Netherlands* was mainly concerned to point out the way in which, throughout the history of the Republic, the stadholders of Orange had subordinated the interests of the Dutch people to their own dynastic gain and to the deceitful claims of England. Toward the end of the pamphlet the author linked classical republican doctrine with the freedom of expression. He exhorted the people of the Netherlands to

> take care of the liberty of the press, for that is the only support of your national liberty. If we have no liberty to speak freely to our fellow-citizens, or to give them timely advice, it will be very easy for our oppressors to act their sinister parts; and it is for that reason that those, who cannot bear to hear their conduct enquired into, are always exclaiming against the liberty of speech and of the press, and could wish that nothing was printed or sold without permission.[41]

While republican members of the magistracy like Lieven de Beaufort[42] had implicitly restricted freedom of expression to politicians, van der Cappellen considered press freedom both a precondition for public debate and open criticism and a democratic means of controlling political power. The pamphlet was reissued thrice in 1781, published again in 1784 and 1795, and translated into French, German, and English.

11. Natural law or human rights

> *Argument*: Man has the "right of unlimited enquiry," the right to speak freely in public, as long as he does not infringe upon the rights of his fellow man.

The argument was common. It surfaces, for example, in 1755 in an essay written by Thomas Hayter (1702–1762), bishop of Norwich (later of London) and a member of the heir-apparent's entourage at Leicester

House, the focus of government opposition led by the Prince of Wales.[43] He posed the question, "How far the Liberty of the Press is connected with the Liberty of the Subject?" Hayter defined liberty in general as "a Freedom from all but natural restraints," and social liberty as "a Freedom from all but legal Restraints." Liberty of speech and its complement, the liberty of the press, are natural rights, which men retain when they leave the state of nature and enter into society. On entering into society, however, men agreed to submit to certain restraints. Members of a polity have consented to the punishment, by the civil government, of "Blasphemy, Perjury and Treason" as the three main offenses against the commonwealth.[44]

In the Dutch Republic, one of the more critical periodicals, *The Thinker* (1764–1775), illustrates the role of "spectators" (the genre first developed in England by Addison and Steele) in disseminating ideas and initiating debates. Soon after its start in 1763, *The Thinker* published a translation from an English periodical, "On the freedom of thinking and writing on religious subjects"; an editor of the *Thinker* subsequently elaborated on it.[45] *The Thinker* posed the question, "whether it is in itself equitable, or possibly even advantageous to Society or Religion, to limit Freedom of the Press as little as possible?"[46] The author applied explicitly to the press the traditional argument from natural law, namely, that freedom of thought and the freedom to communicate ideas had not been renounced when mankind left the state of nature and entered into society.

Such theoretical natural rights were in due course set forth as constitutional human rights. Directly following the fall of the Dutch Republic in January 1795, a committee of four was appointed by the Provisional Representatives of the People of Holland to compose a declaration of human rights. The "Publication of the Rights of Man and of the Citizen," a Dutch version of the French declarations of 1789 and 1793, was formally acknowledged by the States General and almost all Provinces. It consisted of nineteen unnumbered statements. Freedom of expression was affirmed in the fourth statement: "Each person is therefore free to reveal his thoughts and sentiments to others, either through the press or by any other means."[47] On July 13, 1797, the National Assembly, following extensive deliberations, published the blueprint for a new constitution. It listed the rights of man and of the citizen in a prologue. Freedom of action was laid down in Article VI. One of the actions over which the citizen could dispose freely was "making known his thoughts and sentiments by word or writing, or by means of the press."[48] Freedom of expression would be included in all subsequent constitutions formally accepted by Dutch parliaments.

12. Security

> *Argument*: Publication of matters of national concern is necessary to prevent politicians and others from acting treacherously (i.e., to the disadvantage of the state).

Among others, Bishop Hayter pointed out that, without freedom of expression, "any Characters or Designs unfavorable to the Royal Family, or to Liberty, cannot be publickly Known, till it is too late to oppose them."[49] The argument is closely related to arguments 10 and 11, and is often found together with them.

13. History

> *Argument*: Preventive censorship is a legal measure contingent on historical circumstance. For the sake of political stability it is imperative that historical ("ancient") constitutional liberties be preserved. In addition, historical evidence shows that press freedom is not bad for society.

David Hume (1711–1776), who subscribed to the widespread prejudice that liberty of the press is "a peculiar Privilege of *Britain*," did not, when he addressed the issue explicitly, present a very powerful case for that freedom. Hume included an essay "Of the liberty of the press" in his *Essays, moral and political*, the first edition of which appeared in 1741.[50] Why, he asked, should "the unlimited Exercise of this Liberty" be considered advantageous? Hume referred to the popular notion of the ancient constitution, observing that there is "nothing of greater Importance in every State than the Preservation of the ancient Government, especially if it be a free one." The traditional liberties attendant on the ancient constitution of Britain should therefore be preserved. Hume further argued that freedom of the press had few inconveniences, relatively speaking. In contrast, he noted that oral communication—speech—is far more dangerous than communication through print: "A Man reads a Book or Pamphlet alone and coolly. There is none present from whom he can catch the Passion by Contagion." In any case, history ("the Experience of Mankind") shows that press freedom is not bad for society.[51]

14. Social peace

> *Argument*: A free press is a prudential measure in that it prevents people from being driven to extreme group behavior (rioting, rebellion).

Coornhert had opined in 1582: "What will be the effect on people's hearts of the new interdiction concerning a freedom [e.g., of religious expression] that has been pursued for so long and obtained at such high costs?" Surely this would lead to rebellion. It is politically wiser to allow people to hold their beliefs, since they will more readily support a regime that guarantees their freedom.[52] This argument from prudence was common in the seventeenth and eighteenth centuries. An example from Britain is the *Livery-man*. Freedom of speech and freedom of publication, it observes, will prevent people from becoming dispirited or being driven to extremities. The civil authorities will do best to exercise prudence and not react too quickly or too harshly to subdue intemperate conversations or immoderate publications. Libellers must be punished; but they should not be prevented from talking or publishing in the first place.[53]

35

15. Criminal law

> *Argument*: No publication should be prosecuted under criminal law unless its explicit purpose is to incite people to riot or commit any other violent act.

The argument is unique to England. It centers on the legal consequences of the distinction between civil libel and criminal or seditious libel. In the English common law tradition, civil libel was treated as a "tort," that is, as a private, wrongful act for which the injured party could seek remedy in a suit for damages.[54] Criminal or seditious libel was a public offense and, therefore, liable to punishment under the law. A much-debated issue concerned the admission of truth as a defense against a charge of criminal libel. Did defendants possess the right to prove truth in their defense? Criminal libel cases generally followed the rule bequeathed by the Star Chamber, which held that truth could not exonerate a libeler. The chief argument for *not* admitting truth as a defense was that a truthful defamation caused greater damage to public security than a false one.

The single most authoritative eighteenth-century statement on the concept of seditious libel can be found in the fourth volume (on "public wrongs") of the *Commentaries on the laws of England* by William Blackstone (1723–1780), the eighteenth-century scholar of common law. He treated libels together with breaches of the public peace, such as riotous assembly, unlawful hunting, the demolition of sluices, public brawls, forcible entry, and the spreading of false prophecy. In his view, it is irrelevant whether a libel is true or false, "since the provocation, and not the falsity, is the thing to be punished criminally." Blackstone rejected the idea of preventive censorship, but firmly supported the notion of seditious libel.[55]

In practice, the concept of seditious libel could be, and was, easily used as a political instrument to silence opposition. "Sedition" was a pliable concept, and judges could be, and were, influenced or bought. The *bête noire* of eighteenth-century pamphleteers who clamored for abolition of or restrictions to the concept of seditious libel was undoubtedly William Murray, 1st Earl of Mansfield (1705–1793). As chief justice, Mansfield was responsible for a classic formulation of the role of truth in cases of criminal libel, which he expressed in the case against William Shipley (1745–1826), the dean of St. Asaph, in 1784.[56] It is not in the province of a jury, he declared, to inquire or decide on the intent of a defendant, or whether the disputed publication is true, false, or malicious.

The schoolmaster James Burgh (1714–1775), who, as a Presbyterian and a Scot, had firsthand experience of religious and social exclusion in the London society in which he worked, produced perhaps the most penetrating piece of writing of these later years.[57] A prolific writer on radical politics, Burgh was a member of the "Honest Whigs," a club committed to Commonwealthman ideology that included critics of government, such as Richard Price, Joseph Priestley, and Benjamin Franklin. His influential *Political disquisitions* (1775) included a chapter on "the liberty of speech and writing."[58] He claimed exactly the opposite of Blackstone: "In a petition to parliament, a bill in chancery, and proceedings at law, libellous words are not punishable; because freedom of speech and writing are indispensably necessary to the carrying on of business."

If libel cases brought before the court during the 1770s had already aggravated the public's doubts about the liberty enjoyed by the British press, misgivings about the government's policy concerning the press began to be expressed with much greater frequency following the French Revolution. In a heady revolutionary atmosphere nourished by popular radicalism, militant debating clubs, "subversive" publications, antagonism with France, and rumors of Jacobin conspiracies, the British government clamped down on the press. Wherever the government could not obstruct communication, it used informers and spies to monitor it. Such repressive measures by the government did not represent a clear break with eighteenth-century political and legal tradition,[59] but they did constitute an obvious attack on the more libertarian interpretations of the freedom of the press that had become current by the 1780s and 1790s.

In May 1792, the Pitt ministry issued a proclamation against "wicked and seditious writings." It considered Thomas Paine's *Rights of Man* (1791-1792), a defense of the French Revolution against the attacks by Edmund Burke, to be the most offensive. Paine, who escaped to France, was charged with seditious libel for insulting the constitution and the royal family in the second part of his book. His case was pleaded by Thomas Erskine (1750-1823), a rhetorically gifted, ambitious, and expensive lawyer of Scottish descent. Erskine was a Whig, a friend of Charles Fox, and the attorney general to the Prince of Wales. On December 18, 1792, during the Paine trial, Erskine treated judge and jury to a speech in support of the liberty of the press. Written down by a shorthand writer, the address was soon widely available in print. Erskine's "celebrated speech"—a "sublime effort of the human genius," as an Edinburgh editor would have it—was wasted on both judge and jury. Paine was considered guilty as charged (a decision that boosted the sales of *Rights of Man*), while Erskine lost his position as attorney general. Defeated in the Paine trial, Erskine continued his campaign for a free press out of court. Addressing "a meeting of the Friends to the Liberty of the Press" at the Free-Mason's Tavern in London in 1792, he argued that "the liberty of discussing public subjects" belongs to the people. The society thereupon resolved unanimously:

> That the Liberty of the Press is a right inseparable from the Principles of a free Government, and essential to the security of the British constitution.

> That this liberty consists in the free discussion and examination of the principles of free government, and of all matters of public opinion.

> That no writing ought to be considered as a public libel, and made the subject of criminal prosecution, unless such writing shall appear to be published with a design to excite the People to resist the Civil Magistrate, or obstruct the execution of the existing laws.[60]

16. Constitutional law

Argument: Ministers are responsible for acts of government, while the king is immune. It is therefore permissible to openly criticize persons wielding political power.

Before 1813, this argument does not occur in the Netherlands, since there was no parliamentary constitutional monarchy before that date. A crucial figure in initiating the British debate was the London journalist and member of parliament John Wilkes (1725–1797). This charismatic if profligate personality, who drew substantial support from the lower middle classes, began in 1762 to use his periodical *North Briton* to attack the ministry of Lord Bute. Charged with seditious libel (and for obscenity for his *Essay on Woman*, a parody on Alexander Pope's *Essay on Man*), Wilkes was thrown into the Tower of London, but released after a week because of his immunity as a member of parliament.[61] The article in *North Briton* was condemned as libelous, and Wilkes, who in the meantime had left for France, was found guilty. Forced by his debts to return four years later, Wilkes served his sentence. He was by now a popular hero and was soon re-elected to the Commons; his subsequent expulsion in 1769 did not prevent him from becoming mayor of London and finally a member of parliament once again. Wilkes is generally credited with having widened the scope of press freedom during his erratic career in and outside the House of Commons, among other things by compelling parliament to allow the publication of its debates, or at least not to prosecute publishers for doing so. It was only in 1770 that the London press (including Wilkes himself) started reporting extensively and regularly on parliamentary debates, i.e., on political speech.[62]

The Wilkes affair is also interesting because it reveals the connection between press freedom and the principle of ministerial responsibility. Wilkes had the audacity to take that principle for granted by treating—in the infamous *North Briton*, no. 45, published on April 23, 1763—a speech by the king as a statement by his minister. The king, in this reasoning, is immune to criticism (Wilkes had accused the king of lying) because it is his minister who is responsible. Hence, it is wrong to regard comments on the administration as an attack on the throne: "otherwise, no act of a minister could ever be arraign'd," argued the *Monitor*, a contemporary periodical, "and no liberty of the press exist."[63]

Conclusion

A gamut of arguments was invoked over time in defense of freedom of expression. Many if not all of them are recognizable and familiar. The sixteen arguments presented above are interrelated in several ways, even interdependent. We could classify them further, for example, into normative, legal, utilitarian, and cultural groups. The normative group would include those arguments concerned with freedom of choice or freedom of the will and involve issues of anthropology and natural law or human rights (7, 11). Those derived from criminal and constitutional law belong to the legal group (15, 16). The utilitarian group encompasses the realms of education, utility, commerce, security, and social peace (4, 8, 9, 12, 14). Finally, the cultural group includes arguments from normative texts, religion, culture, nationhood, eschatology, politics, and history (1, 2, 3, 5, 6, 10, 13). Obviously, other classifications are possible.

How relevant is knowledge of this broad array of arguments for our understanding of the history of the freedom of expression? It is important, I think, to distinguish between the legal and constitutional aspects of that history, on the one hand, and the intellectual and cultural aspects, on the other. In regard to the former, one important outcome of eighteenth-century arguments was the increase in jurisdiction related to freedom of expression and its inclusion in legal codes and constitutions. The freedom to express oneself in speech or print, as well as the extent to which this freedom was limited in practice because of its inevitable conflicts with other freedoms or with the power claims of governments and rulers, became part of the way modern liberal societies organized and managed themselves. In regard to the latter, this enshrinement of the freedom of expression is a consequence of long-standing intellectual reflection and cultural practice. The eighteenth century stands out, not as marking the origin of liberty, but as a time in which freedom of expression was first subject to relatively widespread public debate. It cannot be said that many, even most, of the arguments listed above were characteristic of the eighteenth century—or, for that matter, the "Enlightenment" with which that century is associated. If we do wish to apply a label that would do most justice to the character of eighteenth-century debates, it would be that of a very "moderate" Enlightenment, one that found relatively broad support and was open to compromise and, therefore, made allowances for culture, religion and tradition.[64] Nor did the eighteenth century bring the subject to "closure." No authoritative thinker, whether Spinoza in the Netherlands or Paine in Britain, nor any legal code from France to the United States, has made the definitive statement. Freedom of expression cannot be absolute; liberal values are subject to discussion, and so they should be, since they are historically produced conventions rather than universal moral or rational principles that, whether we like it or not, are self-evident only to those who propound them.[65] The debate, then, is open.[66]

Notes

1. In the following "man" is used as a synonym for "human being": I have retained the former mainly for reasons of translation.

2. A comprehensive overview of British and American texts may be found in Ralph E. McCoy, *Freedom of the Press: An Annotated Bibliography* (Carbondale: Southern Illinois University Press, 1968) and *Freedom of the Press: A Bibliocyclopedia: Ten-year Supplement (1967–1977)* (Carbondale: Southern Illinois University Press, 1979). In the 1970s Garland Press reprinted much of the source material used for this chapter. For the Netherlands there is no comparable overview; but see my "Between Practice and Principle: Dutch Ideas on Censorship and Press Freedom, 1579–1795," *Redescriptions. Yearbook for Political Thought and Conceptual History* 8 (2004): 85–113.

3. Diane Parkin-Speer, "Freedom of Speech in Sixteenth-Century English Rhetorics," *Sixteenth Century Journal* 12 (1981): 65–72.

4. Heidelberg Catechism, "Sunday" 43, question 112 (cf. www.reformed.org/documents/heidelberg.html).

5. Cf. my *Mutua Christianorum Tolerantia. Irenicism and Toleration in the Netherlands: The Stinstra Affair 1740–1745* (Florence: Leo S. Olschki Editore, 1998).

6. [William Bollan], *The freedom of speech and writing upon public affairs, considered* (London, 1766).

7. Joel D. Meyerson, "The Private Revolution of William Bollan," *The New England Quarterly* 41 (1968): 536–50.

8. Bollan refers to Neh. 9:13, Prov. 16:6, Isa. 5:20, Jer. 9:3, Rom. 2:2, 2 Cor. 13:8. Biblical passages used as handles for censorship (e.g., "Thou shalt not curse the ruler of thy people") include Lev. 19:13, Ex. 22:28, Eccl. 10:20, Ps. 69:12, Job 30:8-9; these are mentioned, e.g., in Edward Coke, *The reports (...)* (London, 1658) V, 125a–126a (Star Chamber case of "L.P." [Lewis Pickering] *de libellis famosis*, 1605).

9. D.V. Coornhert, *Synodus of vander conscientien vryheyt*, 2 vols. n.p., n.d. [1582], II, 127–46. The section refers to the edict of September 22, 1540, against the printing and selling of heretical books.

10. John Milton, *Areopagitica and Other Political Writings of John Milton* (Indianapolis: Liberty Fund, 1999), 3–51, at 8–13.

11. Thomson's preface appears in Thomas Birch's 1738 edition of Milton's *Historical, political, and miscellaneous works*. In 1780 it was reprinted as an appendix to a speech on wasteful government spending by the dissenting minister George Walker (1734? –1807): *Substance of the speech of the Rev. Mr. Walker at the general meeting of the county of Nottingham, held at Mansfield, on Monday the 28th of February 1780* (London, 1780), 9–12. I quote Thomson here from this latter text.

12. Milton, *Areopagitica*, 16.

13. Philopatris [= Charles Blount], *A just vindication of learning* (London, 1679). On Blount, see J.A. Redwood, "Charles Blount (1654–1693), Deism, and English Free Thought," *Journal of the History of Ideas* 35 (1974): 490–98.

14. [Joseph Addison], *The thoughts of a Tory author, concerning the press* (London, 1712), 4–12.

15. Robert Hall, *An apology for the freedom of the press, and for general liberty* (London, 1793); a seventh edition had appeared by 1822.

16. Ibid., 1–15.

17. *Prijsverhandelingen over de edelmoedigheid en de vrijheid van de drukpers* ([Haarlem], 1784), pp. 28–48.

18. "Ontwerp, om de Republyk door eene heilzaame vereeniging der belangen van regent en burger, van binnen gelukkig, en van buiten geducht te maaken," *Verzameling van placaaten, resolutien en andere authentyke stukken* (Kampen, 1793), vol. 50, 185–244, at 220–21 and 238 (§§ 8 and 11).

19. Debates on this theme, including the natural right of subjects to submit petitions and complaints to the king, had already surfaced in the Dutch pamphlet literature of the 1560s and 1570s; see Pieter A.M. Geurts, *De Nederlandse Opstand in de pamfletten 1566–1584* (Nijmegen: Central Drukkerij, 1956), 131–56.

20. Milton, *Areopagitica*, 41.

41

21. This is the main point of Addison's *Spectator* essay of August 7, 1712 (no. 451): censorship in the form of outlawing anonymity "would not only destroy Scandal, but Learning."

22. J. van Dijk, *De vrijheid der drukpers* (Rotterdam, 1786). The argument as to who invented the printing press, the Germans or the Dutch, would continue well into the twentieth century.

23. Milton, *Areopagitica*, 16, 39–51.

24. Ibid., 38, 7, 16.

25. On this theme, see Roger Shattuck, *Forbidden Knowledge: From Prometheus to Pornography* (New York: St. Martin's Press, 1996), 55–76.

26. Matthew Tindal, *Reasons against restraining the press* (London, 1704).

27. *The independant Briton: or, Free thoughts on the expediency of gratifying the people's expectations* (London, 1742).

28. Samuel Johnson, *Lives of the most eminent English poets* (London, 1790; first ed. 1781), I, 154–55 (Life of Milton).

29. Johann Friedrich Reitz, *Oratio de censoribus librorum* (Utrecht, 1751).

30. *Plan, om door middel van de aanstelling van Censores Librorum, de verkooping van quaade boeken te voorkomen* (n.p., 1769); the text of the plan is printed in full in A.C. Kruseman, *Aanteekeningen betreffende den boekhandel van Noord-Nederland in de 17de en 18de eeuw* (Amsterdam, 1893), 390–95.

31. Luzac's "Memorie van consideratien, gemaakt op het nader geredresseerd placaat tegens godslatserlyke boeken en geschriften (...)" can be found in *Nieuwe Nederlandsche jaerboeken* V (1770), part ii, pp. 788–896. On Luzac, see John Christian Laursen and Johan van der Zande, eds., *Early French and German Defenses of Freedom of the Press: Elie Luzac's "Essay on Freedom of Expression" (1749) and Carl Friedrich Bahrdt's "On Freedom of the Press and Its Limits" (1787) in English translation* (Leiden: Brill, 2003).

32. Peter King, *The life and letters of John Locke* (London, 1858; repr. New York: B. Franklin, 1972), 202–209; E. Neville Williams, *The Eighteenth-Century Constitution 1688–1815. Documents and Commentary* (Cambridge: Cambridge University Press, 1970), 399–401.

33. Jonathan I. Israel, *Radical Enlightenment: Philosophy and the Making of Modernity, 1650–1750* (Oxford: Oxford University Press, 2001), 159–75.

34. E.g., [Lieven de Beaufort (1675–1730)] *Verhandeling van de vryheit in den burgerstaet* (Leiden, 1737).

35. Cf. the following academic orations: Christian Heinrich Trotz, *De libertate sentiendi dicendique iurisconsultis propria* (at Franeker, 1741); Paulus Chevallier, *De fructibus, qui ex juste temperata cogitandi libertate in theologum redundant* (at Groningen, 1752); Ladislaus Chernac, *De libertate philosophandi in licentiam non vertenda* (at Deventer, 1776). These addresses are reminiscent of earlier orations on the topic, such as Henricus Bornius, *De vero philosophandi libertate* (at Leiden, 1653).

36. Daniel Defoe, *An essay on the regulation of the press* (London, 1704).

37. There was a German translation: *Cato, oder, Briefe von der Freyheit und dem Glücke eines Volkes unter einer guten Regierung* (Göttingen, 1756–57), as well as a Dutch one: *Brieven over de vryheid, en het geluk des volks onder een goede regeering* (Alkmaar and Amsterdam, 1752–54).

38. [John Trenchard and Thomas Gordon], *Cato's letters or, Essays on liberty, civil and religious, and other important subjects*, ed. Ronald Hamowy (2 vols.; Indianapolis: Liberty Fund, 1995), 110–17; 228–34; 712–17; 717–22 ("Of freedom of speech: that the same is inseparable from public liberty" (Feb. 4, 1720); "Reflections upon Libelling" (June 10, 1721); "Discourse upon libels" (Oct. 27, 1722); "Second discourse upon libels" (Nov. 3, 1722).

39. Leonard W. Levy, ed., *Freedom of the Press from Zenger to Jefferson: Early American Theories* (Indianapolis: Bobbs-Merrill, 1966), xxiii–xxiv. For a critique of Levy's argumentation, see Stephen A. Smith, "The Origins of the Free Speech Clause," *Free Speech Yearbook* 29 (1991): 48–82.

40. Trenchard and Gordon, *Cato's letters*, 110–12.

41. *An het volk van Nederland*, n.p., n.d. [1781]. I have followed the (equally anonymous) English translation: [Joan Derk van der Capellen tot den Pol], *An address to the people of the Netherlands, on the present alarming and most dangerous situation of the republick of Holland* (London, 1782), 136–37.

42. See note 34.

43. [Thomas Hayter], *An essay on the liberty of the press, chiefly as it respects personal slander* (2nd ed.; London, 1755).

44. Ibid., 1–14.

45. With an epigraph borrowed from Tacitus, *Histories* I, 1: "Rara temporum felicitas, ubi sentire quae velis, & quae sentias dicere licet."

46. *De Denker* I (1764), no. 24, 185–92.

47. Wybo Jan Goslinga, *De rechten van den mensch en burger. Een overzicht der Nederlandsche geschriften en verklaringen* (The Hague, 1936), 92–95, 173–75.

48. Ibid., 143–44, 178–79.

49. Hayter, *An essay on the liberty of the press*, 9–14, 18, 29, 33–39

50. David Hume, "Of the liberty of the press," in *Essays, moral and political* (2nd ed., corrected; Edinburgh, 1742), 9–18. Hume's text is available online at http://oll.libertyfund.org/title/704/137468 (accessed June 30, 2010); this is an annotated edition with variant readings originally published as David Hume, *Essays Moral, Political, Literary*, ed. Eugene F. Miller (Indianapolis: Liberty Fund, 1987).

51. Hume, "Of the liberty of the press," 15–16.

52. Coornhert, *Synodus*, II, 127–46.

53. [Anon], *The livery-man: or, plain thoughts on publick affairs* (London, 1740), 9, 31, 50–54.

54. The following is indebted to Alfred H. Kelly, "Constitutional Liberty and the Law of Libel: A Historian's View," *The American Historical Review* 74 (1968): 429–52.

55. William Blackstone, "Of offences against the public peace," in *Commentaries on the laws of England* (Oxford, 1765–69), IV, 150–53 (chapter 11).

56. Shipley was accused of libel for publishing a book on political reform written by his brother-in-law. Thomas Erskine's defense of Shipley which included a plea for expanding the prerogatives of the jury, ultimately led to dismissal of the case (on Erskine, see below).

57. See Carla H. Hay, "The Making of a Radical: The Case of James Burgh," *The Journal of British Studies* 18 (1979): 90–117.

58. James Burgh, "Of the Liberty of Speech and Writing on Political Subjects," in *Political disquisitions, or, An enquiry into public errors, defects, and abuses* (London, 1774–75), III, 246–66.

59. See Clive Emsley, "Repression, 'Terror' and the Rule of Law in England during the Decade of the French Revolution," *The English Historical Review* 100 (1985): 801–25.

60. Cf. *The speech of the Hon. Thomas Erskine, at a meeting of the Friends to the Liberty of the Press, at Free-Mason's Tavern, Dec. 22, 1792* (London, 1793).

61. On Wilkes, see George Rudé, *Wilkes and Liberty: A Social Study of 1763–1774* (Oxford: Clarendon Press, 1962); Peter D.G. Thomas, *John Wilkes, a Friend to Liberty* (Oxford: Clarendon Press, 1996); Arthur H. Cash, *An Essay on Woman by John Wilkes and Thomas Potter* (New York: AMS Press, 2000).

62. Peter D.G. Thomas, "The Beginning of Parliamentary Reporting in Newspapers, 1768–1774," *The English Historical Review* 74 (1959): 623–36.

63. Quoted in Marie Peters, "The 'Monitor' on the Constitution, 1755–1765: New Light on the Ideological Origins of English Radicalism," *The English Historical Review* 86 (1971): 706–27, at 715.

64. Interesting observations on the development of natural rights arguments in terms of both religion and politics are made in Gregory Molivas, "From Religion to Politics: The Expression of Opinion as the Common Ground between Religious Liberty and Political Participation in the Eighteenth-Century Conception of Natural Rights," *History of Political Thought* 21 (2000): 237–60.

65. Cf. John Gray, *Two Faces of Liberalism* (Cambridge: Polity Press, 2000), 105–39.

66. A case in point is the "renegotiation" of notions of blasphemy in contemporary Western society and debates over "the freedom to insult." Any socially workable solution will require a balance between recognizing religious sensibilities and safeguarding an acceptable measure of freedom of expression. For an historical overview of this balance, with a focus on the role of the state in regard to religion, see David Nash, "Analyzing the History of Religious Crime: Models of 'Passive' and 'Active' Blasphemy since the Medieval Period," *Journal of Social History* 41 (2007): 5–29.

Cynicism as an Ideology behind Freedom of Expression in Denmark-Norway

ANCIENT CYNICISM, THE PHILOSOPHY OF DIOGENES OF SINOPE, promoted disregard for tradition and political authority; simple living in accord with nature; and *parrhesia*, or freedom of speech. Diogenes (fourth century B.C.) also coined the term "cosmopolitan" in order to stress that he was not bound by the customs of his hometown. Twentieth-century French philosopher Michel Foucault claimed a place for his own political activism in the history of cynicism.[1] Yet it is not widely known that a number of political actors and thinkers of the eighteenth century also deserve a place in this lineage.

One such person is Johann Friedrich Struensee (1737–1772), prime minister of Denmark-Norway in 1770. In this position he made history by issuing the first official declaration of complete freedom of the press in Europe, in 1770.[2] Note that this was freedom of the press, not freedom of speech, and that Diogenes would not have known what "the press" would later mean. But both speech and the press are part of a larger freedom of expression, of communication, of the liberty to share one's thoughts and feelings. It is not difficult to see how ancient cynical insistence upon freedom of speech would apply by analogy to freedom of the press. And once freedom of the press is established, it is much more difficult to justify limits on freedom of speech. After all, one can always ask: "If I am allowed to say something in print, why can't I say it in speech?"

As a paradigm case of enlightened absolutism,[3] Struensee also issued some 1,800 other decrees in the year and a half he was in office. One problem for interpreting his record is that he did not leave much of a paper trail, and there has been little effort to understand what motivated him, other than the obvious "enlightened values." Two articles he wrote in 1763, however, before coming to power, throw light on his ideological orientation. They are essays in the praise and in the practice of ancient cynicism. It is thus not unreasonable to interpret Struensee's activities in the context of this tradition. If so, we owe the first official declaration of freedom of the press at least in part to a package of ideas first propagated by ancient cynicism. Struensee's two articles were immediately suppressed by the censors, so he had a personal motivation to vindicate these ideas when he came to power.

As a "coda," news of Struensee's decree was publicized in the Danish West Indies during the time that Alexander Hamilton was growing up there, and this news may have spread north toward the American colonies at the time that George Mason was writing the Virginia Declaration of Rights of 1776. To the best of my knowledge, no one has given an ideological source for Mason's decision to include an explicit protection of freedom of the press in the Virginia Declaration, later also included in the Bill of Rights of the U.S. Constitution. The influence of the Danish precedent cannot be excluded.

It should be pointed out that the ancient tradition of cynicism had little of the modern connotation of selfish manipulativeness.[4] Indeed, it was a high moralism, and may therefore be just as pernicious in some ways as selfishness. Others have observed that Struensee was impolitic, insensitive, and arrogant in his pursuit of his ideals. If they have ventured reasons why he might have been so, other than personality quirks, they have attributed these characteristics to his acceptance of many of the principles of Spinozism or of the Voltairean Enlightenment. I do not claim that cynicism was the only or even the major ideological influence on his way of thinking, but his debt to it has not been taken into account in overall assessments of his ideas and influence.

Let us expand upon the elements of ancient cynicism. The first known cynic was Antisthenes, and the most famous was his student Diogenes of Sinope. Later cynics of ancient Greece and Rome included Crates and his wife, Hipparchia, and Menippus the satirist. All were strict moralists. Diogenes lived in a barrel; had no property except for a minimum of belongings such as a staff, a wallet, and a cloak; eschewed comfort; and criticized his contemporaries for their materialism and selfishness. He cultivated self-denial (*askesis*), claimed independence (*autarkia*), and spoke as he pleased (*parrhesia*). He was famous for the slogan "deface the coinage!" a metaphor for rejection of established customs and institutions. He repudiated established political systems and rulers. Anecdotes report him telling Alexander the Great to stop blocking his sunlight.[5]

Putting Alexander down was only one of many examples of a cheeky freedom of speech among the cynics. Antisthenes told the native Athenians that pride in their roots in the soil did not make them any better than snails.[6] "It is strange," he also said, that we "do not excuse evil men from the service of the state" (DL VI.6). He used to taunt Plato with being conceited, and his student Diogenes once trod on a carpet belonging to Plato saying, "I trample on Plato's vainglory" (DL VI.7, 26). When captured and put up for sale as a slave and asked what he could do, Diogenes answered, "Rule men!" (DL VI.29). Besides his rude treatment of Alexander, he also made cutting remarks to Alexander's general Perdiccas. So, *parrhesia* meant fearless speech without respect for others and without regard for their power.

Cynics were cosmopolitans, by Diogenes's neologism. Some cosmopolitans were also nationalists, although of necessity of the moderate and limited sort.[7] But Struensee was more of an anti-nationalist. At home in the court languages of French and German, he did not even bother to learn Danish. While this refusal may have masked a French and German cultural nationalism at the Danes' expense, it revealed a cosmopolitan immersion in two linguistic cultures. In his anti-nationalism, Struensee was also close to Diogenes, who was an anti-political, anti-patriotic, anti-nationalist, individualist cosmopolitan. Diogenes was perhaps proto-anarchist, because he did not respect any political authorities. He was irresponsible, but on high moral grounds: he was suspicious of anyone who claimed the right to order people around.

The ancient cynics usually eschewed participation in conventional politics, even if their public criticism could be considered a form of political action. The cynics did admire some political actors: Cyrus the Great of Persia was a hero to them because of his self-restraint and self-denial. First-century Greek writer and orator Dio Chrysostom's lectures "On Kingship" tried to persuade the emperor Trajan that a good king loves his companions, citizens, and soldiers.[8] Some cynics even participated in politics, for example, general Cercidas of Magalopolis (ca. 290–220 B.C.). The emperor Julian (331–363 A.D.) wrote sympathetic orations about authentic cynicism. Struensee could be considered similar in some ways to these men. He was briefly, if mercurially, successful in politics but came to a catastrophic end.

The cynics were known to the eighteenth century primarily through texts of Diogenes Laertius, Epictetus, Dio Chrysostom, Lucian, Plutarch, and their Renaissance mediators. Étienne de la Boétie (1530–1563), a friend of Montaigne and author of *Discourse on Voluntary Servitude*, used cynic invective, irony, wordplay, and paradoxes to provoke thought and to excoriate the lazy more than to teach any positive lesson.[9] The libertines of the seventeenth century reworked with glee the cynics' multifaceted critiques of religion, sexual norms, and established conventions.[10] As libertinism moved beyond the erudite and private indulgence of the seventeenth century into the more public provocations of the eighteenth, cynicism was closely associated with it. Struensee was accused of libertinism for his rejection of traditional sexual mores. To the extent that he recognized his own place in the libertine tradition, he could relate it to ancient cynicism.

Born in Halle in 1737, Struensee went to August Hermann Francke's pietist Latin school and at age fourteen entered the university at Halle.[11] The pietists were especially concerned with their own direct and individual moral and spiritual relationship with God and Jesus. The pietist element in Struensee's education could have had two contrary effects on his intellectual development, and they could have been simultaneous. Struensee could have absorbed the moral earnestness of the pietists, which was eventually redirected toward cynical moralism. (A variation on this explanation has been applied to Kant, who was raised in a pietist environment and redirected his moral earnestness toward his own highly principled moral theory.) And Struensee could have reacted against ascetic elements of his religious education by becoming a libertine.

Struensee capped his medical studies in 1757 with a thesis entitled *De incongrui corporis motus insalubritate* (Of Harm Caused by Unhealthy Movement of the Body). At the age of twenty, he was appointed city physician of the Danish-ruled but German-speaking town of Altona. His friends in medical and intellectual circles in Altona and nearby Hamburg included the Jewish doctor and clandestine Spinozist Hartog Gerson and the physician Johann Albert Heinrich Reimarus, son of the more famous Hermann Samuel Reimarus.[12] The medical education, along with his Latin education, may have led Struensee to materialist and radical ideas consistent with cynicism.

Together with several like-minded friends, Struensee wrote for or 49 published four periodicals in the humorous and moral-weekly tradition in the years 1760 to 1764. None lasted for long, and two were suppressed by the authorities.[13] It is thus not surprising that one of his first acts when he became prime minister in Denmark in 1770 was to issue a rescript enacting freedom of the press. It was his declaration of cynic *parrhesia.*

Something of the range of Struensee's interests can be seen from the articles he wrote for these short-lived journals.[14] Some were on medical themes, from infant care to fevers to smallpox inoculation and venereal disease. Generally they represented the rationalist "enlightened" approach. He also wrote about metempsychosis and penned a short continuation of Swift's *Gulliver's Travels* in German. His last article was an essay on the respect that an author ought to have for the public.

The main reason for characterizing Struensee as a self-conscious cynic is the two articles he wrote on the cynics that indicate that his attention to them was more than a passing fancy and that he had absorbed their ideas and style in depth.[15] Those who have adopted the cynical attitude, like some postmodernists today, make the humor and amusement to be found in anecdotes about the ancient cynics part of their own lifestyle. These provide examples of a playfulness and perspective that substitutes for the role of rigorous philosophy in more serious lifestyles and guides the cynics in their way of life.

The first of Struensee's articles on the cynics appeared in *Monthly Journal for Use and Pleasure* in 1763.[16] Titled "Reports on Diogenes," it was a kind of pastiche of paraphrases and quotes from Diogenes Laertius and other sources. It included such scandalous sayings as that "women and the education of children ought to be held in common" (64). Less than a decade later, one of the charges against Struensee was that he held the queen in common with the king.

Many passages were anti-clerical. Drawing a parallel between the cynics and the early Christians, Struensee wrote that "The force with which the first monks castigated their flesh . . . is no more extraordinary than that with which Diogenes and his followers did so." (58). Presumably, he would have endorsed a claim he quotes from Diogenes, namely, that "when I think of philosophy and the art of medicine, man seems to me the cleverest of animals . . . but when I cast my eyes on astrology and prophecy, I find no greater fools" (65). Again quoting Diogenes: "The luck of the robber Harpalus . . . nearly forced me to believe that either there are no gods or that they do not concern themselves with our affairs" (66). The denial of Providence was considered an indication of atheism by thinkers like Pierre Bayle, even if it allowed for the existence of gods.

There was a clear political message in the cynics: Diogenes's "biting wit reformed Corinth" (60). Struensee surely thought he could do the same. Diogenes's combination of naturalism and cosmopolitanism is reflected in one quotation: "A well-ruled republic would be the exact likeness of that old city, the world" (64). To the citizens of Sinope who banished him, he answered, "I condemn you to stay in your houses," with the obvious meaning that they would miss out on getting to know the larger world. "You shall stay in Sinope, and I am going to Athens" (66). This is a clear declaration of cynical cosmopolitanism.

Diogenes, according to Struensee, also "concluded rightly that superstition and unlimited absolutism are the most wretched" forces on earth (66). No doubt the humorless authorities in Altona and Hamburg would not find this article very amusing. Stefan Winkle considered it

Struensee's "indirect vindication" of his life and style, published less than ten years before his fall.[17]

The second article was a longer piece "In Praise of Dogs and the Greek White."[18] It is not obviously of cynic inspiration, unless you know that "cynic" means dog and that the ancient cynics claimed to adopt the lifestyle of dogs and compared themselves to them. Appearing shortly after the article explicitly on Diogenes, it is clearly an exercise in the cynical tradition. The epigraph was "Les hommes ne sont pas si parfaits que les chiens" (233). The text went on to assert that the loyalty and sociability of dogs proves that they have souls (234), a provocation to Christians for whom humans are the only living beings to have souls.

Protestants could appreciate anti-Catholic remarks such as that "dogs are gentler than the Holy Father and the Inquisition" (234) or that monks do not observe their vows of chastity (235). But talking about "Christian hate" in the human heart (243), in contrast to the loyalty and love of a dog, would be offensive even to Protestants (236–37). Struensee quoted Rousseau on the equality of classes (Stände) but insisted that only dogs could distinguish the honorable people from the loafers (239).

In the last section of the article he compared a well-known medical remedy, sold by respected Altona physician Johann Unzer, Album Graecum (Greek Album [a white powder or paste]), to dogshit.[19] Fully in the tradition of the ancient cynics, this sort of vulgar attack on a rival physician reflects the humorous "defacing of the coinage" for which Diogenes was notorious. Dog feces, Struensee contended, contained more wisdom than many famous writers and were better medicine than what doctors prescribe. In this tirade, vain nobles, corrupt judges, wealthy landowners, and Panglossian professors come out worse than the excrement of dogs, which has the same effect as the white powder sold as medicine (252). Since Hamburg's Pastor Goeze, who later fought with Lessing, was a user of this remedy, its "humor" cut close to home. Goeze made sure that Struensee's periodical was banned in both Hamburg and Altona, in part for its anti-religious implications, but also for its boorishness.[20] Although it was just the sort of provocation that a cynical cosmopolitan could think was both humorous and merited by the establishment, one can see why even other enlightened intellectuals found it hard to defend publication of this sort of thing.[21]

51

His interpersonal and medical skills enabled Struensee to rise to power. His successful inoculation of the Danish crown prince against smallpox was one of the factors that helped him win the hearts of the king and queen. He was appointed prime minister in 1770 because of their favor. Soon he was sleeping with the queen, with the king's approval because the king, too, was a libertine and spent many nights with prostitutes.

Did Struensee transmit his cynical ideas to his companions in Copenhagen, including the king, the queen, or his ally Enevold Brandt? We do not know. They left no record that offers clues to their thinking. Many political actors leave no paper trail; it is a special feature of the Struensee case that we have evidence of his ideas from his earlier writings.

Struensee's cynicism can also be observed in his ruling style. The ancient cynics were moral elitists, ever challenging the status quo, political leaders, and even ordinary people for their corruption. Struensee was no democrat, actively seeking to encourage political participation. Rather, like most of the ancient cynics, he was consummately unpolitical. He made enemies by speaking too openly of his contempt for others and relied almost exclusively on dictatorial power, issuing more than 1,800 decrees during his short period (1770–1772) in office.[22] He eliminated wasteful holidays, ended monopolies and other economic favoritism, and cut back on military and religious privileges. Some of these may have been useful reforms, but they were carried out with gross insensitivity to real people and their problems. So might Diogenes of Sinope have ruled had he come to power. Struensee carried out some of the cynic policies attributed to the cynic kings Cyrus, Cercidas, and Julian.

It is worth noting that, as much as Struensee enjoyed writing anonymous satirical pieces himself, he was not so happy with them once he came to power. Within a year after his press rescript the attacks on him as prime minister had become so raucous that he issued a new rescript reasserting some control over the press. It required that the author or publisher be named in articles and books and that the publisher know the identity of an author, so that responsibility for libel and slander could be ensured.[23]

As I have mentioned, Struensee never bothered to learn Danish, which was perceived as an affront by Danish nationalists, and even by those who were only moderately nationalist.[24] Of German and not Danish birth, he stood apart, living as a kind of exile in Denmark. He was an outsider, a feature he shared with Diogenes, who lived most of his life in exile from Sinope.

Struensee's power did not last long. On the night of January 18, 1772, a group of conspirators obtained an order from the king for the arrest of his queen and Struensee.[25] Each of the victims confessed in order to save the other, and after a kangaroo-court trial the queen was divorced from the king and exiled to Celle in Hannover. Struensee, convicted of lèse majesté, was beheaded, drawn, and quartered. Many of his reforms were rescinded, including the rescript on freedom of the press.

It is worth noting that, although there were precedents for his concern with freedom of the press, Struensee did not mention them himself. John Milton's English-language *Areopagitica* (1644), for instance, defended freedom of the press against renewal of a press licensing law as a matter of what he called "Christian Liberty." This cause was soon taken up by non- and even anti-Christians. Benedict de Spinoza, whose Latin-language *Theological-Political Treatise* (1670) defended *libertas philosophandi* (the liberty to philosophize), has been called "the most radical of all the cynics" by a modern philosopher.[26] The deist Charles Blount brought these two authors together: he provided the first English translation of the chapter on miracles in Spinoza's *Treatise*, and possibly the first English translation of the entire work (1689),[27] and he published essays in the 1690s that reiterated Milton's arguments.[28]

Pierre Bayle's French-language "Clarification concerning Obscenities" (1702), which defended the right to publish scandalous materials, was published numerous times in several languages in the first half of the eighteenth century. Matthew Tindal's two essays in defense of freedom of the press were published four times between 1698 and 1709.[29] Anthony Collins mentions one of Tindal's books in *A Discourse of Freethinking* (1713), in which he used some of the ironies and railleries that a cynic would appreciate, such as claiming that priests and religious rigorists were actually more atheistic than some of the real atheists of the ancient world.

Written in Altona or Hamburg shortly before Struensee's time there, Johann Lorenz Schmidt's 130-page introduction to his German translation of Matthew Tindal's *Christianity as Old as Creation* (1741) defended freedom of speech and press against persecution, and Schmidt also translated Spinoza into German (1744).[30] Elie Luzac's French-language *Essay on Freedom of Expression* (1749) defended the right to publish works like La Mettrie's atheist and materialist *Man a Machine* (1748).[31] All of these were serious efforts to turn public opinion against persecution and censorship. We do not know if Struensee was familiar with them, but his own experience with having his work banned would have led him to appreciate the need for freedom of the press.

Struensee's philosophical sympathies were with such thinkers as Spinoza, Hume, and Voltaire.[32] Each can be assimilated to ancient cynicism in one way or another, especially in their common goal of "defacing the coinage" and rejecting established religious hierarchies. They identified more with the cosmopolitan "republic of letters" than with national identities. They thought they were writing for the world, while defacing many of the established currencies. I have suggested elsewhere that his perceived association with Spinoza was part of the atmosphere that brought about the coup against Struensee.[33] Demonstrating the influence of the ancient cynical tradition on Struensee does not diminish that of Spinoza, Hume, Voltaire, or others: it complements and supplements them, showing that intellectual history is often complex, multilayered, and subtle.

Struensee's press rescript was rescinded in 1772, but prior censorship was not restored, which meant that Denmark-Norway had more press freedom after Struensee than before. The police could still punish an author or publisher, but the country now met Blackstone's definition of freedom of the press, which was the absence of prior censorship.[34] It is widely accepted that post-publication censorship is more compatible with liberty for it does not have the chilling effect of prior censorship, under which many things will never be considered for publication because they might bring down the wrath of the censors. Lax post-publication censorship might allow works to slip through the cracks, or at least circulate clandestinely.

News of Struensee's declaration of freedom of the press arrived early in the Americas. The *Royal Danish-American Gazette* began publishing at Christiansted, St. Croix, in the Danish Virgin Islands in 1770.[35] Because of liberal residency policies, many of the planters in the Danish islands were English-speaking, justifying an English-language newspaper. In an issue dated January 30, 1771, it was announced that "The King of Denmark has given striking proof of his good sense, in the forbidding any kind of censure to be passed on the contents of such books as may be published in his dominions."[36] More detail was provided some few weeks later on March 9: "The King of Denmark looking on the liberty of the press as one of the most efficacious means to forward the progress of the sciences, has published a rescript, dated at the Chateau of Hirscholm, the 14th of Sept. in which he exempts from every kind of censure all books which shall be printed in his dominions."[37]

A Harvard Law School professor has claimed that George Mason became "the author of the world's first explicit legal protection of freedom of the press" when he wrote the Virginia Declaration of Rights in 1776.[38] What he really meant was that he was not aware of, and had not searched for, any earlier such legal protection elsewhere. Mason, however, could have learned about the Danish example, directly or indirectly through others, from the English-language reports in the English press both in England and in the Virgin Islands. Alexander Hamilton was living in those islands in 1770–1771, and other Founders knew Caribbean planters from whom they might have learned of the Danish decree.

55

Ideas about freedom of the press continued to spread in the years after Struensee's downfall and the Virginia Declaration. In 1781 Joseph II significantly relaxed controls on the press in the Habsburg lands. Carl Friedrich Bahrdt's *On Freedom of the Press and Its Limits* appeared in German in 1787, claiming a wide-ranging human right to freedom of the press.[39] Other writings by Bahrdt qualify him for the epithet "cynic," based on his humor and disrespect for authorities.[40] The French Declaration of the Rights of Man of 1790 provided that "every citizen may speak freely, write, and print, subject to accountability for abuse of this freedom." The First Amendment of the United States Constitution, part of the Bill of Rights, provides that "Congress shall make no law . . . abridging the freedom of speech, or of the press." These declarations coupled speech with the press, clearly conceiving of them as inseparable.

Since then, no modern liberal democracy has ever doubted the importance of freedom of speech and the press until recently.[41]

Granting that ideal types such as the ancient cynicism we have outlined cannot capture the complexity of an individual thinker, and may indeed lead to oversimplifications, there remains something to be gained by bringing out this dimension of Struensee's behavior. One conclusion that emerges from the examples cited is that cynicism has an unfortunate tendency to try to tear down authority and reconstruct society at one stroke. The good thing is that all sorts of problems are addressed; the bad thing is that they are not addressed well. Cynicism makes a fetish of rejecting much-loved customs and national feeling; it can be insensitive to human foibles; and as we have seen with Struensee, it provokes opposition by being perceived as arrogant.

Struensee's pursuit of moral ideals may remind us of English philosopher Michael Oakeshott's assertion that "The pursuit of moral ideals has proved itself (as might be expected) an untrustworthy form of morality."[42] As Oakeshott writes, the "self-conscious pursuit of ideals" dismisses the "morality of habit of behaviour . . . as primitive and obsolete,"[43] allowing the idealists to run roughshod over the concerns of those who live by that morality. Then, "Too often the excessive pursuit of one ideal leads to the exclusion of others, perhaps all others; in our eagerness to realize justice we come to forget charity, and a passion for righteousness has made many a man hard and merciless."[44] Furthermore, "every moral ideal is potentially an obsession; the pursuit of moral ideals is an idolatry."[45]

Oakeshott did not make these assertions in regard to cynical moralism, but these and other elements of his analysis fit nicely as an evaluation of Struensee's politics and his fall. His callous firing of many unnecessary government employees was apparently carried out with the same indifference to their personal lives as the modern-day amoral cynical cosmopolitan's outsourcing of 5,000 jobs seems to be. His abolition of numerous holidays was the sort of moralism that was not likely to appeal to most working people.

In case the reader is prepared to dismiss this critique on the ground that Oakeshott was a political conservative, let us note that political

56

radical Wendy Brown has made a similar case against moralism in politics: "moralism . . . actually marks both analytical impotence and political aimlessness." It is a "depoliticizing form of political discourse."[46]

Parrhesia, of course, can be used by anyone, for any purposes. It is testimony to Michel Foucault's intellectual honesty that, after exploring the genealogy of his own political activism in the cynical tradition, he concluded that we have no way of distinguishing the honest truth-speakers from the chatterers, the flatterers, the selfish, the immoral, the self-deluded, and the ignorant.[47] Good cynicism can mutate into bad cynicism.

In a posthumous publication, Oakeshott admitted his preference for the politics of skepticism while at the same time recognizing that a healthy politics needs some of each of skepticism and faith.[48] Perhaps the same can be said for cynicism. Our example in this chapter suggests that we owe the world's first declaration of freedom of the press in part to ideas and practices from the cynic heritage. While it may be true that most of the time we are better off with more moderate and less moralistic forms of politics that are more attuned to the sensitivities of ordinary men and women, we may indeed benefit from something like ancient cynicism from time to time.

Notes

1. Michel Foucault, *Fearless Speech* (Los Angeles: Semiotexte, 2001).

2. The Netherlands, England, and some other places in Europe had de facto freedom of the press, but had not declared it as a matter of law.

3. See H. Blom, J. C. Laursen, and L. Simonutti, eds., *Monarchisms in the Age of Enlightenment: Liberty, Patriotism, and the Common Good* (Toronto: University of Toronto Press, 2007).

4. See Peter Sloterdijk, *Critique of Cynical Reason* (Minneapolis: University of Minnesota Press, 1987 [orig. *Kritik der zynischen Vernunft* (Frankfurt: Suhrkamp, 1983)], who traces the modern meaning to late nineteenth-century Germany; and David Mazella, *The Making of Modern Cynicism* (Charlottesville: University of Virginia Press, 2007), who dates it to late eighteenth- and early nineteenth-century England.

5. For general introductions to cynic thought, see William Desmond, *Cynics* (Berkeley: University of California Press, 2008); Luis Navia, *Diogenes the Cynic* (Amherst: Humanity Press, 2005); R. Bracht Branham and Marie-Odile Goulet-Cazé, eds., *The Cynics: The Cynic Movement in Antiquity and Its Legacy* (Berkeley: University of California Press, 1996); Heinrich Niehues-Pröbsting, *Der Kynismus des Diogenes und der Begriff des Kynismus* (Munich: Fink, 1979; 2d ed. 1988).

6. The main source of such anecdotes is Diogenes Laertius, *Lives of Eminent Philosophers*, trans. R. Hicks (Cambridge: Harvard University Press, 1929), Book VI, here p. 1. Cited hereafter in the text in standard form.

7. For a variety of ^{efforts} to theorize cosmopolitanism combined with moderate patriotism, see Stephen Nathanson, *Patriotism, Morality, and Peace* (Lanham: Rowman & Littlefield, 1993); Amartya Sen, *Identity and Violence: The Illusion of Destiny* (New York: Norton, 2006); Kwame Anthony Appiah, *Cosmopolitanism: Ethics in a World of Strangers* (New York: Norton, 2006).

8. Dio Chrysostom, *Discourses*, trans. J. Colhoon (Harvard University Press, 1932), vol. 1, Discourses 1–4.

9. Michèle Clément, "'Abrutis, vous pouvez cesser de l'être': Le *Discours de la servitude volontaire* et la pédagogie cynique," *Libertinage et philosophie au XVIIe siècle* 7 (2003): 105–19; idem, *Le Cynisme à la Renaissance* (Geneva: Droz, 2005).

10. Jean-Michel Gros, "La place du cynisme dans la philosophie libertine," *Libertinage et philosophie au XVIIe siècle* 7 (2003): 121–39.

11. For his biography, see Stefan Winkle, *Johann Friedrich Struensee: Arzt, Aufklärer, Staatsmann* (Stuttgart: G. Fischer, 1983, 1989).

12. See Stefan Winkle, *Die heimlichen Spinozisten in Altona und der Spinozastreit* (Hamburg: Verein für Hamburgische Gechichte, 1988).

13. See, generally, Stefan Winkle, *Struensee und die Publizistik* (Hamburg: Christians, 1992).

14. Listed in ibid., 118–20.

15. H. Niehues-Pröbsting missed Struensee in *Der Kynismus* and in his survey chapter: "The Modern Reception of Cynicism: Diogenes in the Enlightenment," in Branham and Goulet-Cazé, *The Cynics*, 329–65.

16. "Nachrichten vom Diogenes," *Monatsschrift zum Nutzen und Vergnügen* (Hamburg, 1763), suppressed by the censor and actually published under the false title *Zur Belustigung* 1 (Hamburg, 1764): 57–67. Hereafter cited parenthetically in text by page number.

17. Winkle, *Struensee und die Publizistik*, 106–107.

18. "Lobrede auf die Hunde und das Album Graecum," *Monatsschrift zum Nutzen und Vergnügen* (Hamburg, 1763), suppressed by the censor and actually published under the false title *Zur Belustigung* 3 (Hamburg, 1764): 233–53. Hereafter cited parenthetically in text by page number.

19. Winkle, *Struensee und die Publizistik*, 43ff.

20. Ibid., 54–69.

21. For a contrast of Struensee with moderate enlighteners, see J. C. Laursen, "Humanism vs. Cynicism: Cosmopolitan Culture and National Identity in Eighteenth-Century Denmark," in Knud Haakonssen and Henrik Horstbøll, eds., *Northern Antiquities and National Identities* (Copenhagen: Royal Danish Academy of Sciences and Letters, 2008), 145–62 and 336–39.

22. See Holger Hansen, *Kabinetsstyrelsen i Danmark, 1768–1772* (Copenhagen, 1916–19).

23. See J. C. Laursen, "Denmark, 1750–1848," in Derek Jones, ed., *Censorship: An Encyclopedia* (London: Fitzroy Dearborn, 2001), 663.

24. See Vibeke Winge, "Dansk og Tysk i 1700-tallet," in Ole Feldbaek, ed., *Dansk Identitetshistorie* (Copenhagen: C.A. Reitzel, 1991), vol. 1, 89–110, and Ole Feldbaek, "Faedreland og Indfødsret. 1700-tallets danske identitet," in ibid., vol. 1, 169–80.

25. See Michael Sonnenscher, *Before the Deluge* (Princeton: Princeton University Press, 2007), 22–23, for a contrast between the Danish and French revolutions.

26. Andre Comte-Sponville, *Valeur et vérité: Etudes cyniques* (Paris: Presses universitaires de France, 1994), 48.

27. See Richard Popkin, *Spinoza* (Oxford: Oneworld, 2004), 122.

28. [Charles Blount], *Reasons Humbly Offered for the Liberty of Unlicens'd Printing* (London, 1693), and *A Just Vindication of Learning and the Liberty of the Press* (London, 1695).

29. [Matthew Tindal], *A Letter to a Member of Parliament, Shewing, that a Restraint on the Press is inconsistent with the Protestant Religion, and dangerous to the Liberties of the Nation* (London, 1698; second impression, 1700), reprinted in *Four Discourses on the Following Subjects... IV. Of the Liberty of the Press* (London, 1709), 292–329; [Tindal], *Reasons against Restraining the Press* (London, 1704).

30. [Johann Lorenz Schmidt], "Vorbericht" to [Matthew Tindal], *Beweis, dass das Christentum so alt als die Welt sey* (Frankfurt und Leipzig [Hamburg], 1741); [J. L. Schmidt, translator], *B.v.S. Sittenlehre widerleget von dem berühmten Weltweisen unserer Zeit Herrn Christian Wolf* (Frankfurt und Leipzig [Hamburg], 1744).

31. J. C. Laursen and J. Van der Zande, eds., *Early French and German Defenses of Freedom of the Press: Elie Luzac's Essay on Freedom of Expression (1749) and Carl Friedrich Bahrdt's On Freedom of the Press and Its Limits (1787) in English Translation* (Leiden: Brill, 2003).

32. See J. C. Laursen, "David Hume and the Danish Debate about Freedom of the Press in the 1770's," *Journal of the History of Ideas* 59 (1998): 167–73; J. C. Laursen, "Voltaire, Christian VII of Denmark, and Freedom of the Press," *SVEC [Studies on Voltaire and the Eighteenth Century]* 2003:06, 331–48; J. C. Laursen, "Télémaque manqué: Reverdil at Court in Copenhagen," in P. Coleman et al., eds., *Reconceptualizing Nature, Science, and Aesthetics* (Geneva, 1998), 147–56.

33. J. C. Laursen, "Spinoza in Denmark and the Fall of Struensee," *Journal of the History of Ideas* 61 (2000): 189–202.

34. William Blackstone, *Commentaries on the Laws of England* (Oxford, 1769), vol. 4, 151–52.

35. The following discussion is taken from J. C. Laursen, "Censorship in the Nordic Countries, ca. 1750–1890: Transformations in Law, Theory, and Practice," *Journal of Modern European History* 3 (2005): 108–9.

36. *Royal Danish-American Gazette* 1.60 (1771), 2.

37. Ibid., 1.71 (1771), 2.

38. Frederick Schauer, "Free Speech and its Philosophical Roots," in T. Daniel Shumate, ed., *The First Amendment: The Legacy of George Mason* (Fairfax, VA: George Mason University Press, 1987), 132; see also Bernard Schwartz, *The Roots of the Bill of Rights* (New York: Chelsea House, 1980 [orig. *The Bill of Rights* (1971)], 233. Such works misled Lynn Hunt, *Inventing Human Rights* (New York: Norton, 2007), whose first mention of freedom of the press (121) is a reference to the Virginia Declaration of Rights.

39. See Laursen and Van der Zande, eds., *Early French and German Defenses of Freedom of the Press*.

40. See Carl Friedrich Bahrdt, *The Edict of Religion. A Comedy* and *The Story of My Imprisonment*, eds. J. C. Laursen and J. Van der Zande (Lanham: Lexington Books, 2000).

41. See the introduction to this volume by Elizabeth Powers.

42. Michael Oakeshott, "The Tower of Babel" [orig. 1948] in *Rationalism in Politics and Other Essays* (Indianapolis: Liberty Fund, 1991), 486.

43. Ibid., 486.

44. Ibid., 476.

45. Ibid.

46. Wendy Brown, *Politics Out of History* (Princeton: Princeton University Press, 2001), 29, 25.

47. Foucault, *Fearless Speech*, passim.

48. Michael Oakeshott, *The Politics of Faith and the Politics of Scepticism* (New Haven: Yale University Press, 1996). See J. C. Laursen, "Oakeshott's Skepticism and the Skeptical Traditions," *European Journal of Political Theory* 4 (2005): 37–55.

*A*lexander Radishchev's *Journey from St. Petersburg to Moscow* and the Limits of Freedom of Speech in the Reign of Catherine the Great*

ALEXANDER RADISHCHEV'S JOURNEY FROM ST. PETERSBURG TO *Moscow* is arguably the most notorious book in Russian history. Published in 1790, it immediately attracted the attention of the state authorities, which banned the book, seized and destroyed all known copies, and sentenced its author to death. The ban lasted seventy-eight years until its repeal by Tsar Alexander II in 1868. Even after the ban was lifted, overzealous censors continued to confiscate and destroy copies of Radishchev's *Journey* for many years. To quote one of Radishchev's biographers, "No book in Russia or Europe was so long and so thoroughly suppressed."[1]

Suppressed under the tsars, under the Soviets Radishchev's *Journey* was elevated to the status of a holy text and its author enshrined as the founding father of the Russian revolutionary intelligentsia. Studying the *Journey* and its author became a cottage industry for historians and literary scholars. Perhaps no other work has been so exhaustively mined, particularly for its criticisms of the evils of tsarist Russia, for its harsh indictment of serfdom, for evidence of the corrupting influence of the ruler's court and the rapacious inhumanity of the noble landlords. It would seem that there is nothing more to be said about this most studied of texts.

Surprisingly, however, there is one theme that has not been fully explored, namely the book's discussion of freedom of speech. This is all the more noteworthy since Radishchev's *Journey*, I would propose, presents the most uncompromising and forcefully argued defense of freedom of speech in eighteenth-century Russia, a defense that crosses over into what can only be seen as a truly radical vision of free speech that was as ill-suited to and unwelcome in Radishchev's homeland as it would have been possibly everywhere else in Europe at the time.[2] My interest here is threefold: first, to examine Radishchev's ideas of freedom of expression, particularly alongside one of their main sources; second, to place Radishchev's ideas in the broader context of freedom of speech in eighteenth-century Russia; and third, to offer a few observations on how the Radishchev affair illuminates some more general issues concerning the problematic nature of free speech in Russia over the past two hundred years.

62 Alexander Radishchev was born in Moscow in 1749 into a wealthy noble family of Tatar descent with a long history of service to the princes of Muscovy and the Russian tsars. He spent the first seven years of his life on his father's estate of Verkhnee Obliazovo in the Saratov province before returning to Moscow in 1757 to live with his mother's relatives. In 1764, Alexander left Moscow for St. Petersburg to enroll in the Imperial Corps of Pages along with forty other bright boys chosen for the honor by Catherine the Great herself. Radishchev remained at the Corps for two years, until Catherine selected him to join an elite group of young men to continue their education at the University of Leipzig.

Radishchev lived in Leipzig from 1766 to 1771, studying ancient and modern languages, moral philosophy, history, and law. It was during these years that Radishchev came in contact with the ideas of the Enlightenment through the works of Voltaire, Montesquieu, and Rousseau, as well as Hobbes, Spinoza, Leibniz, and Montaigne.

Upon his return to St. Petersburg, Radishchev joined the civil service as a clerk in the Senate. Several years later he moved to the Commerce Collegium, a body responsible for collecting economic and trade statistics, where he served with distinction up until the publication of the *Journey* in 1790, the same year he was appointed chief of the

St. Petersburg Custom House. Radishchev's literary efforts began not long after his return to Russia. In 1773, he published his first book, an edited translation of Gabriel Bonnot de Mably's *History of Ancient Greece* (1766). Although he would later write verse, biography, essays, and history, Radishchev's name and main historical significance are linked to his *Journey*.[3]

Radishchev began writing the *Journey* in 1780, eventually finishing it at the end of 1788. In the spring of 1789, he submitted the manuscript to the St. Petersburg police for publication approval, which was granted on July 22 by Nikita Ryleev, the city's chief of police.[4] Radishchev then turned to finding a publisher, which proved to be a more difficult matter. He first contacted a printer in Moscow, who refused, supposedly after familiarizing himself with the text and being too afraid to take on such an explosive book. Discussions with other publishers also led nowhere. In the end, Radishchev decided to set up his own small press at home and print it himself.[5] The most notorious book in Russian history, it turns out, was printed by a vanity press. The first copies appeared in local bookstores at the end of May 1790. Radishchev, for reasons that remain not fully explained, published the book anonymously and even told booksellers to keep his identity a secret. The book was an immediate sensation, and within weeks all the copies had been sold.[6] Such was the curiosity about this incendiary work that the *Journey* was passed around in a hungry frenzy among family and friends.

The *Journey* has been alternately described as a travel account, a polemic, a novel, an *Erziehungsroman*, a *conte philosophique*, and a "sentimental journey."[7] It is all of these things, yet at its heart it is an attack on social injustice, particularly the great sin of serfdom, presented in the form of an imagined travel account. In its role as an abolitionist tract its closest equivalent in literature would be *Uncle Tom's Cabin* (1852) by Harriet Beecher Stowe. Radishchev said the book was inspired by Lawrence Sterne's *A Sentimental Journey Through France and Italy* (1768) and Guillaume Raynal's *Histoire des deux Indes* (1770). The latter book's troubled reception, later ban, and public burning, should have given Radishchev pause.

True to the Sentimentalist spirit of the age, the *Journey* is awash in tears, redolent with vapors, and overflowing with flushes, sighs, moans, and wails. The reader follows the narrator on his way from St. Petersburg to Moscow and is made a witness to his indignation as he encounters example after example of injustice, turpitude, and corruption. Most of these examples come by way of various traveling companions, overheard conversations, books and documents found abandoned in dingy inns or lying forgotten in the dirt. The narrator is never the one denouncing Russia's social ills, but presents himself merely as a reporter for what he hears and reads while on his journey.

And what he reports amounts to a damaging indictment of Catherine the Great's Russia. It is a land where arbitrary power rules, where laws are nonexistent or openly ignored, where the rich and mighty oppress the poor and honest, where people are bought and sold and denied their humanity, and where the unctuous flattery of courtiers blinds the vain ruler to the troubles in her realm. More than a critique of specific abuses, the *Journey* amounts to a sustained indictment of the Russian social and political system itself.[8]

And Radishchev didn't stop there. Sections of the book can easily be read as a call to arms. The serfs are incited to rise up against their masters, and, in one of the book's most shocking sections, Radishchev appears to endorse regicide, even praising Cromwell: "But you have taught generation after generation how nations can avenge themselves; you had Charles tried in court and executed."[9]

"Torzhok," the longest chapter named after a minor provincial town sixty kilometers west of Tver, has the least to say about conditions in Russia, which may in part explain why it has attracted less attention than other parts of the book. It begins with an encounter at the post station between our narrator and a man on his way to St. Petersburg to petition for the right to set up a printing press in his local town. Their meeting sets the stage for a lengthy discussion on the evils of censorship and, in mildly disguised form, a presentation of Radishchev's ideas on freedom of speech.

Our narrator is surprised upon hearing of his fellow traveler's journey to the capital because, as he says, the empress had granted the right to establish private presses in 1783. True, replies the frustrated publisher, but that does not equal the freedom to publish, for censorship, he claims, remains and is keeping the citizenry in a state of intellectual infancy:

[T]hat which may be printed is still under watch and ward. Censorship has become the nursemaid of reason, wit, imagination, of everything great and enlightened. But where there are nurses, there are babies and leading strings, which often lead to crooked legs; where there are guardians, there are minors and immature minds unable to take care of themselves. If there are always to be nurses and guardians, then the child will walk with leading strings for a long time and will grow up to be a cripple. . . . Everywhere these are the consequences of the usual censorship, and the sterner it is, the more disastrous are its consequences.[10]

The publisher proceeds to give the usual criticisms of censorship of the period: that God and His truth are too powerful to require the puny help of earthly defenders; that persons unjustly attacked in the press can adequately find redress through civil law; that public morality is undermined not by pornography but by our lustful desires that lead us to engage in debauchery; that out of fear of accidentally allowing something dangerous into print, censors are prone to prohibit that which is truly beneficial and so inhibit "the progress of reason"; and that, being as we are the "children of Eve," censorship excites our curiosity all the more, drawing us inexorably to that which is forbidden.[11]

65

But, this critic of censorship continues, the various reasons given to justify censorship are just smoke screens intended to hide its true purpose:

[I]n prohibiting freedom of the press, timid governments are not afraid of blasphemy, but of criticism of themselves. He who in moments of madness does not spare God, will not in moments of lucidity and reason spare unjust power. He who does not fear the thunders of the Almighty laughs at the gallows. Hence freedom of thought is terrifying to governments. The freethinker who has been stirred to his depths will stretch forth his audacious but mighty and fearless arm against the idol of power, will tear off his mask and veil, and lay bare its true character. Everyone will see its feet of clay; everyone will withdraw the support which he had given it; power will return to its source; the idol will fall. But if power is not seated in the fog of contending opinions, if its throne is founded on sincerity and true love of the common weal, will it not rather be strengthened when its foundation is revealed? . . . Let the government be honest and its leaders free from hypocrisy; then all the spittle and vomit will return their stench upon him who has belched them forth; but the truth will always remain pure and immaculate. He whose words incite to revolt (in deference to the government, let us so denominate all firm utterances which are based on truth but opposed to the ruling powers) is just as much a fool as he who blasphemes God. Let the government proceed on its appointed path. . . . But woe to it if in its lust for power it offends against truth. Then even a thought shakes its foundations; a word of truth will destroy it; a manly act will scatter it to the winds.[12]

The people, not the censors, should decide the merit of ideas: "[T]he censorship of what is printed belongs properly to society. . . . Leave what is stupid to the judgment of public opinion; stupidity will find a thousand censors. The most vigilant police cannot check worthless ideas as well as a disgusted public can. They will be heard just once; then they will die, never to rise again." "Vast and boundless," he adds, will be the usefulness ushered in by "freedom of the press."[13]

The critic leaves our narrator with the following parting words, ones that paint a radiant future in which truth, honesty, and wisdom prevail:

If everyone is free to think and to proclaim his thoughts to all without hindrance, then naturally everything that is thought out and discovered will become known: what is great will be great, and truth will not be obscured. The rulers of nations will not dare to depart from the way of truth lest their policy, their wickedness, and their fraud be exposed. The judge will tremble when about to sign an unjust sentence, and will tear it up. He who has power will be ashamed to use it only for the gratification of his lusts. Secret extortion will be called extortion, and clandestine murder—murder. All evil men will fear the stern glance of truth. Peace will be real, for there will be no ferment in it. Nowadays only the surface is smooth, but the ooze that lies at the bottom is growing turbid and dims the transparency of the water.[14]

Radishchev's thinking on freedom of expression was shaped by a variety of sources. Prominent among them was Johann Beckmann's *Beiträge zur Geschichte der Erfindungen*, published in five volumes in Leipzig between 1786 and 1805. Radishchev draws heavily from Beckmann's work in a section of "Torzhok" under the heading "A Brief Account of the Origin of Censorship," which outlines a history of censorship beginning with the ancient Greeks. This grand tour of censorship includes observations on Frederick the Great and Joseph II of Austria, whom Radishchev criticizes for pursuing contradictory and ultimately harmful policies that hindered free speech. Radishchev had also familiarized himself with the constitutions of several American states—Pennsylvania, Delaware, Maryland, and Virginia—and he quotes specific language on the people's right to freedom of speech and writing and on the inviolability of the press. Paraphrasing section 14 of the Virginia Declaration of Rights, Radishchev notes, "The freedom of the press is the greatest bulwark of liberty."[15]

Under interrogation Radishchev later confessed that he had first gotten the idea for this chapter in 1786 from an essay by Johann Gottfried Herder titled "On the Influence of the Government on the Sciences, and the Sciences on the Government."[16] Radishchev's debt to Herder has been commented on before, but what has escaped notice is the degree to which Radishchev altered Herder's views, going well beyond Herder's notion of freedom of expression.

Herder wrote his essay in 1779 for a contest sponsored by the Berlin Academy of Science. His work had an even older provenance, however, that is significant for our interests. The origin of Herder's essay has been traced to 1769, when he seized upon the idea of composing a political treatise for Catherine the Great. Writing with what he called "the fiery quill of Rousseau and the sparkling wit of Montesquieu," Herder had hoped to catch the ear of the empress and influence her plans to reform the Russian empire.[17] Although Herder never completed his essay, he did eventually get his wish to speak to the Russian empress, albeit through the much sharper pen of Radishchev.

At the beginning of the "Torzhok" chapter the critic exhorts the reader to listen to Herder and provides a lengthy quotation—with ellipses added by Radishchev—from a section of his essay titled "General Observations on How the Government Influences the Sciences":

> The best means for promoting good is noninterference, permission, freedom of thought. Any inquisition is harmful to the realm of learning: it makes the air stifling and smothers the breath. A book that has to pass

through ten censors before it sees the light of day is no longer a book, but a creature of the Holy Inquisition, very often a mutilated unfortunate, beaten with rods, gagged, and always a slave. . . . In the province of truth, in the kingdom of thought and spirit, no earthly power can or should pass judgment; the government cannot do it, much less its hooded censor. In the realm of truth he is not a judge, but a party, like the author. . . . All improvement can take place only through enlightenment; neither hand nor foot can move without head and brain. . . .

The better grounded a state is in its principles, the better organized and the brighter and stronger in itself, the less danger it incurs of being moved and swayed by the winds of shifting opinion, by any pasquinade of an overwrought writer; all the more readily, then, it will grant freedom of thought and freedom of writing, through which truth will ultimately be victorious. Only tyrants are suspicious; only secret evildoers are fearful. An openhearted man, who does good and is firm in his principles, lets anything be said about himself. He walks in the light of day and turns to his own advantage even the worst lies of his enemies. . . . All monopolies of thought are harmful. . . . The ruler of a state must be almost without any favorite opinion of his own in order that he may be able to embrace, tolerate, refine, and direct toward the general welfare the opinions of everyone in his state: hence great rulers are so rare.[18]

It would seem, then, that Herder was a supporter of a radical conception of freedom of expression and thought. Yet the Herder Radishchev gives us is not the one we find in his essay. Radishchev artfully marked his editing of Herder's text with ellipses, a move that tricks the reader into thinking he has been given a fair rendering of the original text. In fact, Radishchev removed important words and phrases from the above passage that strip away Herder's moderating tone.

In the first sentence, for example, Radishchev silently removed the words "to work for a good cause" ("eine gute Sache zu treiben") after "permission," thus removing all limits on the noun; further on he silently removed Herder's qualifying words "with certain restrictions for each situation and condition" ("mit einiger Einschränkung nach seiner Situation und Lage") in his discussion of the freedom granted by the state to thought and writing.

These are but minor omissions, however, and the Herder of his essay differs in fundamental ways from the Herder of Radishchev's *Journey*. Here, for instance, is Herder:

> I do not at all recommend an unrestrained insolence or an indifference toward ideas, particularly when they unmistakably impinge on the wheels of state, when they undermine its very principles and disturb its aims and its happiness. Well-being is more important to humanity than wild speculation, the well-being of the many than the potential happiness of one. I believe, therefore, the state may, in fact must, prohibit certain branches of knowledge as well as certain amusements and pursuits. . . . Not everything may be permitted to bloom everywhere.[19]

Herder repeats the idea again later in his essay to give it the required significance:

> It is indisputable that there are misuses of the sciences that can only be described as insolence, arrogance, and licentiousness and so without a doubt damage a society's traditional turn of mind. He who would excuse open blasphemy or, what is tantamount to it, slander against sound reason, respectability, and virtue not only excuses them, but in fact glorifies them. The state is not merely free to act, it is obligated to act to defend its members and to preserve itself.

If we permit, Herder asks, "blasphemous, voluptuous, scandalous writings," who will be hurt? Not the thinking man capable of casting aside such harmful writings, but society's weakest, most defenseless members—"the vain milksop, the weak woman, the inexperienced youth, . . . the innocent child." As a result, the state will be "corrupted." "The state is the Mother of all its children; it must see to the health, strength, and purity of all. . . . Should he [the writer] give license to his feverish fantasy or to an eruption of irrationality, so must the state be free to treat him as sick and insane."[20] These last few words would have particular relevance for Radishchev.

Herder goes so far as to endorse surveillance over state officials, noting that it is dangerous to permit "young polygraphs in its offices, Anacreons in its departments, critics in its courts, and novelists in its communication trenches." This too went straight at Radishchev, the writer–civil servant. And so did one final caution from Herder, namely, that anonymous works should never be allowed, for removing the onus of personal responsibility encourages "overreaching" in one's writings that can only have the "most harmful influence."[21]

The differences between Herder's vision of freedom of speech and Radishchev's are striking. So different are they, in fact, that it raises the question why Radishchev made explicit reference to Herder in "Torzhok" and quoted him so liberally, only to distort him so thoroughly. This discrepancy is something scholars have yet to explain and that I too cannot account for, other than to point out Radishchev's familiarity with German thought and the likelihood of his looking to it for inspiration. What has been noted, however, even if not fully appreciated, is how radical was Radishchev's model of free speech. His biographer has called it "the first of its kind in Russia,"[22] but one could go further. Such a notion of unlimited freedom would have stood out in most if not all of Europe. Even the French Declaration of Human Rights (1789) extended freedom of opinion only so far that it "does not disturb the public order established by law." In 1791, two constitutional articles were adopted that outlawed "incitement to commit an illegal act and discrediting of public officials," although these were subsequently repealed.[23] In England, all dramatic performances had to pass through the censors before they could be staged, and libel laws were often used to curb politically unpopular speech, particularly attacks on the powerful and well connected.[24] And in the United States, the freedoms enshrined in the First Amendment were not absolute, but limited by "the rights of others . . . and by the demands of national security and public decency."[25] And, of course, one must also point out the curbs on freedom of expression imposed by the Sedition Act of 1798.

What Radishchev proposed in his *Journey*, then, is best described as extreme, naïve, and unworkable, especially in a country like Russia.[26]

The idea of freedom of expression did not exist in Russia before the second half of the eighteenth century. Although Peter the Great famously began a breakneck process of modernization in the early 1700s, it did not extend to encouraging his subjects to speak their minds. Far from it.

During his visit to London in 1698 the tsar was shocked by the freedom of opinion afforded English lawyers. "I, too, have that ilk at home," he growled, "I will hang them all as soon as I get back."[27] Dissent of any kind under Peter was to be swiftly and brutally suppressed.

In 1701, Peter issued an edict prohibiting monks from keeping ink or paper in their cells; writing was allowed only in the refectory and only with the knowledge and approval of their superior. Over time the restrictions increased. In 1718, Peter forbade everyone in his realm, save religious teachers, from writing behind locked doors. Anyone with knowledge of such an offense was obligated to report it to the authorities or face a charge of sedition.[28] For the tsar-reformer, the printed word was meant to serve the state.

Spoken, as opposed to printed, speech was just as jealously restricted. No unauthorized discussion of the person of the ruler or of the state's policies and actions was permitted lest it be interpreted as criticism. Such talk went by the term *slovo i delo Gosudarevo*—"the Sovereign's Word and Deed"—and was considered treason punishable by death. Slovo i delo remained law until 1762, and for decades it was used to torture and execute many unfortunate souls found guilty of speaking too freely.[29]

Despite some loosening under the empress Elizabeth in the middle of the century, this restrictive environment remained largely intact until the reign of Catherine the Great. Her thirty-four-year reign marks a high point in the history of freedom of expression in Russia and is justly seen as a period of exceptional toleration and the expansion of civil liberties. Never before had Russians enjoyed such liberty to speak their minds, profess their beliefs, and share their opinions free of fear.

This new spirit of toleration was noticed soon after Catherine seized the throne in 1762. The empress sponsored a publication of the *Encyclopédie*, then banned in France; she helped translate Jean-François Marmontel's *Belisaire* (1767), an uncompromising condemnation of absolute monarchy, and saw that it was published; she endorsed the publication of an essay by Beardé de l'Abbaye that argued for the complete emancipation of Russia's serfs, over the objections of members of the Free Economic Society, which had commissioned the essay.[30]

The shift in attitude was noticed by all. George Macartney, the British envoy, nervously observed that "the administration of the

71

present Empress . . . has been extremely mild and gentle; perhaps too mild, too gentle for the rough nature of her subjects." The historian August Ludwig Schlözer (1735–1809), who resided in St. Petersburg in the 1760s, credited Catherine with ushering in a new epoch in Russia in which the state's previous "fear of publicity" and "of the press" had become a thing of the past.[31]

A watershed moment was Catherine's convening of the Legislative Commission in 1767. Although other attempts had been made to codify Russia's Byzantine legal code, this was the first such commission to encourage the free groups (chiefly the non-serf population) in Russian society to express their opinions on a variety of civil and legal matters. Catherine expressed her own opinions in her *Velikii Nakaz*, or *Great Instruction* (1767), which endorsed a liberal policy on freedom of expression, proclaiming that such freedom was the natural right of citizens and that it was the state's duty to preserve this right. She wrote in the *Instruction* that the extent of freedom of expression and the level of learning and knowledge in a society were directly related and that possible offenses against this freedom (i.e., libel, lèse majesté) should be treated not as high treason but as misdemeanors. Catherine's proposals on freedom of expression were quite simply revolutionary, amounting to what has been called "the first articulate statement of the principles of this aspect of freedom, conceived as one of the civil liberties, in the history of Russia." Catherine the Great, writes the historian K. A. Papmehl, "was the first ruler in Russian history who was conscious of the concept of freedom of expression and of its positive value."[32]

So bold were Catherine's ideas on protecting and encouraging freedom of expression that they met considerable resistance from the ecclesiastical and political elite. Their resistance is telling, for it highlights the fact that freedom of speech in Russia was born as a gift from the ruler as part of her program to modernize and enlighten the empire. This freedom was not wrested from the state as a concession to the undeniable authority of a rising literate public, but granted unexpectedly from on high by a monarch in a moment of generosity. As such, this freedom could be taken back, and it later would be.[33] Still, many educated Russians embraced this new liberty and came to view it as a right of citizenship, although most of Radishchev's contemporaries would not have gone as far in their understanding of the outer limits of this freedom.

Radishchev makes reference to Catherine's *Instruction* in "Torzhok." "Let anyone print anything that enters his head," says the critic of censorship. "If anyone finds himself insulted in print, let him get his redress at law. I am not speaking in jest. Words are not always deeds, thoughts are not crimes. These are the rules in the *Instruction for a New Code of Laws*."[34]

Actually, this is not what Catherine wrote in the *Instruction*. Rather, she made a clear distinction between spoken and printed words, giving much greater freedom to the former and noting that the latter, being "more durable" than mere words, can be considered high treason if they in fact "lead to the crime of high treason." "Slanderers," she also declares, "ought to be punished."[35] Just as Radishchev had rewritten Herder, so too did he rewrite Catherine.

Radishchev is correct, however, to point out the lack of a defense of freedom of speech in law. The Legislative Commission failed to codify and endorse a new set of laws for the empire. In the end, Catherine's lofty rhetoric about civil liberties remained just that, and freedom of speech never gained legal protection in her reign. For the next century, the limits of expression would chiefly be determined by the wishes of the tsar and the prevailing attitudes of his ministers, and, despite periods of general liberalism, none were as sustained or as expansive as that under Catherine.[36]

73

Thus, it is something of a paradox that the most extreme attack on censorship appeared at a moment of unprecedented tolerance. Although perhaps not. Under no previous ruler would anyone in Russia have thought to write, much less publish, such a work as Radishchev's *Journey*; under subsequent rulers, few would have dared to.

Having asserted the right to freedom of speech in her *Instruction*, Catherine helped to foster the spread of ideas, with her edict of 1783 giving private individuals the right to establish printing presses, with the sole requirement that the local police, known as the Board of Public Morality (*uprava blagochiniia*), be notified and shown all books for inspection prior to publication.[37]

The edict of 1783 raises the subject of censorship. Unbelievable though it may seem, no state system of censorship in the juridical sense existed in Russia until the end of the eighteenth century. When Peter the Great began establishing printing operations at the beginning of the century there was no need for official censorship since all presses were controlled by the state. The one exception was presses controlled by the church, whose publications were overseen by the church administration. Over time, a system developed whereby the Holy Synod oversaw the publications from all church and monastic presses, the Senate those of the official presses, and the Academy of Sciences those of its own presses. Thus, throughout the century no formal mechanisms existed for reviewing printed material before its publication, and until the 1780s most books and newspapers and journals appeared without ever passing through a censor's approval. Those in control of the presses operated according to what has been called the "three-fold limiting clause" that sought to suppress or, more often, amend works inimical to the established church, the political order, or accepted standards of decency.[38]

74

Of course, rulers, including Catherine, sometimes intervened. Catherine, for example, banned the import of books on Tsar Peter III, murdered during her coup of 1762, and sought to root out persons spreading rumors of this coup and plots against her. Nonetheless, the empress ignored a report commissioned by the Senate in 1763 on establishing concrete guidelines for what books should be prohibited from publication. The instances when Catherine made use of her censorial authority are rare; her actions could be at times incoherent, but she did not endorse a strict policy of censorship; if anything, the desire to censor, ban, and expurgate was strongest among her administrators and officials, who looked to Catherine as the arbiter in their quarrels.[39]

Such arbitration became especially acute after 1783 when the number of books being published rose dramatically. Worried church hierarchs, government officials, and local police petitioned Catherine to crack down on what they saw as a flood of dangerous, suspect literature, harmful to public morality. Catherine typically resisted their pleas. Eventually, in 1787, she did order inspections made of the country's booksellers, although only fourteen titles out of over 140,000 were removed from sale, and these were soon permitted to return to the market.[40]

This liberal climate changed, but only gradually, with the outbreak of the French Revolution. In 1789 and 1790, Russian newspapers carried the shocking news of the events in France. The *St. Petersburg Gazette* even published a translation of the entire text of the Declaration of the Rights of Man.[41] With time, however, Catherine, like many, came to view the upheavals in France as the result of the writings of the *philosophes* and the nefarious deeds of freemasons. The stories coming out of France became ever more frightening and spoke of spreading anarchy. In addition, Russia was fighting two bloody wars, one against Sweden in the Baltic and another against the Ottoman Empire along the Black Sea coast.

It was at this moment of heightened international crisis that Radishchev chose to publish his radical book, a copy of which reached Catherine's hands sometime in late June. She spent the rest of the month reading it carefully, marking up the text with her comments, underlining entire passages, and filling in the margins with questions for the author. Although busy fighting two wars, Catherine was sufficiently agitated to find the time to write out ten tightly lined pages with her reaction to the book. "The purpose of this book is clear on every page," she stated, "its author, infected and full of the French madness, is trying in every possible way to break down respect for authority and for the authorities, to stir up in the people indignation against their superiors and against the government. He is probably a Martinist or something similar." To her secretary Alexander Khrapovitskii she called Radishchev "a rebel, worse than Pugachev."[42]

"Torzhok" particularly upset Catherine, and she filled its pages with angry remarks, pointed questions, and heavy underlining. "[H]e speaks quite boldly and insultingly here about authority and government," she fumed, "which, it is evident, are despised by the author. . . . The author does not love monarchs, and wherever he can vilify love and respect for monarchs, he does so with rare audacity and greedy relish."[43] Yet interestingly, even though she had underlined almost the entire chapter, she made no comments about his words on censorship, other than to call his treatment of it abusive.

After having read the first thirty pages of the *Journey*, Catherine sent for Chief of Police Nikita Ryleev to ask how he could have permitted

75

such a book to be published. Ryleev sheepishly confessed that he had not bothered to read the book, given its innocuous title.[44] Ryleev's confession is worth noting, since it highlights the general laxity toward censorship following the edict of 1783. The police had been charged with inspecting all material before it was published, but few took their responsibility seriously. This attitude was a result of the great number of books now being published, too many for the local police to read, and a general sense that the empress wished to encourage, not restrict, the spread of the printed word.

By now Radishchev had gotten wind that his book had displeased the authorities, including the empress, and had begun frantically burning all his remaining copies at home in his kitchen. He had barely finished when the police came to arrest him on June 30. Radishchev was locked up in the Peter and Paul Fortress directly across the Neva River from the Winter Palace. During the final days of June and the first week of July Catherine wrote out a series of questions for the interrogators to put to Radishchev.[45]

Radishchev now sought to distance himself from his book, claiming that he had never intended to incite a rebellion or undermine authority. He had written the book before the troubles began in France, he said, and thus it had nothing in common with them; nor was he a Martinist, as freemasons were then called in Russia. He had written out of vanity, out of a desire to win fame as a daring author, and to make money. The sole reason for anonymous publication, he insisted, was due to his own timidity and not because he wanted to hide from the ideas expressed in his work. When asked about his interaction with the police prior to publication, Radishchev admitted to surreptitiously adding pages to the manuscript after receiving publication approval, even though he knew this was against the law. He recanted comments expressed in the book about the evil and stupidity of censorship, adding that he now recognized it was needed to protect figures such as himself, who were "confused in their thoughts" and suffering from "weak reasoning."[46]

In the end, Radishchev claimed temporary insanity and threw himself on Catherine's mercy. Yes, he admitted, his words were "vile" and "depraved," his book was a "monster," but it was not entirely his fault "for he had lost his reason." "For a time I was insane and beset by wild, outrageous behavior."[47]

On July 13, Catherine issued an ukase to the St. Petersburg Criminal Court to judge Radishchev's crime and deliver a sentence. His crime, as she saw it, was twofold: first, he published a book that undermined social peace and respect for the authorities and was filled with indignant and insulting words directed against the person of the empress; and second, he knowingly added many pages to the text after it had received police approval.[48] Eleven days later, the criminal court, citing a number of edicts and official statutes, found Radishchev guilty of insulting the honor of the ruler, of publishing an anonymous libel, and of printing a work without prior permission of the local police. He was sentenced to death by beheading. The end of the war with Sweden later that summer saved Radishchev: in a spirit of magnanimity, Catherine commuted his sentence to ten years exile in Siberia.[49]

Radishchev ends "Torzhok" with the narrator climbing back into his carriage to continue his journey to Moscow. As he does so, he begins to tell us about censorship in Russia, but then abruptly stops mid-sentence, saying: "You will find out some other time what happened to the censorship in Russia." Radishchev himself found out about censorship not long after writing these words. He had characterized Russia as a land ruled not by laws but by powerful people, and his own fate proved the point. His *Journey* had angered the powerful, most importantly the empress, which is what doomed him, not the particular laws referred to at his sentencing. The laws had been consulted after the fact and used to give the entire affair an appearance of careful procedure and legality.

77

Catherine eventually did establish a system of censorship, but not until October 1796, a month before her death. Citing the need "to put an end to various inconveniences resulting from the free and unrestricted publication of books," the new law rescinded the right of private individuals to own presses and established censorship committees in every major city and town with the authority to examine all domestic and foreign books prior to publication.[50] In the end, something closer to Herder's vision of freedom of expression, not Radishchev's, was adopted in Russia.

The Radishchev affair left a stain on Catherine's legacy that has yet to fade and has led some historians to cast her rule, unjustly, in a dark light. For when compared with the reigns of her predecessors and successors, Catherine's is deservedly seen as exceptionally tolerant, liberal, enlightened. With few exceptions, the nineteenth century in Russia was markedly more hostile to freedom of expression. Not until 1905 was freedom of speech given legal sanction, and then only after a bloody revolution. This window of openness proved to be short-lived; for most of the twentieth century the printed and spoken word was held prisoner. The collapse of the Soviet Union in 1991 gave reason for optimism that freedom of expression along the lines of what is known in the West might take root in Russia. Recent developments in Russia, however, most notably the Kremlin's neutering of the mass media and the murder of more than a dozen journalists in the past seven years,[51] suggest that anything resembling Radishchev's vision of free speech remains an unfulfilled dream.

Notes

* I would like to thank Professors Marcus Levitt and Irina Reyfman for their insightful comments on an earlier draft of this paper.

1. Ya. L. Barskov, *Materialy k izucheniiu 'Puteshestviia iz Peterburga v Moskvu' A. N. Radishcheva* (Moscow-Petrograd, 1935), 2:334; P. N. Berkov, "K tsenzurnoi istorii 'Puteshestviia' Radishcheva," in *Radishchev: stat'i i materialy*, ed. M. P. Alekseev (Leningrad, 1950), 290–93, 301; Allen McConnell, *A Russian Philosophe: Alexander Radishchev, 1749–1802* (The Hague: M. Nijhof, 1964), vii, 71; A. N. Radishchev, *Puteshestvie iz Peterburga v Moskvu. Vol'nost'*, ed. V. A. Zapadov (St. Petersburg, 1992), 482–84. The first complete edition was not published in Russia until 1905.

2. McConnell gives only a page to freedom of speech in his treatment of the *Journey*. See 96–97.

3. Details from McConnell; David M. Lang, *The First Russian Radical: Alexander Radishchev (1749–1802)* (London: Allen & Unwin, 1959); and Roderick Page Thaler, ed. and intro., *A Journey from St. Petersburg to Moscow*, trans. Leo Weiner (Cambridge, MA: Harvard University Press, 1958).

4. The origins of the *Journey* have been traced back as far as 1772. See Zapadov, *Puteshestvie*, 495–96; D. S. Babkin, *Protsess Radishcheva* (Moscow-Leningrad, 1952), 27–38.

5. Babkin, *Protsess*, 27–28.

6. Ibid., 154, 168.

7. McConnell, *A Russian Philosophe*, 71–72, 87; Andrew Kahn, "Self and Sensibility in Radishchev's *Journey from St. Petersburg to Moscow*: Dialogism, Relativism, and the Moral Spectator," in *Self and Story in Russian History*, ed. Laura Engelstein and Stephanie Sandler (Ithaca: Cornell University Press, 2000); G. P. Makogonenko, *Radishchev i ego vremia* (Moscow, 1956), 438–78.

8. McConnell notes (79, 81) that this indictment makes the *Journey* different from past critiques, which were careful not to attack the system, but merely to point out abuses for correction.

9. *Journey*, 199–200. I have slightly modified Werner's translation. McConnell, *A Russian Philosophe*, 87–88.

10. *Journey*, 164–65.

11. Ibid., 166–71.

12. Ibid., 168–69.

13. Ibid., 171.

14. Ibid., 171–72.

15. Ibid., 184–85, 273. Radishchev's most probable source was *Recueil des lois constitutives des colonies angloises [sic], confédérés sous la dénomination d'États-Unis de l'Amerique-Septentrionale*, comp. and trans. Regnier (Philadelphia and Paris, 1778).

16. Babkin, *Protsess*, 189.

17. Little is known of Herder's plans and sketches for what this treatise might have looked like, other than a "Skizze zu einer Abhandlung über die Bildung der Völker." Johann Gottfried Herder, *Werke*, vol. 3, ed. Wilhelm Dobbek (Berlin, 1969), 410–11; Rudolf Haym, *Herder nach seinem Leben und seinen Werken* (Berlin, 1885), vol. 2, 117–25.

18. *Journey*, 165–66; Herder, *Werke*, 307, 310. All ellipses are Radishchev's.

19. Herder, *Werke*, 307–308.

20. Ibid., 350–51.

21. Ibid., 352.

22. McConnell, *A Russian Philosophe*, 96. Two other notable endorsements of freedom of speech are much more restrained and limited. See "O glavnykh prichinakh, otnosiashchikhsia k prirashcheniiu khudozhestv," originally published in the *Moscow Monthly Edition (Moskovskoe izdanie)* (February 1781). Reprinted in Makogonenko, ed., *N. I. Novikov—Izbrannye sochineniia* (1951), 414–16; also in *N I Novikov i ego sovremenniki* (1961), 213–15. See also the translation of "Bielfeld's Dissertation on Superfluous Arts and Sciences," published in Novikov's *Industrious Man at Rest* in 1784-85.

23. Quoted in K. A. Papmehl, *Freedom of Expression in Eighteenth-Century Russia* (The Hague: Nijhof, 1971), 125–26 n. 42; Hannah Barker and Simon Burrows, eds., *Press, Politics, and the Public Sphere in Europe and North America, 1760–1820* (Cambridge: Cambridge University Press, 2002), 185.

24. James Van Horn Melton, *The Rise of the Public in Enlightenment Europe* (Cambridge, 2001), 20, 32, 64–66, 132, 138, 140–41, 172–73. On theater censorship, see Paula Fichter's essay in this volume.

25. Robert E. Cushman, *Civil Liberties in the United States. A Guide to Current Problems and Experience* (Ithaca: Cornell University Press, 1956), 2.

26. Papmehl calls Radishchev's ideas on censorship and freedom of the press "extreme" and "a trifle specious." *Freedom of Expression*, 124, 126.

27. Ibid., 2.

28. Ibid.

29. Ibid., 4–6.

30. Ibid., 33–36, 44–45.

31. Ibid., 41–42.

32. Ibid., 42–43, 47–56. The relevant sections of the *Instruction* are in Chapter 20, Nos. 480–84. W. F. Reddaway, ed. *Documents of Catherine the Great: The Correspondence with Voltaire and the Instruction of 1767, in the English Text of 1768* (Cambridge, 1931), 287–88. For a more negative assessment, see John P. LeDonne, *Absolutism and Ruling Class: The Formation of the Russian Political Order, 1700–1825* (New York: Oxford University Press, 1991), 169–77.

33. Papmehl, *Freedom of Expression*, 53–60, 68–69, 126.

34. *Journey*, 167. Radishchev refers to the work by its full title.

35. Reddaway, *Documents of Catherine*, article 485.

36. See Charles A. Ruud, *Fighting Words: Imperial Censorship and the Russian Press, 1804–1906* (Toronto: University of Toronto Press, 1982); Marina Tax Choldin, *A Fence Around the Empire: Russian Censorship of Western Ideas under the Tsars* (Durham: Duke University Press, 1985); Kathleen Parthe, *Russia's Dangerous Texts: Politics Between the Lines* (New Haven: Yale University Press, 2004).

37. Papmehl, *Freedom of Expression*, 90–92; Gary Marker, *Publishing, Printing, and the Origins of Intellectual Life in Russia, 1700–1800* (Princeton: Princeton University Press, 1985), 219.

38. Papmehl, *Freedom*, 20, 82–83; Marker, *Publishing*, 212–13; and, most recently, A. Iu. Samarin, "'Pod kakim prismotrom i tsenzuroiu pechatanie knig proiskhodit': tipograficheskoe delo i tsenzura v Rossii epokhi prosveshcheniia," *Novoe literaturnoe obozrenie* 92 (2008): 356–75.

39. Papmehl, *Freedom of Expression*, 36–40; Zapadov, ed., *Puteshestvie*, 606.

40. Papmehl, *Freedom of Expression*, 113–19; Marker, *Publishing*, 219–25.

41. Marker, *Publishing*, 226; M. M. Shtrange, *Russkoe obshchestvo i frantsuzskaia revoliutsiia 1789–1794 gg.* (Moscow, 1956), 47–53.

42. *Journey*, 11, 239; Babkin, *Protsess*, 33–35, 151, 156–64.

43. *Journey*, 247–48.

44. Babkin, *Protsess*, 27–38, 318.

45. See *Journey*, 239–49.

46. Babkin, *Protsess*, 168, 170, 173, 181, 186; Papmehl, *Freedom of Expression*, 125 n.41; V. P. Semenikov, *Radishchev—ocherki i issledovaniia* (Moscow-Petrograd, 1923), 32.

47. Babkin, *Protsess*, 53–54, 174, 166–90.

48. Radishchev gave vague and contradictory answers about which sections had been added after he had received the censor's approval. See Zapadov, *Puteshestvie*, 498.

49. Ibid., 196, 237–50.

50. Marker, *Publishing*, 228–31; Papmehl, *Freedom of Expression*, 121–23.

51. Reporters without Borders ranked Russia 141 out of 173 countries, between Mexico (140) and Ethiopia (142), in its annual Press Freedom Index for 2008. See http://www.rsf.org/article.php3?id_article=29031. Accessed December 9, 2008. Insightful discussions include Michael Specter, "Letter from Moscow: Kremlin, Inc." *The New Yorker* (Jan. 29, 2007): 50–63; Jamey Gambrell, "Putin Strikes Again," *New York Review of Books* (July 19, 2007): 74–75; and David Remnick's 2008 *New Yorker* article, "Letter from Moscow: Echo in the Dark," available at http://www.newyorker.com/reporting/2008/09/22/080922fa_fact_remnick. Accessed December 9, 2008.

Paula Sutter Fichtner

Print vs. Speech: Censoring the Stage in Eighteenth-Century Vienna

ARTICLE 11 OF THE FRENCH DECLARATION OF THE RIGHTS OF Man in 1789 and the First Amendment to the Constitution of the United States protect the freedom to speak and publish. Neither document, however, qualitatively distinguishes spoken words from those that are written. Direct speech and its equivalent on paper are aligned closely enough to make them sound like two sides of a single civil right. Speech, however, and the right to speak openly is listed first, and for good reason. If nothing else, it is a power given to humankind generally; even the mentally disabled express themselves orally. Scholars who study the relationship of orality and the written word point out that language evolved as a means of spoken rather than written communication.[1]

Our minds also take meaning from para-verbal elements in speech acts, such as intonation, pauses, facial expressions, and gestures. Environment plays a role in helping us understand what we hear as well: we converse and listen in countless varieties of settings that clarify and reinforce the content and intent of what is being said. Indeed, our brains seem organized to absorb and process information that comes at us from several sources at once.[2] Far less encumbered by the linear logic of print, speech is also prone to suggestive ambiguities that are difficult to evaluate and even harder to control.

Nevertheless, institutional supervision of the written word was routine in early modern Europe, especially as a technique for enforcing confessional orthodoxies. Intellectual and spiritual life in the Habsburg empire was no exception. Programmatically and personally committed to checking and reversing the spread of the Protestant Reformation, governments of the devoutly Catholic house of Austria and the clerical hierarchy that worked closely with it regularly censored printed materials throughout the dynasty's central European lands.[3]

The execution of this policy, however, was at best imperfect and by no means precluded the free exchange of opinion and ideas in public settings among Habsburg subjects. Down to the middle of the eighteenth century, the unconstrained word flourished on popular comic stages in and around Vienna and other theaters throughout the monarchy. Managers of these facilities took it as an article of faith that their chief job was to amuse, the more heartily the better. Farce, with extensive impromptu commentary by performers, dominated the repertoire. Should an impresario want to increase his box office take, improvised performances were his surest strategy. Around 1761, a company of players from Württemberg, the Menningers, drew big enough audiences in Baden, not far from Vienna, to mount burlesques and improvised skits on a daily basis. The director of the German theater in the Moravian capital of Brno scheduled an extemporaneous production in 1770 simply to coax more people to his establishment. Josef Anton Stranitzky, the acknowledged father of Viennese popular comic theater and a comedian himself, always made room in his scripts for extemporization.[4]

Habsburg governments knew that they ruled a theater-loving public, especially in Vienna. And they were willing to cater to public taste. In 1712, a period when the dynasty's armies were crushing the once-dangerous Ottoman empire in the Balkans, the court thought that its peoples had sacrificed so much that their preference for comedy should be respected. As late as 1741, some government officials also thought that such distraction kept audiences from even less desirable behavior.[5]

Particularly cherished was the "*Hanswurst*" figure, a stereotyped peasant who originally made heavy use of the Salzburg dialect of German when entertaining audiences with impromptu and earthy commentary on a variety of topics. Stranitzky developed and played this

82

figure to the hilt, using his talents to cultivate personal bonds with those who came to see and hear him. At the end of his acting career, he personally beseeched his public from the stage to accept his successor, Gottfried Prehauser, one of the preeminent comic actors of Vienna in the eighteenth century.[6]

All classes of society enjoyed these antics, even when performances took place in outlying taverns and farm sheds. Part of their attraction was linguistic accessibility; the stage tongue was usually German, unlike the Italian and French that were spoken in circles around the Habsburg rulers themselves and used in court-sponsored theaters. It was an Italian company that in 1708 opened the first public stationary theater ever built in Vienna, the Theater at the Carinthian Gate.[7]

Comprehensibility aside, improvised theatricals delighted audiences for two other reasons. Actors' off-the-cuff remarks often voiced the social, political, and economic resentments that troubled the Habsburg version of the Old Regime, but that rarely worked their way into corrective policy. Should criticisms be openly aired, it was done in more supervised settings where great care was taken to avoid suggesting remedies that would subvert political or religious authority. School dramatic presentations, a common feature of Jesuit and Benedictine instruction by the seventeenth century, were training grounds for future courtiers and diplomats who had to learn how to speak in a variety of settings. Students often took the opportunity to criticize or poke fun at the establishments of their lands, but none of this circulated beyond the semiprivate stages of their academies.[8]

83

Stranitzky, however, in a secular setting, could criticize obliquely but wickedly. Very few of his theatrical concoctions survive in written form, aside from one compilation of his scenarios, *Ollapatrida des durchgetriebenen Fuchsmundi* (*The Reeking Stew of the Much-tried [Mr.] Foxy-mouth*). Published in 1722, it shows him at his mischievous best, so much so that it became a handbook for the comic theater throughout all of Germany. One sequence has a sergeant haranguing a lad into joining the army. The young man frequently interrupts the officer to inquire about the possibility of being wounded; the sergeant does not rule that out, but assures him that such injuries lead to promotion and glory. Throughout their exchange, the young man imagines one of his body parts after another being maimed or altogether destroyed in combat. Yet, upon losing an arm and a leg he is told that he is eligible for the cavalry. How, he asks his perfervid interlocutor, can anyone be a horseman in such a condition?[9]

The political and social edge in on-stage commentaries of Hanswurst and his numerous *Doppelgänger* was even more overt. Performing usually in the suburbs around Vienna and in the local dialect, they often grumbled about the Habsburg government, the aristocracy, and the Roman Catholic clergy, who were collectively responsible for the common man's lot in life. To outraged noblemen who railed against him, *Hanswurst* was known to reply, "but we can still talk." Parody, which normally stirs up irreverent thoughts about its targets, was also common to these productions, thus adding to their critical purpose.[10]

The title of Stranitzky's collection was taken over from a Spanish dish of boiled meat and vegetables, *Olla podrida*. Translated literally as "stinking pot," it had made its way into Habsburg court cuisine in the seventeenth century.[11] It also reflected another feature of the impromptu theater that captivated audiences: it was uproariously and unashamedly vulgar. Only a few lines from Strantizky's *Ollapatrida* are needed to make the point. Fuchsmundi, a picaresque figure who morphs from identity to identity as the central protagonist of the skits, assures a girlfriend that he will be as devoted to her as an apothecary is to his enema equipment (*clistir-spritz*). Crude though they were, these productions attracted government officials, even visitors to the city such as Lady Mary Montague, the cosmopolitan wife of Great Britain's ambassador to Constantinople. On her way to the Porte to join her husband, she stopped in Vienna where she not only attended these antics, but, with the aid of an interpreter-translator and her own literary background, found them irresistibly comic. She attended a take-off on the Amphytrion story, which she knew from English, Latin, and French sources, curious, she said, to see what an Austrian theater would do with it. She soon found out. The language, she wrote in a letter, was something that the English common folk would not tolerate in a market crier. Furthermore, players dropped their trousers in full view of men and women from the upper niches of society who sat in the front rows.[12]

By the middle of the eighteenth century, the general public in German-speaking Austria was in its own way as much an arbiter of theatrical taste as it was in France and England. Audiences were growing, and more commercial theaters were opening to accommodate them, particularly in and around Vienna. At the same time, however, the quality of popular judgment and intellectual expectations of audiences were being questioned.[13] Some Germans, eager and anxious to have their native cultural production approach standards allegedly routine in England and France, were increasingly dissatisfied with what passed for good theater in central Europe. As early as the sixteenth century, Martin Luther had railed against a prototype of the ribald *Hanswurst* or *Pickelherring*, as he was called in Saxony and points north. Municipal officials in Vienna had complained for decades about the idleness and rough behavior that such theatrical performances encouraged.[14]

A loose censorship of plays had been operating in Vienna since the beginning of the eighteenth century. The first open refusal of the Habsburg government to allow a performance came in 1707, when a company from Württemberg tried to put on *Die hohe Vermählung zwischen Maria Stuart und Heinrich Dar[n]ley, König von Schottland und Frankreich (The Noble Marriage of Mary Stuart and Henry Darnley, King of Scotland and France.)* The exact nature of the regime's "certain objections" (*gewisse Bedenken*) to the play was not specified, though they may have concerned the part that called for public execution of a head of state, in this case the briefly reigning Henry.[15]

By 1750, however, officials at even the famously lethargic Habsburg court were ready to go on the offensive against the lowlife tone of the local theater. Driving the change was the character of Empress Maria Theresa, who ruled the family empire from 1740 to 1780. Though flexible toward political and economic experiments that promised to contribute to the survival of her dynasty, she was stubbornly prudish, especially in questions of public behavior. She abhorred the vulgarity and obscenity of Hanswurst; she also fretted over the competition to her recently established court theater coming from popular stages where he performed. The empress banned Hanswurst productions completely between 1752 and 1754, though not successfully. She did not, however, give up. Previous censorship of the theater in Vienna had been delegated by the imperial administration to a municipal office. In 1765, Maria Theresa transferred this responsibility to the court censorship commission (*Zensurhofkommission*). This body, however, found it impossible to discriminate between acceptable and unacceptable impromptu speech on stage. The comic theater, therefore, went on.[16]

The empress's other goal, shared by her son and successor, Joseph II, was more didactically positive: to foster good moral and intellectual tone by raising standards in the theater. To this end, playwrights and actors were to follow the model of contemporary French social comedy, which explored the lives, manners, and conversational conventions of the upper classes. Language usage, therefore, became the central issue of theatrical reform. The leading champion of this program in the German-speaking world was not an Austrian, but a professor at the University of Leipzig: Johann Christoph Gottsched. *Eine lateinische Magnifizenz*, or the "literary pope of Leipzig," as not always worshipful writers dubbed him, Gottsched dedicated much of his professional life to purging the German language of convoluted Baroque oratory and making word choice the crucial element in rhetoric. One of his major works, *Ausführliche Redekunst, (The Complete Art of Rhetoric)* went through five printings from 1736 to 1759. Persuasive speech, he argued, was speech that conformed closely to the situation being described or analyzed and followed a logical progression.[17] With random remarks completely out of place in this setting, he was, in fact, adapting the techniques of the expository essay to the theater.

Maria Theresa herself had cordially received the scholar and his wife on a visit to Vienna in 1749. She, her eldest son, and some of their key administrators took up Gottsched's rhetorical mission very seriously, insofar as it applied to the stage. They set about banishing wide-ranging impromptu discourse and all of the vulgarity that went with it from German stages throughout the Habsburg empire.[18]

Performers, on the other hand, were thoroughly convinced that off-color suggestive behavior and language were just what audiences wanted to see and hear in theaters. In Vienna, the great Stranitzky paid close attention to getting the maximum effect from every word and gesture used. He studied speech idiosyncrasies and their associations to heighten the comic impact of Hanswurst's impromptu commentaries.

For Stranitzky it was not enough that the character, an adaptation of the Italian Arlequino, spoke the German dialect of Lower Austria with which he was probably most familiar. It lacked, he said, the vocabulary to get across a "well-turned phrase, a spoof, or a joke" (*eine glückliche Fraze, einen Possen, eine Zotte*). He therefore drew upon speech patterns found in Bavaria and Salzburg—then an independent prince-bishopric—which he thought were more effective. His audiences responded accordingly. The Vienna public found the Salzburg or Bavarian peasant in costumes associated with nearby Lower Austria not only funny, but even more amusing when the Hanswurst figure shifted artlessly from one regional pronunciation and vocabulary to another.[19]

Maria Theresa was accustomed to controlling theaters; she would shutter them totally in 1765 as part of an official year of mourning for her deceased husband. It was making censorship work when stages were accessible that was hard. Even with written texts before them, censors could not predict what performers would say when they were on stage. Scenarios (*Das Buchl*) were often published and sold at the city's box offices. Outlines of extemporaneous remarks could be sketched out beforehand, and often were. But neither of these practices revealed what an audience actually heard once the show began. Well aware that their popularity depended upon their talents as improvisers, actors held forth gladly while on stage on topics utterly unrelated to such scripts as they had.[20]

But reading scripts of theatrical productions before they were performed was the obvious way to carry out the government's cultural mission, especially when it had the enthusiastic endorsement of Gottsched's followers in Vienna. Among them was Joseph von Sonnenfels, one of the eighteenth-century's most tenacious cultural busybodies.[21] Advisor on many matters to both the empress and Joseph II, he was certainly no intellectual philistine. In fact, he was widely read and aesthetically sensitive, with a keen ear for music. He was one of the strongest supporters of the great composer Christoph Willibald Gluck. He also had a strong family background in linguistic matters. His father, born Perrin Lippman, later to become Aloys von Sonnenfels as a Jewish convert to Catholicism, was an expert in the tongues of the Near East, which he taught at the University of Vienna.[22]

The younger Sonnenfels was passionately dedicated to improving the theatrical culture of the Habsburg empire through the discipline of the written word. In his opinion, plays were worthwhile only when they reached printed form, a conviction that may have been formed by his private intellectual habits. His great esteem for the playwrights of classical antiquity had come from reading their works and not merely from seeing them on stage. In all likelihood, he had also acquired his considerable familiarity with contemporary drama—Italian, French, and English—in his library rather than in live performance. But armed with personal conviction and the support of Maria Theresa and the future Joseph II, Sonnenfels began his war of print against improvised theatrical speech in the 1760s. He argued his case in Briefe über die wienerische Schaubühne (Letters on the Theater in Vienna), first published in 1768, and in Der Mann ohne Vorurteil (The Unprejudiced Man), a periodical he brought out episodically between 1765 and 1775. His intention was to criticize impromptu digressions by performers out of public existence. In the process, however, he would inadvertently explain much about the communicative mechanisms and power of the spoken word that would have persuaded eighteenth-century constitution writers to prioritize speech over written expression.[23]

88

The point of departure for Sonnenfels' attack was his scorn for the intellectual emptiness of impromptu speech from the stage. Good theater, he said, should be read, a task, not accidentally, in which censors were theoretically expert. Maria Theresa herself, whose formal education was limited, allegedly read through all plays proposed for her court theater. Sonnenfels also deplored mentally lazy performers who wanted to say the first thing that came into their heads rather than to memorize several hundred verses or page upon page of prose, often in a foreign language. Just as bad was the public affection for such "garbage," as he called it, so entrenched that audiences assaulted the critics who came to these performances and actors cursed them from the stage. In a revision of his Briefe in 1784, he singled out for praise a well-known actor, Christoph Gottlob Stephanie, for abandoning the easy comforts of extemporization and accepting roles in "properly written pieces." As for critics, he thought that, when serious, they were agents of theatrical improvement.[24]

But actors did not confine themselves to the spoken word alone. They often underscored or signaled meaning with gestures that distorted even good plays beyond recognition. Therefore, according to Sonnenfels, a performer's body language and general demeanor should bear some relationship to the subject on stage. Great theatrical language, he said, taking his cue from Gottsched, underscored the ideas and conceptual structure of a play. In 1765, *Der österreichische Patriot*, a periodical very close to Sonnenfels, fleshed out this thought. A good play, it argued, flows naturally from the action; it cannot be changed at will.[25] The logic of this prescription was clear: actors who resorted to impromptu remarks and spectacular gesticulation were drawing attention to them, rather than the text of what they were performing.

At the turn of the nineteenth century, Joseph Oehler (1763–1836), a learned Viennese publisher, said that the theatrical aim of Sonnenfels's weekly *Mann ohne Vorurtheil* was to promote reading and to wipe out extemporaneous commentary.[26] Theater professionals in Vienna had sensed this larger purpose as soon as Maria Theresa banned Hanswurst episodes in 1752 for two years. Most performers, though not all, did not take kindly to speech reform of any sort. Johann Friedrich Weiskern, one of the most skilled, thoughtful, and articulate actors in Vienna, made the point obliquely as early as 1754. In his *Des wunderangenämen Sprach=Mundahrt=und Schreibrichtigkeit=Verbessers . . . Sendschreiben aus der anderen Welt an einen philosophisch-hochdeutschen Sprachlehrer dieser Zeit . . .* (*A Message from the Other World of a Language Reformer to Modern Teachers of German Speech*), the protagonist remarks that language reform has usually created more problems than it solved, especially when inspired by ambitious academics.[27]

But it was the imposition of the standards of the written word on speech that provoked deep outrage. The Sonnenfels program was fully under way in 1768, the year that M. v. J., a self-described theatrical producer vehemently alerted Habsburg officials to the troubles that actors and their employers faced in meeting new performance requirements on their stages. Sonnenfels, fumed M. v. J. in the Wednesday supplement of the *Wiener Diarium*, the court newspaper of the time, was behaving like some critic driven by "the rage of a writer with the purpose of cutting to pieces men, whose work could justifiably make many nations proud." Theatrical producers and managers were under particular pressure. Where, said M. v. J., were impresarios to find actors who could perform all of the mental chores that the official's commitment to the written theater imposed on them? Gottfried Prehauser, a famous comedian of the time, was a superb choice for a part that the producer had in mind. But he did not think it fair to ask a man who was almost seventy years old to memorize lines, a job that would force him to invent a second nature. Whoever was advising Sonnenfels on this matter would, in M.v J.'s opinion, probably have lost his wits by the time he reached that advanced age or perhaps collapsed entirely. The least Sonnenfels could do was to pay for the seats that his censors occupied in theaters. A second letter, published in the Diarium of August 3, 1768, was even more direct. Sonnenfels and/or his advisors, wrote M. v. J., were well read, but singularly lacking in judgment.[28] Maria Theresa briefly relented enough to allow some popular comedies, but only if they used written texts that had no double entendres and obscenities. Comedians who flouted the rules were to be punished. Censors did get outlines of extemporaneous interludes from theater managers, but no specific dialogue.[29]

A few theater managers trimmed plays to the official version of Gottsched's standards, but more of them worried about the effect language purification would have on their box-office receipts. Comic actors who cooperated with official standards soon found their careers in jeopardy. One of Vienna's most popular players, Josef Kurz, created a Hanswurst-like character, Bernardon, so popular that the actor once performed the same skit thirty times nonstop. When the actor subjected written versions of his impromptu commentary to government censors, they lost all of their double entendres and crude humor. Audiences were bitterly disappointed. Even playwrights committed to reform of the Viennese theater had to make compromises if they wanted an appreciative public. Among them was Christian Gottlob Klemm, who had come from Saxony to promote the Sonnenfels agenda. By 1767, however, he was apologizing for concessions to Viennese taste in some of his pieces, which he found necessary to have an audience for his work performed in the Habsburg capital.[30]

Sonnenfels became the official theater censor in 1770. According to a not wholly unsympathetic actress, Christiana Huber, he planned to monitor not only stories (Fabel) but dialogue itself.[31] In March, he presented a *Promemoria* on the subject to Joseph II, the future emperor, who acted as co-regent in these matters for his mother. All stage improvisation was to be forbidden; performers would be arrested for the first offence and banned from the public stage if they did it again. Comic elements in plays could follow the patterns of the old *Posse* (farce), but only if propriety was observed. All scripts had to be submitted for government vetting one month ahead of performance. The decree was to apply not only to Vienna, but throughout the monarchy.

Like Sonnenfels, Joseph was a sworn enemy of intellectual and moral vacuity. The emperor-to-be accepted these measures readily and told Sonnenfels to follow through with them in local theaters. Indeed, the archduke had some recommendations of his own. While the actual policing of the program was delegated to the provincial administration of Lower Austria, censors were to be very busy people. Joseph directed them to supervise not only the content of a piece, but also its presentation on stage. Actors were expressly warned to avoid not only spontaneous commentary and improvisations, but also direct address to audiences. Nor were they to make any changes in texts that had been approved. Censors also had to keep a sharp eye on performers to make sure that their gestures did not violate sound morals.[32]

Sonnenfels worked overtime to advance his goals—he sat in on rehearsals and disburdened himself of advice about productions as well as texts.[33] By 1772, the state presence in Vienna's theaters was fairly heavy. A couple of low-level bureaucrats along with a police official now routinely attended performances, still free of charge. In case of disorder, the army could be brought in from a local post. Entrances to government-subsidized stages, such as the court theater, were also heavily guarded.[34]

Sonnenfels himself, however, was no longer supervising the stage for the Habsburg government, having been dismissed in 1770 for reasons not altogether clear. Nevertheless, he left the job happy to think that he had banned extemporaneous interpolations in the German-speaking theaters of the Habsburg lands.[35] The enforcement of these measures, however, may have been more haphazard than he would have liked. Some provincial authorities readily complied, especially when they had influential local support, as in Graz, but others dragged their feet. The chief censor in Prague, for example, was too busy with other duties to attend plays, so he requested an assistant.[36]

Comic companies throughout Vienna gleefully memorialized Sonnefels's fall from grace. The Menningers, once again playing outside of the city in 1770, tried to put on a poorly disguised satire of the official called *The Learned Fool*. Upon the intervention of Franz Karl Hägelin, Sonnefels's successor, they drew in their claws a bit. The piece came to the stage more evasively entitled *Der Geschmack der Komödie Ist Noch Nicht Bestimmt (The Taste of Comedy Is Not Yet Settled)*.[37] But the thirst for vengeance was strong. Carl Stephanie Junior, the son of the actor whom Sonnenfels had respected deeply, came up with a play in 1773 called *The Fashionable Scold, or I Know Better*. The hero is the arrogant, not always transparent, Mr. Hader, who rethinks everything nine times and whose learning on questions of dramaturgy, theater, dance, opera, medicine, trade, correct German speech, and etiquette makes him ridiculously self-important. Impromptu popular comedy thus continued, in part encouraged by Joseph himself in one of the many progressive episodes that characterized his career before and immediately after he became emperor. Acting as his mother's regent in 1776, he allowed new theaters to open freely. Many more suburban theaters sprang up and productions of all kinds, popular comedies included, increased substantially.[38]

In 1781, after a year on his own as emperor, Joseph issued a sweeping decree on censorship that granted the press and publishers a remarkable degree of latitude. Steering a path between total license and repression that might frustrate his ambition to develop Vienna as a center of the book trade, he was anxious to make sure that worthwhile books and journals did appear. Authors did have to put their names on what they wrote, but only works offered for sale were to be monitored. He had, however, already begun to regret his expansive theatrical policy. What was spoken in the theater had to be watched much more closely because of its much larger public and the immediacy of its impact.[39]

Even in his progressive moods, Joseph was first and foremost a confirmed monarchist who made no distinction between the welfare of his peoples and the interests of the house of Habsburg. One of his chief targets both as regent and as ruler in his own right was anti-intellectualism among clergymen, especially those whose homiletic styles were often quite similar to practices that he and Sonnenfels had deplored on stage. It was not unusual in seventeenth-century German churches, Catholic and Protestant alike, for entire sermons to be built around gesticulation and mimicry. The pulpit oratory of the talented and popular Habsburg court preacher Abraham a Sancta Clara (1644–1709) was a dazzling fusion of moral uplift with allegories, personifications, puns, pictures, imagined dialogues, and seemingly impromptu rhymes. He also used liturgically suspect props while preaching; an envelope he waved at a sermon on All Saints Day presumably helped him convince the faithful that he had received a message from the afterlife. Sensitized as they were to this style of preaching, audiences throughout the Habsburg empire could be expected to examine body language for information about the texts and subtexts not only of plays but also of homilies. Committed to persuasion by reason rather than emotion, Joseph II and Sonnenfels consulted such reports of pastoral physical behavior before congregations to make sure churches were not furthering religious irrationalism in the population.[40]

Nevertheless, eager as Joseph was to rid his empire of obscurantist vestiges of the Old Regime, he had no intention of yielding monarchical control over Habsburg lands, a policy that was challenged on a number of fronts in the 1780s, at first domestic, then from revolutionary France. In fact, he rather quickly saw what Sonnenfels had once written: that extemporaneous commentary on stage of any kind was difficult to control. Therefore it could be as dangerous politically as it was morally. Watching actors poke fun at the Habsburg regime on stage could, at the very least, weaken audience respect for the government's power to punish. Joseph therefore had no trouble retaining a policy that required plays to be free of anything that "offends in the slightest religion, the state, or good manners" in order to improve public taste. Such material was altogether out of place in a "capital city" and the seat of a court.[41]

Joseph also took very seriously a Sonnenfels prescription that appeared in Der Mann ohne Vorurteil: words heard from the stage affected audiences quite differently than printed texts. Theatrical language, and all of the physical action associated with it, worked directly on the emotions and senses of the auditor. Gottfried Prehauser was famous for miming his impromptu remarks so explicitly that even people innocent of German understood him. A theater censor had to imagine the effect that gesture, intonation, stage sets, props, and costuming would have on an audience.[42] Suppressing body language alone was therefore seen as a major step in reforming the Austrian theater. For example, an anonymous piece in the *Allgemeiner Theater Allmanach* triumphally noted in 1782 that expressions of true emotion on stage had replaced making faces; ridiculousness and exaggeration were less frequent, too. Representations of human life, the essay concluded, were now more than melodramatic sound and fury.[43]

In Franz Karl Hägelin, who held the position of censor from 1770 until his death in 1804, Joseph had the perfect man for the job. Born in Freiburg im Breisgau, then in the westernmost part of the Habsburg lands, he had studied at the University of Halle, a center of German Protestant pietism that laid great stress on popular literacy. His first work with the Habsburg government had concerned educational reform.[44] Those who knew Hägelin said he was a cultivated and progressive spirit—in a word, a man of the eighteenth-century Enlightenment or, at least, its German variant. He was not beyond using the name of Rousseau in supporting his arguments. Aesthetically sophisticated as well, he knew a considerable amount about the arts, including the history of the European theater. Like Sonnenfels and the emperor, however, he believed that all plays, regardless of genre, had to have a moral purpose if they were not to threaten the state. Even light entertainment, such as musical theater, should offer "respectable (*ehrbare*) distraction" or "healthy" (*unschädlich*) uplift.[45]

The years between 1785 and 1804, when Hägelin died, were politically chaotic. Joseph's intrusive centralism drove the Austrian Netherlands and Hungary into outright revolt. His successors, Leopold II and Francis II (the latter as Francis I of the new Austrian empire following the collapse of the German Holy Roman Empire in 1806), faced ideological and military revolutionary challenges from France.[46] Within this context, Hägelin applied himself to keeping the theater in Vienna and throughout the monarchy as uncontroversial as he could. In the process he, like Sonnenfels before him, thought long and hard about the reasons for monitoring impromptu speech and curbing it when needed; he also sensed the sharp distinction between the powers of speech and print.

Hägelin summarized his thoughts on these matters in 1795 in an extended memorandum on censorship. Though intended for Hungary, the document echoed ideas and policies then current in Vienna and the rest of the Habsburg empire.[47] Twenty-five years of keeping an eye on actors had taught him that it was very difficult to control what they actually said and the impact of their words. Not only was the theater open to the entire public, but the spoken play was much more compelling than the written word. What was spoken on stage was reinforced very often by sight and sound, making it possible to manipulate intentionally a listener's affective side. A specific emotional event is the result. Reading alone did not do this. Audiences also reacted very differently to language that expressed simulations of real life than they did to words spread along the printed page. It was also hard to anticipate reactions to what was heard from the stage, even after written texts had been vetted and amended. Depending on their social class, people could interpret words quite differently. *Double entendres* would be obvious to some, and escape others. Even after a text had been cleaned up quite nicely, impromptu onstage remarks, suggestive intonations in words and phrases, breaks in oral delivery, or pauses that signaled double meanings might recontaminate them.

95

The memorandum encouraged playwrights either to avoid words with undesirable social overtones or vulgar connotations or to find alternatives. "Ehebruch" (adultery) was off-limits in Hägelin's stage vocabulary because it called to mind a practice that corrupted a basic social institution. While he admitted that this particular sin of the flesh could have a place in serious drama, it should be called "betrayal" and not "wearing horns" or "donning horns," because such behavior was no joking matter.[48]

With the excesses of the French Revolution and alarming domestic unrest at home in mind, Hägelin was also looking at stage commentary far more politically after 1795. Censorship of the theater in his hands, and of his successors, took on a more topical cast, as not only the subtexts and tone of words but also their daily contemporary referents became crucial. New regulations that Hägelin drew up forbade using the terms liberty, freedom, and Enlightenment on stage. Nor could performers mention tyranny and despotism, presumably because some in the audience would associate Habsburg government with these practices. Rulers were never to abdicate, wrote Hägelin; therefore *King Lear*, as played in Vienna, ended happily for the much-tried monarch. Friedrich Schiller's *Maria Stuart* could not be performed at all because it called for the on-stage execution of a ruler. *Wilhelm Tell*, which Schiller based on the historical rebellion of some Swiss cantons against Habsburg rule, was banned from the Austrian theater until about twenty years after the French Revolution and thereafter performed only after an anonymous adapter had cleaned it up. Hägelin's prescriptions applied to opera libretti as well. Until 1848, the closing quartet of Mozart's *Don Giovanni* did not celebrate freedom ("Es lebe die Freiheit/Die Freiheit soll leben" [Long Live Liberty/Liberty must live], but joy ("Long live joyfulness/Joyfulness must live").[49]

Like all in the Habsburg empire who had confronted the issue of impromptu speech from the stage before him, Hägelin also concluded that such liberties with speech from the stage would end only when

actors were forbidden to take them and when censors or police in the audience made sure that performers obeyed. Supervision of the theater, therefore, tightened. It was also more cumbersome, so much so that the best that operators of commercial theaters could hope for was that censors would work quickly. All scripts had to be read fully. The producer would first submit the text, written out by a copyist, to appropriate officials. The latter would then read the manuscript, paying especially attentive to *double entendres* that were potentially indecent. They would then ink out all offending passages and return the revised piece to the theater for performance. While Habsburg governments were perfectly happy during the Napoleonic era and even after for their subjects to distract themselves at plays and public musical entertainments, they were especially watchful with dialect houses because they drew large audiences. The growth in literacy in the Habsburg empire in the first decades of the nineteenth century brought tighter monitoring of written materials too, but police still vigilantly lurked in and around theaters to make sure that nothing said onstage overstepped the bounds of propriety and good taste or questioned Habsburg rule. After 1803 commissars sat in on dress rehearsals and all performances, beginning with the first, to see that good taste and political correctness prevailed.[50]

Sonnenfels and Hägelin did not eradicate Vienna's tradition of popular comedy and its linguistic self-indulgence. Indeed, the so-called *quod libet* interludes and overtly topical parodies convulsed audiences at the plays of Austria's classic comic writers, Ferdinand Raimund and Johann Nestroy, in the post-Napoleonic era. Neither of these authors allowed the public to forget that the resources of the spoken word surpassed those of its written counterpart. One of Nestroy's most enduring creations, *Der böse Geist Lumpazzi vagabundus* (*The Malevolent Spirit Lumpazzi vagabundus*), has three central protagonists, two of whom cannot read but get through life quite nicely through native cunning, good luck, and marvelously facile tongues.[51]

Compared with what passed as popular comedy in the preceding century, however, the plays of Raimund and Nestroy were highly literarized. Both paid much more attention to the subtleties of character and social setting than did their predecessors. Raimund was especially subtle at probing character and the psychological dynamics that drove it, even as he called attention to the ridiculous side of society and the human condition generally. Indeed, Raimund and Nestroy's variant of popular theater had been tamed so much so that by the end of the century some of their stage works had entered the repertory of the august court theater.[52] As for the dim-witted crudity of the old-fashioned *commedia dell'arte* Austrian-style, its negative associations still endure in Vienna today. A leading Austrian daily, the *Kurier*, wrote in 2006 of two aides of the late Jörg Haider's populist political movement, the Alliance for the Future of Austria, that they were incapable of performing even minor roles at Tschauner's, the only stage for old-fashioned improvised theater, vulgar wisecracks, Austrian dialect and all (*Stehgreiftheater*) that remains in the city.[53]

But eighteenth-century controversies over the freely spoken and, often, unrefined word in the Viennese popular theater have more than local resonance. At the very least they show that both Habsburg rulers and their officials clearly recognized that speech was a sufficiently powerful instrument to require far more stringent regulation than published material. Its multidimensionality in public settings, especially the theater, created grave problems for those anxious to control cultural and, somewhat later, political behavior. The written word, on the other hand, was not only much easier to supervise; it was also an instrument through which speech itself could be curbed.

Driven first by a vision of public self-improvement, then by contemporary political pressures, Maria Theresa, Joseph II, his brother Leopold, and their bureaucrats demonstrated that the spoken word and the written word had quite different effects in the public arena. Though both were active agents of individual communication, their capacities to persuade and to mold behavior and values worked on different sides of the psyche and intellect. Of the two, speech was by far the more powerful, and therefore the more in need of supervision. The printed word and the uttered one were not wholly antagonistic, but their compatibility was conditional rather than necessary. Thus, when the writers of eighteenth-century constitutions and their successors listed speech and the opportunities for free speech first among the civil rights of self-expression, they were not simply following a formula. They were acknowledging a primal aspect of the human condition.

Notes

1. E.g., R. Graeme Dunphy, "Orality," in *Early Germanic Literature and Culture*, ed. Brian Murdoch and Malcolm Read (Rochester, NY: Camden House, 2004), 103.

2. Wolf Singer, "Zum Problem der Willensfreiheit," in *Die Freiheit des Denkens*, ed. Konrad Paul Liessmann (Vienna: Zsolnay, 2007), 126–27, 130.

3. For the German-speaking community generally, see Josef Benzing, *Die Buchdrucker des 16. und 17. Jahrhunderts im deutschen Sprachraum* (Wiesbaden: Harrassowitz, 1963).

4. Johann Heinrich Friedrich Müller, *Theatral-Neuigkeiten* (Vienna: Gehlen, 1773), 211; Johann Heinrich Friedrich Müller, *Genaue Nachrichten von beyden Schaubühnen und andern öffentlichen Ergötzungen* (Pressburg: Löwen, 1772), 110; W. E. Yates, *Theatre in Vienna: A Critical History, 1776–1995* (Cambridge: Cambridge University Press, 1996), 4.

5. Carl Glossy, "Zur Geschichte der Wiener Theatercensur, " pt. 1, *Jahrbuch der Grillparzer Gesellschaft* 7 (1897), 241.

6. Joseph Oehler, *Geschichte des gesamten Theaterwesens zu Wien* (Vienna: Oehler, 1803), 116–17.

7. Hilda Haider-Pregler, "Nachwort," in Josef Sonnenfels, *Briefe über die wienerische Schaubühne* [Vienna 1765] (rpt. Graz: Akademische Druck- und Verlagsanstalt, 1988), 400 n. 89; Glossy, "Theatercensur," 244. Cf. *Der österreichische Patriot*, July 5, 1765, 365; Christiane Huber [untitled], in Müller, *Genaue Nachrichten*, 37.

8. Hermann Stauffer, *Erfindung und Kritik. Rhetorik im Zeichen der Frühaufklärung bei Gottsched und seinen Zeitgenossen* (Frankfurt am Main: Lang, 1997), 217 n. 31; Leslie Bodi, *Tauwetter in Wien. Zur Prosa der österreichischen Aufklärung 1781–1795* (Frankfurt am Main: S. Fischer, 1977), 138–39.

9. Joseph Anton Stranitzky, *Ollapatrida des durchgetriebenen Fuchsmundi. . .* [n.p., n.d.], 19–21; Oehler, *Theaterwesen*, 100.

10. Peter Branscombe, "The Beginnings of Parody in Viennese Popular Theatre," in *From Perinet to Jelinek: Viennese Theatre in its Political and Intellectual Context*, ed. W. E. Yates, Allyson Fiddler, and John Warren (Oxford: Peter Lang, 2001), 10, 23. Citation in Ernst Wangermann, *The Austrian Achievement 1700–1800* (New York: Harcourt, Brace, Jovanovich, 1973), 52–53.

11. Renate Wagner-Wittula, *Imperial Austrian Cuisine*, trans. Mark Hackworth and Paul Heinrichs (Salzburg: Residenz, 2006), 46.

12. Simon Williamson, "The Viennese Theater," in *Schubert's Vienna*, ed. Raymond Erickson (New Haven: Yale University Press, 1997), 215–16; Oehler, *Theaterwesen*, 90–91; Stranitzky, *Ollapatrida*, 241. Williamson incorrectly identifies Stranitzky as Johann.

13. James Van Horn Melton, *The Rise of the Public in Enlightenment Europe* (Cambridge: Cambridge University Press, 2001), 160–61.

14. Anon., *Der Österreichische Patriot*, Feb. 10, 1766, 312.

15. Glossy, "Theatercensur," 241–42, 246–47; Franz Hadamowsky, *Wien. Theatergeschichte von den Anfängen bis zum Ende des Ersten Weltkriegs* (Vienna: Jugend und Volk, 1988), 236; Müller, *Genaue Nachrichten*, 10–11.

16. Franz Hadamowsky, "Zur Quellenlage des Wiener Volkstheaters von Philipp Hafner bis Ludwig Anzengruber," in *Die österreichische Literatur. Ihr Profil im 19. Jahrhundert (1830–1880)*, ed. Herbert Zeman (Graz: Akademische Verlagsanstalt, 1982), 583; Melton, *The Rise of the Public*, 188–89.

17. Josef von Sonnenfels, *Briefe über die wienerische Schaubühne* (1768; rpt. Vienna: Konegen, 1884), 99–100; Otto Rommel, *Die Alt-Wiener Volkskomödie. Ihre Geschichte vom Barocken Welt-Theater bis zum Tode Nestroys* (Vienna: Schroll, 1952), 382; Stauffer, *Erfindung und Kritik*, 127, 131, 227; Manfred Rudersdorf, ed., *Johann Christoph Gottsched in seiner Zeit* (Berlin: de Gruyter, 2007), ix; Hadamowsky, *Theatergeschichte*, 236.

18. Oehler, *Theaterwesen*, 137; Rüdiger Otto, "Nachleben im Bild: ein Überblick über posthume Bildnisse und Beurteilungen Gottscheds," in Rudersdorf, *Johann Christoph Gottsched*, 377.

19. "Der Bauer aus dem Gebürge, eine Nachahmung des Arlequin Sauvage auf die hiesigen Sitten gerichtet," *Wiener Diarium*, Jan. 10, 1768, unpaginated; Oehler, *Theaterwesen*, 96–97.

20. Glossy, "Theatercensur," 239, 246–47, 252–53; Oehler, *Theaterwesen*, 126, 128, 144; Yates, *Theatre in Vienna*, 11.

21. On Sonnenfels generally, see Hilda Haider-Pregler's excellent "Afterword" to her edition of *Briefe über die wienerische Schaubühne* (see note 7 above), and idem, "Die Schaubühne als 'Sittenschule' der Nation. Joseph von Sonnenfels und das Theater," in *Josef von Sonnenfels*, ed. Helmut Reinalter (Vienna: Österreichische Akademie der Wissenschaften, 1988), 191–244.

22. Sonnenfels, *Briefe*, 124–25, 137; Paula Sutter Fichtner, *Terror to Toleration: The Habsburg Empire Confronts Islam, 1525–1850* (London: Reaktion, 2008), 121.

23. Glossy, "Theatercensur," 278–86; Yates, *Theatre in Vienna*, 9–10.

24. " . . . dennoch die Gemächlichkeit des Extemporirens der Absicht aufopfert, regelmässige, ganz niedergeschriebene Stücke statt des Unraths . . . " Sonnenfels, *Briefe*, xi, 14–15, 42–43, 82, 201; Glossy, "Theatercensur," 336.

25. Sonnenfels, *Briefe*, 38, 41, 92; *Der Österreichische Patriot*, July 5, 1765, 640.

26. "Der erste bestand in einer allgemeinen Verbreitung der Lektüre: und der zweyte in Abschaffung des Extemporierens," Oehler, *Theaterwesen*, 196–97.

99

27. Philip von Zesen [pseud. Johann Friedrich Weiskern], *Des wunderangenämen Sprach=Mundahrt=und Schreibrichtigkeit=Verbessers . . . Sendschreiben aus der anderen Welt an einen philosophisch-hochdeutschen Sprachlehrer dieser Zeit . . .* (Vienna: Schilg, 1754), unpaginated. On Weiskern, see Haider-Pregler, "Nachwort," 401 n. 90.

28. *Wiener Diarium*, July 27, 1768, no. 60, unpaginated; *Wiener Diarium*, Aug. 3 1768, no. 62, unpaginated; Paul P. Bernard, *Jesuits and Jacobins: Enlightenment and Enlightened Despotism in Austria* (Urbana: University of Illinois Press, 1971), 38.

29. Rommel, *Volkskomödie*, 384; Glossy, "Theatercensur," 246–53.

30. Rommel, *Alt-Wiener Volkskomödie*, 382; "Die Huberin," in Müller, *Genaue Nachrichten*, 16–18; Christian Gottlob Klemm, *Beyträge zum deutschen Theater* (Vienna: Trattner, 1767), unpaginated.

31. "Die Huberin, " in Müller, *Genaue Nachrichten*, 13.

32. The texts of the Sonnenfels memorandum and Joseph's amplification of it are in Haider-Pregler, "Die Schaubühne," 229 n. 116, and 231 (see note 21 above); Hadamowsky, *Theatergeschichte*, 227–28.

33. Haider-Pregler, "Nachwort," 412 n. 113, 415, 417.

34. Müller, *Genaue Nachrichten*, 103–4.

35. Glossy, "Theatercensur," 262; Sonnenfels, *Briefe*, 410–11; Robert Kann, *A Study in Austrian Intellectual History* (New York: Octagon, 1973), 220–21. Franz A.J. Szábo, *Kaunitz and Enlightened Absolutism, 1753–1780* (Cambridge: Cambridge University Press, 1994); 205–8, follows Kann in suggesting that Sonnenfels ran afoul of Imperial Chancellor Franz Kaunitz over the question of German versus French classical plays at the court theater (*Burgtheater*). That Sonnenfels did have considerable respect for the model of the French social comedy argues for some scholarly rethinking of his allegedly hostile attitude toward the French theater. Haider-Pregler covers the question more thoroughly in "Die Schaubühne," 236–39, without being able to answer it definitively. She appears to discount the Kaunitz story altogether.

36. Müller, *Theatral-Neuigkeiten*, 149–50, 152–53, 184–85, 188, 196.

37. Haider-Pregler, "Nachwort," 420–23.

38. Branscombe, "Beginnings," 24; Bodi, *Tauwetter*, 102.

39. Bodi, *Tauwetter*, 45, 56.

40. Ibid., 39, 103, 135–37; Irmgard Weithase, *Zur Geschichte der gesprochenen deutschen Sprache* (Tübingen: Niemeyer, 1961), vol. 1, 132–39.

41. Bodi, *Tauwetter*, 41, 43, 48–49; Yates, *Theatre in Vienna*, 9–10

42. Haider-Pregler, "Nachwort," 374, 412 n. 113.

43. Oehler, *Theaterwesen*, 182; *Allgemeiner Theater-Almanach von 1782* (Vienna: Gerold, 1782), 222.

44. Glossy, "Theatercensur," 267, 275–76, 297–98.

45. Ibid., 273, 301, 326–28, 338.

46. Yates, *Theatre in Vienna*, 23.

47. Glossy, "Theatercensur," 297; for the full text of the 1795 memorandum, see 298–340. See also Yates, *Theatre in Vienna*, 25–27.

48. Glossy, "Theatercensur," 327.

49. Yates, *Theater in Vienna*, 23, 28, 32–33. On censorship in the Habsburg monarchy generally in the last years of the eighteenth century, see Ernst Wangermann, *Von Joseph II. zu den Jakobinerprozessen* (Vienna: Europa Verlag, 1966); Gerda Lettner, *Das Rückzugsgefecht in Wien 1790–1792* (Frankfurt am Main: Campus, 1988); Ernst Wangermann, *Die Waffen der Publizität. Zum Funktionswandel der politischen Literatur unter Joseph II.* (Vienna: Verlag für Geschichte und Politik/Munich: R. Oldenbourg, 2004).

50. Glossy, "Theatercensur," 340; Yates, *Theatre in Vienna*, 28–29; Bodi, *Tauwetter*, 45.

51. Melton, *The Rise of the Public*, 188–89; Johann Nestroy, "Der böse Geist Lumpazi vagabundus oder das liederliche Kleeblatt," in *Nestroys Werke*, ed. Otto Rommel (Berlin: Deutsches Verlagshaus Bong, [1908]), pt. 1, 50–51.

52. Haider-Pregler, "Nachwort," 428.

53. Franz Schuh, " '. . . und sprach sich als Ratsvorsitzender dafür aus, die Freiheit von Zensur nicht aufs Spiel zu setzen.' Zur Komödie der Meinungsfreiheit," in *Freiheit des Denkens*, 315 (see note 2).

The Crisis of the Hispanic World: Tolerance and the Limits of Freedom of Expression in a Catholic Society[1]

Applying the what-where-when test to loftier abstractions produces even more shattering results. . . . Take "free speech." What variety? In what age? In what country? I know of no more effective method for dragging abstractions out of the stratosphere into the market place.

> Stuart Chase, *The Tyranny of Words*

And then there's another question: the question of who we are to decide what are the truths and what are the lies. It's so easy to think we have superior knowledge, that our understanding is better. We love to correct the errors of the past in terms of what we now think is true. But who's going to correct our errors?

> Peter Kingsley, *In the Dark Places of Wisdom*

Ilustración *and Religion: Enlightenment in a Catholic Context*

BEFORE ITS SUDDEN DISINTEGRATION, IN THE FIRST DECADES OF the nineteenth century, the Spanish monarchy had ruled for three centuries over a vast territorial entity that extended to both sides of the Atlantic and that was united by strong political and cultural links. Indeed, despite the enormous distances separating the mother country from her American possessions and some viceroyalties from others, and in spite of the great variety of contexts, climes, and circumstances, written sources reveal that the elite classes of this huge and heterogeneous human and territorial group shared a handful of basic beliefs. And among these beliefs, the authority of Catholicism was without doubt the most significant. Catholicism was truly the very center of the system, on account of its capacity to inform, shape, and determine the behavior of its adherents. Not for nothing was the political entity to which we refer known for centuries as "the Catholic monarchy."

Any analysis or reflection regarding freedom of expression in the Hispanic world of the eighteenth century must begin by recognizing that even the most enlightened and reformist groups moved within the coordinates of a Catholic dogma that was very rarely questioned. Thus, some historians have used the epithet "Catholic Enlightenment"[2]— borrowing this classification from a branch of German historiography— and it would not be unreasonable to speak of "Catholic liberalism" when describing the first Iberian-American constitutionalism of the era of revolutions and wars of independence.[3] Nevertheless, despite the general acceptance of a Spanish Enlightenment, this intangible religious framework suffices to evidence the gulf separating the Iberian *Ilustración* from the French *Lumières*, the German *Aufklärung*, or the Anglo-American *Enlightenment* (labels that, incidentally, are often employed in a more normative than strictly historiographic sense). It is worth emphasizing, however, that Catholic vocabulary could be employed rhetorically by both defenders of tradition and advocates of reform (and, later, even by revolutionaries). It was more the case, then, of a cultural and intellectual repertoire of argumentative resources, rather than an ideology, as this term is traditionally used in social sciences.

Certainly, insofar as both shared a common cultural legacy, the Iberian-American area formed part of another much larger cultural entity that might be called Euro-America, though the differences between this "other Western world"—Latin America—and Protestant Europe and North America were considerable.[4] It is therefore inappropriate to embark on a study of the social realities of the Hispanic world employing categories and analytical models created as a result of historical experiences largely alien to that world. I refer, for example, to the much debated and controversial Habermasian theory regarding the development of the public sphere. It would be a mistake mechanically to apply this model to Latin American societies. The enormous incongruities in the constitution and evolution of a modern public sphere in the various countries of Latin America suggest adopting a very different approach.[5]

A good starting point would be to understand the agents involved in their own terms, as these terms and notions were, after all, those that shaped and made sense of their world.[6] For instance, concepts like *public, criticism, censorship, tolerance,* or *public opinion* were not used in the same way in the English-speaking and Spanish-speaking areas (and, furthermore, within each of these linguistic zones they were not employed in identical fashion). It is obvious, for example, that the notions of *público* or *opinión pública* in the late eighteenth century did not mean exactly the same thing as *public* or *public opinion,* and one must take care to identify these and other "false friends" when advancing a comparative approach.

As Annick Lempérière has shown, in the Hispanic monarchy the   105
legal-political order was viewed as presided over by a trinity that might seem unusual from a contemporary North Atlantic perspective: God, the king, and the public (*el público,* understood, in the Spanish of that time, to mean both *people* and *republic*).[7]

Probably the major difference between the English- and Spanish-speaking world, from the perspective that interests us here, could be summarized as follows: while for the English-speaking world religious diversity was a lived fact for almost two centuries—if at times a somewhat uncomfortable one—with very few exceptions Hispanic communities continued to be monolithically Catholic. The dogmatic mentality was so widespread that it was not unusual for Protestants of other European nations to be referred to as "the Northern heretics." This fundamental disparity alone—born of a differing historical evolution since the early sixteenth century—suffices to explain many things, among others the extraordinary difficulty liberal Hispanics had in accepting freedom of conscience and of worship. Indeed, these were generally not even considered legitimate political objectives. It follows that attitudes toward freedom of speech and limits on this freedom depended largely upon these basic cultural tenets.[8]

Nor, from a chronological point of view, does the traditional dating of the French, British, or North American Enlightenments coincide exactly with this movement in the Hispanic countries. In the latter there took place a moderate, eclectic, and delayed Enlightenment, the most significant political and cultural manifestations of which occurred in the late eighteenth and early nineteenth century, thus in the period of the American and French revolutions.[9] This belatedness, due partly to the Catholic world's lack of openness toward the scientific revolution of the seventeenth century and the slow reception in Spain of the advances of this revolution, was essentially the consequence of an obstinate resistance to the acceptance of new ideas. The large majority of the population appears in any case to have persisted in its loyalty to traditional values, while among the Church and the monarchy the resistance to the Enlightenment was first and foremost led by a number of powerful minorities in the most traditionalist sector of the Church, above all by the Inquisition. One should also keep in mind the intellectual inertia prevalent in some universities, where scholasticism still enjoyed a notable presence in the mid-eighteenth century.

Some of this resistance began to be partially lessened with the beginning of the reign of Charles III, in 1759, but the Enlightenment was in any case directed above all to promoting moderate reform and encouraging scientific-technical teaching, economic improvements, and the diffusion of useful knowledge.[10] In comparison with their restless French, British, or North American neighbors, the Spanish and Spanish-Americans appeared far less inclined to express political nonconformity or religious dissidence. Friar Benito J. Feijoo, one of the sternest critics of popular superstitions and without a doubt the chief promoter of the new science (Cartesianism as well as Newtonianism) in the Iberian-American world during the first half of the eighteenth century, advocated *non ultra sapere quam oportet sapere* ("know no more than it is necessary to know": Rom. 12:3), thus removing the mysteries of divinity from the realm of investigation and opinion.[11] And the learned Gregorio Mayans, an active "republic of letters" who engaged in regular correspondence with intellectuals, editors, and booksellers all over Europe, was extraordinarily cautious when dealing with questions of religion. In midcentury, for instance, he voiced his disapproval of the politico-sociological standpoint adopted by Montesquieu in the *Esprit des lois,* on the grounds that, as a book that dealt in part with religion, this work was more dangerous than Machiavelli's.[12]

Debates in the 1780s over Tolerance and Freedom of Expression

Despite the fact that over 10,000 Spaniards managed to print part of their work during the eighteenth century, very few of the authors who wrote in defense of freedom of expression appealed for an extension of that freedom into a debate over affairs of government, and fewer still trespassed in their arguments upon the territory of religious belief.[13] There existed two mechanisms controlling such a debate: one civil, a preliminary censorship; and the other ecclesiastical, the court of the Inquisition, which could act post-publication against suspicious texts. The Inquisition had specialized in the inspection of works imported from abroad, and still retained part of its capacity to intimidate, though it was an institution in decline. We know, for example, that not only did the Holy Office fail to prevent the circulation in Spain of the major works of the French *philosophes,* but also that their anathemas often stimulated the success of certain books, which were specially sought after precisely because of their prohibition.[14] More important was the official control of the printing of books and newspapers, namely the system of prior permission, which included government censorship via a printers' judge commissioned by the Council of Castile. The judge, depending on the subject of the text, submitted the originals for mandatory examination by one or two censors, whose level of enlightenment and openness to the introduction of new ideas might vary considerably.[15] Nonetheless, it would be wrong to regard this censorship as merely an instrument for the repression of ideas threatening throne or altar, as is often claimed. Censorship by the Royal Academy of History, for example, served as a mechanism for both social integration and the creation of a common memory. The academics/censors ensured the improvement and correction of literature in an enlightened sense, striving to direct and channel the activity of the world of letters according to certain criteria of literary quality, didacticism, patriotism and public benefit.[16]

Toward the middle of the century, a few isolated voices, for instance, Miguel Antonio de la Gándara and Juan Enrique de Graef, advocated the "natural freedom" to write and the benefits of allowing people to "*discurrir [libremente] sobre materias de gobierno*" ("discuss [freely] affairs of government").[17] "Discussion is a free country. *Lex Christi est lex libertatis,* and curtailing in excess this natural freedom is a major setback to literary progress," wrote the former, in a tone not unreminiscent of John Milton's *Areopagitica.* As a result, he continued, "writers would enjoy more freedom sensibly and respectfully to discuss, write, challenge and criticize, and thus clarify and purify . . . debatable issues . . . ecclesiastical controversies, moral questions, political discourse . . . in short, all that which pertains to reason and is independent of Dogma."[18]

From the decade of the 1780s onward, coinciding with an incipient political press and a growing and generalized sense of constitutional crisis, the literati intensified their advocacy. For instance, the learned economist Valentín de Foronda addressed the Historico-Geographical

Academy of Valladolid on the subject of the freedom to write, protesting against the absurd "ban on telling the truth" and claiming, among other things: "If each person has not the freedom to write and speak his opinion on any matter, independently of the dogma of the Catholic religion and the will of the government, all our knowledge will be forgotten forever."[19] (Two decades later, the same Foronda, at that time consul in Philadelphia, noted that "freedom of the press as it is enjoyed here [i.e., in the United States] is not freedom, but rather an unlimited licence, a frenzy. Nobody is respected: France, England, Spain and their governments are endlessly insulted and mocked. Their own president, Mr. Jefferson, is continually knocked down, trampled upon, vilified.")[20]

It was in the eighties (a moment of effervescence when, as several of the period's intellectuals recorded, much was written though far less published)[21] that there also began a debate concerning tolerance, which would be inseparable from the subject of freedom of expression. Upon the announcement in 1787 of the imminent translation of *Suma filosófica* by the Neapolitan Dominican Salvador María Roselli, several Spanish scholars reacted against what they regarded as an obsolete and unacceptable defense of scholasticism and intolerance. While civil censorship was quite reticent in its attitude toward the publication of this work, because it was regarded as backward (note that here, as on so many other occasions, the censors adopted an enlightened position, defending "modern philosophy" rather than the "peripatetic"), Manuel de Aguirre, an officer and political writer, published several articles advocating religious toleration in Madrid's *Correo de los Ciegos*. These were in turn condemned by the Inquisition (among other accusations, for being aimed "at establishing absolute freedom of conscience and independence from the Supreme Powers"). Aguirre—who described himself as a "Christian citizen" and, at the same time, a "Catholic Christian"—railed against Roselli and openly advocated tolerance, adducing that "unanimity of opinions" is an impossible objective and that, if that era "rightfully deserves to be called the Age of Reason [*Siglo de las Luces*]," it was a result of "having abandoned opinions and principles as horrible as intolerance." Aguirre maintained that "healthy politics" recommended the rejection of "the terrible monster of Intolerance, disguised in the respectable cloak of religion," and observed that those nations where tolerance reigned were more prosperous than intolerant countries (he mentioned in particular France, England, and "the rising and already powerful American republic").[22]

109

The publication of Aguirre's text prompted an immediate reply in the pages of the journal *Espiritu de los mejores diarios*. An anonymous Sevillian author countered Aguirre's thesis, claiming that it was wise policy "not to have accepted the terrible monster of tolerance disguised in the respectable cloak of piety and evangelical meekness."[23] "Intolerance," concludes the author, "is a fundamental law of the Spanish Nation; the populace [*la plebe*] neither established it, nor should it abolish it."[24] Despite what might be inferred from this last sentence, the "populace" of the Hispanic world of the period was not in the least interested in abolishing intolerance. As foreign as it might seem to our democratic mentality, this eulogy of intolerance was far more in tune with popular sentiment than the Voltairian theses of its opponents, who were very much in the minority.

Several reasons were given in favor of maintaining the Inquisition and of a policy of official intolerance, but the principal argument was nearly always the same: the Holy Office "has saved us from the enormous disaster that has struck other Kingdoms, from that terrible monster of heresy that begins by distancing His creatures from obedience to

God" and that culminates in "universal anarchy." Furthermore, eternal truth is unconditional and cannot be relativized: "The Catholic Religion is and always should be intolerant, but its intolerance is not cruel, it is not bloodthirsty; all its severity is firmly dedicated to maintaining that outside the faith there is no salvation."[25]

The year 1786 saw the initial publication of Pedro Montengón's *Eusebio*, one of the most successful novels in the Hispanic world in the late eighteenth and early nineteenth century. In this didactic work with a strong moral content, the author adopted a position that clearly favored tolerance, albeit in a passage in which the protagonist, Eusebio, is on a study trip to London. Here he remarks upon the plurality of the sects established in Great Britain and the terrible ills resulting from "the English civil wars," caused by the "enthusiasm and fanaticism of the sectarians [*religionarios*], until they were calmed by benign and discreet tolerance, absolutely necessary in order to maintain political and civil order in a country where many sects are active."[26]

110

This exaltation of tolerance with reference to a foreign country is also present in the writings of Leandro Fernández de Moratín. Traveling through Germany, the Spanish playwright observed that in the city of Neuwied there reigned "the most absolute religious tolerance," as a result of which industry and commerce had benefited enormously, following the arrival of "craftsmen, manufacturers and merchants from all over," who were members of the broadest selection of faiths (Jews, Calvinists, Catholics, Quakers, etc.).[27] The relationship between tolerance and economic growth had already been noted by several Spanish writers, economists, and travelers (e.g., Antonio Ponz, in his visit to the Low Countries ten years earlier). This was an argument to which the educated class was very sensitive, painfully aware as most of its members were of Spain's backwardness in scientific and technological fields in comparison with other countries of western Europe. Indeed, during an earlier trip to Great Britain, Moratín had sung the praises of the freedom of speech enjoyed by the English. Even an enlightened minister of the Holy Office, Dr. Antonio J. Ruiz de Padrón, during a visit to Pennsylvania in 1788, when he met Benjamin Franklin, George Washington, and several Protestant ministers, openly admitted that the Inquisition was not necessary to protect the Catholic faith, and recognized the advantages of freedom of the press and tolerance for "a nation of religious but free men," as in Spain.[28]

On August 27, 1788, the *Correo de Madrid* published an article entitled "Sentiments and Reflections of a Philosopher on the Birth of a Prince," which emphasized that rulers should pay heed to the opinions of their subjects, especially men of letters, and should even listen to unpleasant criticism. "The printed word, the gift of a divine hand, will teach you the office of King, the art of putting persuasion before legislation. It will tell you bitter truths in a sweet voice: with the printing press, sentences lose their most caustic points, and even when patriotic expression (which becomes inflamed despite itself) is not always moderate, will you be any less powerful for having once listened to liberal and republican language?"[29]

The end of 1788 brought the death of Charles III, an enlightened king, whose reign, on balance, is usually judged positively. His successor, Charles IV, would have to confront the gravest of circumstances, at a moment when Bourbon France, a country of reference for the Spanish elite and a traditional ally of Spain via "family pacts," was in turmoil. In spite of attempts by the king's reformist minister, the count of Floridablanca, to establish a "cordon sanitaire," which, with recourse to the Inquisition if necessary, would prevent the entry of propaganda and news from the neighboring country, the revolutionary hurricane had an extremely destabilizing impact on Spain over the next couple of decades.[30] This impact, however, was not because the Spanish aspired to follow the example of their French neighbors—this was not the case—but was due rather to the vicissitudes of high politics, both domestic but, above all, foreign policy. The war against the Jacobin Convention (1793–1795) and, subsequently, an unequal alliance with the French Republic dragged Spain into a disastrous naval war against England, which led to the loss of much of the Spanish fleet at the Battle of Trafalgar. The definitive dynastic crisis occurred with Napoleon's intervention in the peninsula. From the spring of 1808 onward, six long years of patriotic war would leave the country in ruins. In Spain these exceptional circumstances produced the beginnings of a new liberal order, while on the American side the monarchy witnessed independence and the loss of many of its overseas territories.

During these years of extraordinary historical acceleration, the intelligentsia on both sides of the Hispanic Atlantic were subject to considerable tension, and they radicalized their controversies around a handful of political concepts: liberty, nation, sovereignty, independence, representation, reform, constitution. Freedom of the press and public opinion occupied a prominent place. Francisco de Cabarrús, in his *Eulogy of Charles III*, which coincided with the start of the French Revolution, imagined the king—whom he described as a "true philosopher"—offering some practical advice on government to his son and heir: among his recommendations, the elderly king warned the future Charles IV to free himself of the disastrous influence of passions "by means of education, and, amid the clash of passions and disputes, you will see the bright light of the torch of public opinion which will guide you safely onwards."[31]

The writer León de Arroyal, meanwhile, extremely and often bitterly critical of the monarchy, penned a letter, dated July 13, 1789, in which he referred to the benefits of freedom of expression. Speaking once more about England, Arroyal observed that "freedom to think, freedom to write, and freedom to speak create, even in the lower classes, a spirit of confidence and mutual interest, which we can barely comprehend."[32] The encomiastic tone of this idealized description apart, the end of the last sentence is particularly revealing: "*which we can barely comprehend*" suggests the huge distance between the social mentality predominant in a traditional and confessional monarchy like Spain and the social customs of a mixed, limited, and pluralist monarchy like England. The freedom of expression and the degree of tolerance enjoyed by the English and some other foreign nations might have suited the particular circumstances of those countries, but were almost inconceivable in a society as politically and, above all, religiously uniform as the Catholic monarchy.

In order truly to appreciate the depth of the politico-cultural rift separating these two worlds, it is best to consider the discourse of the apologists for intolerance. Only in this way can we, as historians, listen to and understand their reasoning, so far removed from our own mentality and values. In this respect, Friar Francisco Alvarado's arguments in response to the way some foreigners criticized Catholic intolerance are revealing of the essence of this dogmatic mentality: "Are we in Spain, or in Holland and North America? Who governs here—the Gospel, or Zuinglio, Quesnel and Puffendorf? Let us take this step by step, and ... clarify something which even children here are aware of. Which tolerance are we talking about? That of another religion, or that of people who are unfortunate enough to profess it? If we are speaking of tolerance of another religion, Catholicism is as intolerant as light is of darkness, and truth is of lies."[33]

The Turn of the Century: Between Enlightenment and Liberalism

Several decisive years intervened between the writings of Arroyal and Alvarado, during which the impact of the French Revolution and the war against Bonaparte served to radicalize both sides of the quarrel. In turn, with regard to freedom of expression, and depending on one's expectations, feelings at the turn of the century were very divided. For some, the tolerance of the Spanish authorities concerning political issues went too far; for a minority of men of letters—and the more radical their opinions, all the more so—tolerance clearly did not go far enough.

"What in society should be the limits of opinions and the word and writings that express them?" This question was posed by radical economist Cabarrús in 1792. He immediately supplied an answer: "The same as those of actions: that is, [whatever is in] the interest of society. My freedom ends when I offend either the pact which ensures me that freedom or the other guarantors thereof."[34] In 1797 a Madrid newspaper, widely read throughout the monarchy and echoing a report by the Economic Society of Bern, regretted in an editorial the lack of "good books on economy," thereby "depriving us of the knowledge necessary to improve our nation by means of debate."[35] While one Madrid newspaper led its first edition with an expressive quote from Livy—"*Quid, si vox libera non sit, liberum esse?*"("Are we who cannot speak really free?")—a popular rhyme complained that in Spain "there now reigns freedom/ of opinion and conscience/ and amidst so much turmoil/ and such obstinacy/ Religion is offended/ with downright insolence."[36]

If the situation in the mother country was fairly insecure in this respect, all the evidence suggests that the restrictions on freedom of the press—particularly in the wake of the French Revolution—were greater still in the American territories. During his travels through Spanish America, between 1799 and 1804, Alexander von Humboldt, lavish in his praise of the institutes, academies, societies, and educational centers set up by the Spanish crown in New Spain or New Granada, was extremely critical of the repressive attitudes to the printed word of the colonial authorities, fearful as they were of the revolution.[37] From the point of view of newspaper circulation, in such a vast monarchy there were inevitably enormous differences between some territories and others. For example, while Mexico and Peru had had printers since the sixteenth century and Guatemala since the mid-seventeenth century, the first printing presses reached Chile at the height of the revolutionary crisis.[38]

Victorián de Villava, who would shortly be appointed Court District Attorney (in Charcas in Peru), wrote in 1784 to protest the lack of freedom of expression and the impossibility of discussing certain political issues in public, complaining that it was still "an act of treason to question and examine the pros and cons of different forms of government."[39] However, there is ample evidence that those decades saw an intense politicization of fairly broad sectors of Hispanic society.[40] In fact, the increase in the newspaper- and pamphlet-reading public, patrons of cafes, and participants in social gatherings (tertulias), alarmed traditionalists, who were distrustful of the appearance of the sort of educated middle class that was formed by a growing sector of pseudo-intellectuals (pseudo-sabios) or, as they were also called in traditionalist pamphlets, semi-scholars (semi-doctos], hungry for news and eager to participate in public debate. Such changes in cultural consumption—a hunger for news and an eagerness to participate in public debate—would soon be conceptualized as the advent of public opinion by those who desired to promote reforms.[41] The wave of politicization and ideologization extended to very diverse fields of literary output, including drama and poetry. Poets like Gaspar M. de Jovellanos, Nicasio Álvarez de Cienfuegos, Manuel J. Quintana, or Francisco Sánchez Barbero, among others, extolled the virtues of fraternity and peace among men and dedicated enthusiastic odes to freedom, equality, the printed word, and other typically enlightened and liberal values.[42]

After October 1807, and above all after May 1808, events on the peninsula followed a rapid course. Beginning with disagreements and scandals within the royal family, and followed by the Spanish uprising against Napoleon and the rejection of José I Bonaparte—in the name of a "captive" prince, Ferdinand VII, regarded by most as the legitimate king—the country entered a phase of war and revolution in which there existed freedom of the press de facto, at least in those areas liberated from the French armies. As successive authorities—provincial committees (*juntas provinciales*), the national government (*Junta Central*), the regency, parliament (*Cortes*)—declared themselves on the side of the patriots, so too did the calls intensify for freedom of the press to be legally recognized.[43] And as soon as the Cortes met in Cádiz, one of its first tasks was to draw up a decree of "political freedom of the press" (*Decreto de libertad política de la imprenta*), which it did on November 10, 1810. In the preamble it was declared that "the ability of citizens to publish their thoughts and political ideas serves not only to limit the arbitrariness of those who govern, but is also a means of enlightening the nation as a whole, and is the only path toward knowledge of true public opinion." These words offer an accurate summary of the arguments most often employed by the liberals of the period. Freedom of the press was basically understood to be: (1) a means of controlling the authorities; (2) a way of encouraging enlightenment and improving education in general; and (3) a channel for shaping public opinion. Nothing was mentioned in that law concerning freedom of spoken expression or assembly, perhaps because its authors felt that non-written expression was more likely to be influenced by passion and, therefore, did not contribute to a genuinely enlightened debate. Furthermore, control of religious issues was left to ecclesiastical censors.[44]

While the poet José Mor de Fuentes dedicated one of his poems to freedom of the press, the author of a widely read pamphlet wrote, following d'Holbach: "Nothing is more unjust than preventing citizens from writing or speaking about objects that are fundamental to their happiness."[45] In Spanish America, however, there was considerable resistance to the application of this new law. In fact, the viceroy of New Spain did not accept it until the parliament, following the promulgation of the Constitution, expressly ordered him to do so, in October 1812.

The arrival of freedom of the press in Mexican territory, as noted by a conservative voice of the time, had an immediate effect: "seditious and incendiary leaflets were handed out even in the poorest and humblest houses."[46] Following independence, practically all the constitutions of the new Spanish-American states included one or more articles recognizing freedom of the press and expression.

The Spanish Constitution of 1812, promulgated by the Cadiz Cortes, guaranteed freedom of the press in article 371: "Every Spaniard is at liberty to write, print, and publish his political ideas without need of any licence, revision or approval whatsoever prior to its publication, subject to the restrictions and responsibility established by law." (Significantly, this article is included in chapter IX of the constitutional text, which is concerned with public education.) Although the legislation does not refer to freedom of speech, only to print, one sector of journalists insisted on linking both as *natural* freedoms: "If speech is free, then so must be the written or printed word, for in the end the written and the printed are but the materialization of speech itself, and printing is no more than rapidly repeating and multiplying one same copy."[47]

It is noteworthy, however, that the new constitutions categorically proclaimed the confessional nature of the state and, thus, religious intolerance in a manner which, from our perspective, appears incoherent. For instance, according to article 12 of the Spanish Constitution: "The religion of the Spanish nation is and forever shall be the one, true, Roman, apostolic, Catholic religion. The nation protects it with wise and just laws and forbids the exercise of any other." Almost identical articles, alongside ones guaranteeing press freedom, are to be found in the various constitutions of Mexico and other newly formed republics in Hispanic America.

Moreover, unlike the majority of the Spanish-American insurrectionists, Spanish liberals did not even consider the possibility of a republic. In the Europe of the early 1800s, this form of government had, in the eyes of liberals, been discredited by the excesses of the Jacobin Convention. Was it not a monarchy—that of England—which had for over a century been the model of the freest society, in the eyes of the "friends of freedom"? For the Spanish, as for most Europeans in the century of Enlightenment, a good monarchy was without a doubt the best regime.[48]

116

Moreover, it was almost impossible to imagine the establishment of a republic in a nation that had since time immemorial been a monarchy and whose territories extended across several continents. Under these conditions, the problem for the first Spanish liberals was, as expressed by one of the most prestigious newspapers of the day, how to become "free without being republicans."[49] The solution that these liberals found was to design a constitution that established a republican monarchy. With its proclamation of national sovereignty, unequivocally placing parliament at the center of the political system and strictly limiting the executive functions of the monarch, the Constitution of 1812 could be regarded—and was in fact interpreted as such by a good many observers—as a system that was monarchic in form but decidedly republican in essence.

Constitutionalism and Catholicism: The First Hispanic Liberalism

The Constitution of Cadiz is quite a radical political code. It included separation of powers and granted suffrage "to all men [i.e., males], except those of African descent, without need for education or property," which in terms of franchise made it a more democratic system than any of "the existing representative governments, such as those of Great Britain, the United States and France."[50] At the same time, it was a confessionally Catholic code, which categorically rejected religious freedom (art. 12). The considerable influence of this constitutional text beyond Spain's borders—it was taken as a model for revolutionaries from many countries—can probably be attributed to its hybrid character, at once radical and Catholic, monarchic and liberal. Thus, that "singular amalgam of the Holy Spirit and the spirit of the century, between Jacobinism and the Catholic religion," as the traditionalist Carl Ludwig von Haller ironically decribed this constitution, enabled it to penetrate and spread across Europe and Spanish-America.[51]

117|

The Catholic confessionalism that pervades article 12 of the Constitution and, in general, all Hispanic liberalism has been a subject of debate among historians. From a normative perspective and also following the traditional history of ideas, some authors have argued that liberalism and intolerance are conflicting and incompatible terms and that therefore no authentic liberalism existed in the Hispanic world during the early decades of the nineteenth century. Again, if we look at the matter through the eyes of those involved, this phenomenon may be better understood.

Fundamentally, for those who participated in the Hispanic revolutions it seems to have been something fairly simple, almost obvious, that the nation was Catholic and was proud to declare itself so by means of the new constitution. Its representatives were acknowledging an empirical reality: Spanish culture was removed from faith as an individual experience but also from religious pluralism. The same could be said of Mexico, Peru, Chile, Colombia, Venezuela, and so on. When it came to taking sovereignty from the king and declaring itself sovereign, each nation quite naturally assumed its Catholicism (which was, undoubtedly, in the vocabulary of today, the very foundation of its "identity"), and looked to the new constitutional state to protect and preserve at all costs what was considered a most valuable asset—indeed, the most valuable of all. Liberal historiography has found it difficult to explain this confessionalism, but for the vast majority of those who experienced these events, religious tolerance was neither an aspiration nor a concern. With very few exceptions, this issue did not feature in their political agenda. It is *we*, not they, who regard as incoherent the behavior of Hispanic liberals and republicans two centuries ago.

This self-investiture of a Catholic nation, of a nation of Catholics who declared themselves sovereign, had significant practical consequences, particularly in the area of freedom of expression. With its commitment to upholding the exclusivity of Catholicism within all the new republics, the nation was implicitly assuming a constitutional mandate to prohibit and restrict public expression of other religious beliefs. At the same time—and this was of immediate cause for alarm for defenders of the traditional faith—this new bond between religion and a nation that professed its intention to protect the faith with "wise and just" laws was evidence that the Inquisition no longer had a role to play in the state. Civil law was thus inforced vis-à-vis the Church of Rome.[52]

Unlike the American and French revolutions, the Hispanic revolutions took place within a largely non-secular context, in which politics and religion were not yet considered separately. In other words, in the Hispanic political culture, forged in the main by ecclesiastics, it was

118

virtually impossible to conceive of a totally secular sovereignty.[53] On the question of the relationship between church and state and religious freedom, there were, of course, significant differences between traditionalists and liberals. What the latter saw as reasonable freedom was anathematized by the former as a form of unacceptable licence, "libertinism" or "licentiousness," of uncontrolled passions. There were also differences in the degree to which theological culture permeated one region or another (on the whole, there can be little doubt that the republic of letters existed more independently of religion in the Iberian peninsula than in the New World). But certain general characteristics of the Catholic worldview were shared by nearly everybody. The renunciation of the idea of an authority completely devoid of religious foundation enables us to appreciate the reasons behind an intolerance that to most early nineteenth-century Hispanic liberals seemed perfectly acceptable. If, as María Teresa Calderón and Clément Thibaud have argued, religious legitimacy of political power represented an insurmountable horizon for the people of the Kingdom of New Granada of the time, then we begin to identify the crux of the issue. Basically, for the peoples of the former Spanish territories in America, taking their first steps along the path of political modernity, *intolerance* literally meant *the unity of the body politic*; tolerance, on the other hand, signified disunion, illegitimacy, even civil unrest.[54] Paradoxically, the religious intolerance consecrated in the Constitution of 1812 was seen as the most efficient means of subjecting the Church to the authority of a newly established state striving to control and direct a complex judicial and political order, comprised of a multitude of *corpora*.[55] Religious pluralism was in no way considered to be a social value or an asset, but rather a threat to cohabitation (a threat similar to, but even greater than, the plurality of interests).

119

Thus, this was a liberalism built upon Christian dogma, which followed in the wake of the moderate Catholic Hispanic Enlightenment.[56] One of the leading Spanish ideologists of this constituent moment, Francisco Martínez Marina, composed at the beginning of the nineteenth century a republican discourse in which *virtue* and *citizenship* were indissociable from the Gospel. This was a "civic Christianity," which even had a place for a hint of "civil religion."[57] It goes without saying that, for this confessional liberalism, freedom of expression was wholly subordinate to other more significant values, such as religion, upon which depended the common good and social order. In short, we are talking about *Catholic* liberalism and republicanism, which omitted dogma from the realm of opinion and restricted freedom of press and of speech to matters of a political nature, which were subject to debate and open to diversity of opinion. Even in this sphere, however, the goal of most political commentators of the time was to anchor public opinion in a position that did not threaten the unity of the nation's body politic.[58]

A few years later, however, the situation began to evolve rather more quickly, at least within certain elite sectors. Upon Ferdinand VII's return to Spain in May 1814, the constitution was immediately abolished, and the liberals were persecuted and imprisoned. Many went into exile, to France or England, where they met other exiles from Spanish America (several of the latter had also settled in the United States). One of the reformist leaders, the Spanish poet Manuel José Quintana, noted from his imprisonment in Pamplona that the traditionalists,

who accused liberals of being "rebellious, subversive and seditious," had attempted to "prove that the main proponents and founders of the Constitution were intent on destroying the Monarchy and the Catholic religion, in order to establish in Spain a republican government and tolerance of every faith."[59] The accusation was, of course, untrue, but it indicates the degree to which any questioning of the monarchy or of Catholicism was regarded as high treason.

In contact with French, North American, and British liberals, Hispanic exiles in London, Paris, or Philadelphia began to accept that tolerance was something positive—or, at least, a lesser evil—and that even in a Catholic country its implementation would not necessarily have disastrous consequences. In this respect it is very significant that the first article of the "Constitutional Act of Spaniards of Both Hemispheres," an alternative text to the 1812 Constitution proclaimed by a group of liberals during a thwarted conspiracy in 1819, recognized toleration of different faiths as one of the "fundamental bases" of the new social contract: specifically, the text refers to "religious freedom, or the right to worship God according to one's conscience."[60] A year later, in 1820, when the Constitution of Cadiz had been re-established, one of the Spanish liberals involved in this conspiracy wrote that "speech, writing, printing, or any other means already or not yet invented to communicate one's thoughts more or less quickly are mere instruments which have no intrinsic morality. Certainly they can be abused; but, if this is the case, punish the criminal and respect the faculty."[61] From 1834 onward, with the definitive triumph of liberalism on the peninsula, numerous political texts insisted that publicity and freedom of the press constituted "the soul of representative governments."

In the meantime, in the countries of the former Spanish territories in America during the early years of independence, "debates as to how 'free' the press should be dominated the political discourse of the 1820s." In practice, however, *de iure* or *de facto*, there were "constant restrictions to the freedom of the press."[62] Nonetheless, throughout the nineteenth century, among a sector of the liberal elites of the Hispanic world, there was a growing conviction, associated with widespread freedom of the press, that tolerance of religious opinions was inevitable, at least in principle.[63]

Let me conclude by highlighting an example of this gradual acceptance—albeit for a long time it represented a minority view—of respect for plurality of faiths.[64] In 1827, barely five years after his country's independence, the Mexican liberal José María Luis Mora, in *Discourse on Freedom of Thought*, advocated "absolute and total freedom of opinion." It is useless, he argued, to attempt to eradicate opinions by means of repression. Freedom, claimed Mora, is necessary for the advancement of science and of societies in general. In particular, "opinions about doctrines must be completely free," as only in this way, via "absolute freedom to speak and write," is it possible to have an obstacle-free debate in which errors are refuted by superior arguments. Only "free discussion" of this kind, he concludes, produces the truth "and true public opinion."[65]

There were also various Spanish liberals who, in their later years, looked back on the constitutional work of the Parliament of Cadiz and judged its confessional content to have been a regrettable error attributable to the circumstances of that time. For instance, the main speaker and political leader of the Cortes of Cadiz, Agustín Argüelles, wrote twenty years later from exile in London that article 12 was "a grave, disastrous error, the cause of many ills, but inevitable nonetheless."

> It consecrated religious intolerance once again . . . [to avoid] the theologi-
> cal fury of the clergy. . . . That is why it was considered prudent to leave
> it to time, to the progress of knowledge, to the enlightened controversy
> of writers, to subsequent and gradual reforms by future parliaments, to
> correct, without conflict or scandal, the intolerant spirit which prevailed
> throughout much of the ecclesiastical state.[66]

There is reason to believe, however, that the motives that led the liberals
of Cadiz to adopt religious uniformity was not merely opportunism or
a desire to avoid alienating the clergy and, thereby, immediately losing
support for the other reforms. It was instead a question of culture. In
my opinion, what led early Hispanic constitutionalists—whether liberals or republicans—solemnly and almost unanimously to proclaim the
centrality of Catholicism was neither fear, prudence, or opportunism,
but a more profound yet simpler fact: most of the agents who took part
in these events shared a Catholic culture that was so deeply embedded
in their societies that an acknowledgment of freedom of conscience was
ruled out in advance.

Notes

1. This chapter is part of the work of the Research Group on *Intellectual History of Modern Politics* (Bilbao, IT-384-07), financed by the Department of Education, Universities and Research of the Basque Government, as well of the Research Project on *Conceptual History, Constitutionalism and Modernity in the Ibero-American World. Fundamental Languages and Politico-Legal Concepts* (HAR 2010-16095), financed by the Ministry of Science and Innovation, Government of Spain.

2. Over thirty years ago, Mario Góngora applied the concept of Catholic Enlightenment to the study of Hispanic American societies. See the chapter "Gallicanism and Catholic Enlightenment," in *Studies in the Colonial History of Spanish America* (Cambridge: Cambridge University Press, 1975), 187–205.

3. According to José Carlos Chiaramonte, "'Spanish Enlightenment' (or) 'Hispanic American En-lightenment' . . . was in fact a set of reformist trends which, depending on the particular vision of iusnaturalism at stake, might drink from such diverse sources as the council tradition of Catholi-cism, Catholic Episcopalism and Jansenism, as well as some of the enlightened European schools of thought" (*La Ilustración en el Rio de la Plata. Cultura eclesiástica y cultura laica durante el Virreinato* [Buenos Aires: Editorial Sudamericana, 2007], 14). After a long period of disdain, the "Spanish Enlight-enment" became the subject of historiographic study a little over half a century ago: Luis Sánchez Agesta, *El pensamiento político del despotismo ilustrado* (Madrid: Instituto de Estudios Políticos, 1953. I shall quote from the 1979 Universidad de Sevilla edition); Jean Sarrailh, *L'Espagne éclairée de la seconde moitié du XVIIIe siècle* (Paris: Klinksieck, 1954; Spanish version: *La España ilustrada de la segunda mitad del siglo XVIII* [Mexico City: FCE, 1957]); Richard Herr, *The Eighteenth-Century Revolution in Spain* (Princeton: Princeton University Press, 1958; Spanish version: *España y la revolución del siglo XVIII* [Madrid: Aguilar, 1964]); Antonio Elorza, *La ideología liberal en la Ilustración española* (Ma-

drid: Tecnos, 1970); Francisco Sánchez-Blanco Parody, *Europa y el pensamiento español de siglo XVIII* (Madrid: Alianza, 1991); idem, *La Ilustración en España* (Madrid: Akal, 1997); idem, *La mentalidad ilustrada* (Madrid: Taurus, 1999). A general view of this historiographic recovery can be found in my own work: "Du mépris à la louange. Image, présence et mise en valeur du Siècle des Lumières dans l'Espagne contemporaine," in *Historiographie et usages des Lumières*, ed. Giuseppe Ricuperati (Berlin: Berlin Verlag–European Science Foundation, 2002), 133–58. For a brief informative synthesis of the Hispano-American Enlightenment, see Luis Alberto Romero, "Ilustración y liberalismo en Iberoamérica, 1750–1850," in *Historia de la teoría política*, ed. Fernando Vallespín (Madrid: Alianza, 1991), vol. 3, 448–85.

4. The systematic application to that "other West" of the abstract models pertaining to the dominant or canonic core of Western modernity makes nearly everything in these countries appear extravagant, anomalous, and peripheral.

5. Annick Lempérière, "Habermas à l'épreuve du monde hispanique, " unpublished text. My thanks to the author for kindly allowing me to consult her manuscript.

6. With reference to the late 18th and early 19th century, we can speak of a single discursive system in the Hispanic Atlantic. Not only was the political vocabulary practically the same in Spain and in America (Rafael Lapesa, *Historia de la lengua española* [Madrid: Gredos, 1980], 434), but—more importantly—the conceptual models corresponded to a Catholic vision of public life. And this applied to the colonial period, to the emancipation movement, and to the first steps taken by the newly independent republics. Annick Lempérière, *Entre Dieu et le roi, la République. Mexico, XVIe–XIXe siècle* (Paris: Les Belles Letttres, 2004); see also Carlos A. Forment, *Democracy in Latin America, 1760–1900* (Chicago: University of Chicago Press, 2003), 49 ff., 79 ff., 90 ff.).

123

7. François-Xavier Guerra, Annick Lempérière et al., *Los espacios públicos en Iberoamérica. Ambigüedades y problemas. Siglos XVIII–XIX* (Mexico City: FCE, 1998); Javier Fernández Sebastián and Joëlle Chassin, eds., *L'avènement de l'opinion publique. Europe et Amérique XVIII–XIXe siècles* (Paris: L'Harmattan, 2004). In recent years numerous researchers have initiated a new line of investigation in comparative conceptual history of the Iberian-American world, paying special attention to semantic problems. Our approach is summarized in my article "*Iberconceptos:* Toward a Transnational History of Political Concepts in the Iberian-American World: A Brief Account of an Ongoing Project," *Isegoría* 37 (2007): 165–76 (http://foroiberoideas.cervantesvirtual.com/ news/news.jsp?tipo=1&menu=2). It would be interesting if Latin American, European, and North American scholars would at some point engage in joint reflection, from a transcultural point of view, on the significant differences in the way our respective societies and linguistic areas conceptualize political life.

8. For succinct comparison of the respective scope of the Enlightenment in Anglo-America and Spanish-America, in terms of printing, newspapers, and public debate, see John H. Elliott, *Empires of the Atlantic World: Britain and Spain in America, 1492–1830* (New Haven and London: Yale University Press, 2006). I quote from the Spanish version: *Imperios del mundo atlántico. España y Gran Bretaña en América (1492–1830)* (Madrid: Taurus, 2006), 483–89. For an analysis of the language and discourse of legitimization of empires, it is useful to refer to the works of Anthony Pagden, among others: *Spanish Imperialism and the Political Imagination: Studies in European and Spanish-American Social and Political Theory 1513–1830* (New Haven and London: Yale University Press, 1990); and *Lords of All the World: Ideologies of Empire in Britain, France, and Spain* (New Haven and London: Yale University Press, 1995).

9. According to José Carlos Chiaramonte (see n. 3), it is even debatable whether the historiographic concept of "Enlightenment" as a category of periodization is appropriate for the cultural history of the region: *La Ilustración en el Río de la Plata*, 13–14. It may be worth noting that, although the

expresssions "Siglo de las Luces" and "Siglo ilustrado" ("Age of Reason," "Age of Enlightenment") were already in use in the 18th-century Hispanic world, both terms were employed much more frequently in the 19th century to refer to that same century.

10. See my summary "[La Ilustración en] la Península Ibérica," in *Diccionario histórico de la Ilustración*, ed. Vincenzo Ferrone and Daniel Roche (Madrid: Alianza Editorial, 1998), 340–51 (in Italian and French: *L'Illuminismo. Dizionario Storico* [Roma: Laterza, 1997]; *Le Monde des Lumières* [Paris: Fayard, 1999]).

11. Although clearly in favor of the autonomous development of a scientific sphere open to criticism and separate from theology, the Benedictine points out that "Criticism should not go so far as to investigate the secrets of Divine Providence" (Benito Jerónimo Feijoo, "Disertación sobre la Campana de Velilla" [1733], in *Teatro crítico universal* [1726–1740] [Madrid: Real Compañía de Impresores y Libreros, 1778], vol. 5, 395).

12. Letter from Gregorio Mayans to Asensio Sales, June 16, 1753; Antonio Mestre, "Los libreros ginebrinos y la Ilustración española," in *Livres et libraires en Espagne et au Portugal (XVIe–XXe siècles)* (Paris: CNRS, 1989), 62.

13. One was allowed to debate ecclesiastical organization and forms of social expression of religiousness, as did the so-called Jansenists, but it was not possible to question dogma itself; Joël Saugnieux, *Le jansénisme espagnol du XVIIIe siècle: ses composantes et ses sources* (Oviedo: Universidad de Oviedo, 1975).

14. Marcelin Defourneaux, *L'Inquisition espagnole et les livres français au XVIIIe siècle* (Paris: PUF, 1963). (The title of the Spanish version of this book is misleading, as it mistakenly includes the word "censorship": *Inquisición y censura de libros en la España del siglo XVIII* [Madrid: Taurus, 1973]).

15. Francisco Aguilar Piñal, *Introducción al siglo XVIII. Historia de la Literatura Española*, ed. R. de la Fuente (Barcelona: Júcar, 1991), 118 ff.

16. María Luisa López-Vidriero, "Censura civil e integración nacional: el censor ilustrado," en *El mundo hispánico en el siglo de las Luces* (Madrid: Editorial Complutense, 1996), vol. 2, 855–67; Manuel Lucena Giraldo, "Historiografía y censura en la España ilustrada," *Hispania* 65/3, no. 221 (2005): 973–89; Lucienne Domergue, *La censure des livres en Espagne à la fin de l'Ancien Régime* (Madrid: Casa de Velázquez, 1996).

17. The meaning of the Spanish verb *discurrir* is ambiguous. Originally it literally referred to the act of walking or traveling through different places. However, the word very soon became a metaphor for thinking, speaking, or writing about something. While in certain contexts it may have been close in meaning to verbs of thinking, meditating, discussing, speaking or writing, in the 18th century it referred above all to speaking or writing about a subject.

18. Miguel Antonio de la Gándara, *Apuntes sobre el bien y el mal de España* (Naples, 1759), ed. Jacinta Macías Delgado (Madrid: Ministerio de Economía y Hacienda, 1988), 194–95. In the mid-eighteenth century, Juan Enrique de Graef, writing in the pages of a Seville newspaper, openly defended the right of simple "individuals" to break the monopoly of the court circles and "discuss matters of government" (*Discursos Mercuriales Económico-Políticos (1752–1756)*, ed. F. Sánchez-Blanco (Seville: Fundación El Monte, 1996), 79–80. All translations from Spanish are by the author.

19. This speech would be published nine years later in a Madrid newspaper: *Espíritu de los mejores diarios que se publican en Europa*, no. 179 (May 4, 1789), 1–14 (included in Valentín de Foronda, *Escritos políticos y constitucionales*, ed. Ignacio Fernández Sarasola [Bilbao: Universidad del País Vasco, 2002], 101–14). The echoes of Foronda's discourse were still to be heard in Hispanic America much later: in the early days of the process of independence of Río de la Plata, for example, it was

revived by the Buenos Aires leader Mariano Moreno ("Sobre la libertad de escribir," *Gaceta de Buenos Ayres*, no. 3 [June 1810]; quoted in J. C. Chiaramonte, *La Ilustración en el Río de la Plata*, 110).

20. Valentín de Foronda, *Apuntes ligeros sobre los Estados Unidos de América Septentrional* (Philadelphia, March 12, 1804), in *Escritos políticos y constitucionales*, 116.

21. "In the present day, whilst at liberty to meditate and to write, still one is not free to publish," wrote Jovellanos, one of the outstanding Spanish literati (quoted in F. Aguilar Piñal, *Introducción al siglo XVIII*, see 124 n. 13). Many texts from the time did indeed remain unpublished (though some of the more important pieces circulated in manuscript), and would only be published years later, after the triumph of the liberal revolution. Various late-18th-century authors were very aware of the need to modulate the degree of radicalism in their discourse, depending on the medium employed, the reader, the literary genre, and the size of the audience. Besides the degree of sophistication of the means used to communicate—spoken, written, or published—an additional factor was the anticipated degree of diffusion of the message in one form or another. In this respect, regarding Jovellanos' work, note what one author has termed his "layers of thought": the ideas expressed by the Spanish jurist and writer were not the same as those voiced as a journalist, nor obviously was the language of his private correspondence identical to that of his personal memoirs or equivalent to the daring and markedly utopian tone of his moral poetry (L. Sánchez Agesta, *El pensamiento político del despotismo ilustrado* [see note 3 above], 187 ff.). Such reserve was attributable not only to self-censorship but also to a certain "fear of the masses" (J. C. Chiaramonte, *La Ilustración en el Río de la Plata*, 35–37).

22. *Correo de los Ciegos*, nos. 161, 162, and 163, corresponding to May 7, 10, and 14, 1788. Manuel de Aguirre, *Cartas y discursos del Militar Ingenuo al Correo de los Ciegos de Madrid*, ed. Antonio Elorza (San Sebastián: Patronato José María Quadrado, 1974), 47–59 and 307–30.

23. L. D. P. L. B., "La intolerancia civil" [Seville, June 3, 1788], in *Espíritu de los mejores diarios que se publican en Europa*, April 6, 1789, 1062–63, emphasis in original. The complete text, entitled *La intolerancia civil. Reflexiones sobre sus perjuicios y utilidades*, was published in three successive volumes of the journal (175, 176, and 177), on April 6, 13, and 20, 1789.

24. Ibid., 1066 and 1116.

25. Ibid., 1060–61.

26. "This stifled furious discord, humanized dissident hearts," he wrote, "[and] turned their senseless rage into tame indifference, a thousand times preferable to the furious envy which drove them to the slaughter and destruction of their fellow men" (Pedro Montengón, *Eusebio* [4 vols., 1786–88], ed. Fernando García Lara [Madrid: Cátedra, 1998], 540–41). In another passage Montengón praised the Quakers, who in similar fashion were tolerant of the Catholic beliefs of Eusebio (ibid., 96).

27. Leandro Fernández de Moratín, *Viaje a Italia* (1793–97), ed. Belén Tejerina (Madrid: Espasa-Calpe, 1991), 124. See also Hans-Joachim Lope, "La Alemania de 1793 vista por Leandro Fernández de Moratín," in *Actas del VII congreso de la AIH* [Venice 1980], ed. G. Bellini (Rome: Bulzoni, 1982), 691–97.

28. Leandro Fernández de Moratín, *Apuntaciones sueltas de Inglaterra* [1793] (Barcelona: Bruguera, 1984), 92–95. Antonio José Ruiz de Padrón, *Dictamen del Doctor don Antonio José Ruiz de Padrón, ministro calificado del Santo Oficio, abad de Villamartin de Valdeorres, y diputado en Cortes por las Islas Canarias, que se leyó en la sesión pública de 18 de enero sobre el Tribunal de la Inquisición*, printed in Cádiz and reprinted in Mexico City (Oficina de Jáuregui, 1813), 32–38. This Spanish priest not only claimed that "science and the arts are as incompatible with the Inquisition as light is with darkness," but also admitted that "the Inquisition is contrary to the spirit of the Gospel." Ironically, a few decades

later, Alexis de Tocqueville, in a well-known passage of *Democracy in America* (1835, vol. 1, part ii, ch. 7), stressing the enormous pressure exerted by public opinion on writers, drew an unfavorable comparison between North American society and Spain under the control of Inquisition: "I know of no country in which there is so little independence of mind and real freedom of discussion as in America. . . . In America the majority raises formidable barriers around the liberty of opinion; within these barriers an author may write what he pleases, but woe to him if he goes beyond them. . . . The Inquisition has never been able to prevent a vast number of anti-religious books from circulating in Spain. The empire of the majority succeeds much better in the United States, since it actually removes any wish to publish them."

29. Reformist minister Campomanes, himself an outstanding economist and writer, ordered the confiscation of the copies two days later (see Esteban Conde Naranjo, *El Argos de la Monarquia. La policia del libro en la España ilustrada (1750–1834)* [Madrid: CEPC, 2006], 443–44). As can be deduced from this extract, one of the factors most appreciated by the defenders of freedom of expression was the possibility of communicating complaints and claims to the authorities, thus advising them of certain unpleasant truths with a view to correcting errors of government. According to one Argentine writing in the mid-nineteenth century, in the Andean region some of these complaints reached the ears of the governors via certain women, who took advantage of the anonymity afforded by their attire: "It should be noted that in those days in Peru, the skirt and cloak were a far more effective guarantee of freedom of expression than is the freedom of the press today in the modern world. Against the words of these muffled women there was neither anger nor violence, neither courts nor trials, and everybody, from the Viceroy down, was prey to the exemptions accorded to a woman's mysterious identity. In *fiestas*, audiences, indeed in every public act, these women surrounded seats of the Viceroys, the judges and other leading figures, grabbed the backs of their chairs and hurled words, reproaches, jokes or praise at their faces as freely as you like. The extraordinary characteristic of a country, which would seem pure invention (though recorded by the most responsible chroniclers) had it not persisted until our own days!" (Vicente Fidel López, *La novia del hereje o la Inquisición de Lima* [1854], [Buenos Aires: Carlos Cañavalle, 1870], vol. 1, 147).

30. Lucienne Domergue, *Le livre en Espagne au temps de la Révolution Française* (Lyon: Presses Universitaires de Lyon, 1984). By the same author: "Propaganda y contrapropaganda en España durante la Revolución francesa (1789–1795)," in *España y la Revolución Francesa*, ed. Jean-René Aymes (Barcelona: Crítica, 1989), 118–67.

31. Francisco de Cabarrús, *Elogio de Carlos III de España y de las Indias* (spoken at the Madrid General Economic Society on July 25, 1789) (Madrid: Sancha, 1789), xii, xxiii, xxviii–xxx, xlvi and xlviii. In a later work, the same author continued to advocate "freedom of opinion," " the communication of ideas," and " the advancement of knowledge," and praised the role of discussion, deliberation, and other "assistance to legislator and judge resulting from the instantaneous clash of opinions" (Francisco de Cabarrús, *Cartas sobre los obstáculos que la naturaleza, la opinión y las leyes oponen a la felicidad pública . . . al Señor Don Gaspar de Jovellanos, y precedidas de otra al Príncipe de la Paz* [1792], I quote from the edition of J. Esteban and J. A. Maravall [Madrid: Fundación Banco Exterior, 1990], 40, 73 ff.).

32. León de Arroyal, *Cartas politico-económicas al conde de Lerena* (1786–1790), ed. Antonio Elorza (Madrid: Ciencia Nueva, 1968), 163.

33. Fray Francisco Alvarado, *Cartas criticas del Filósofo Rancio* (1811–1813) (Madrid: Impr. de E. Aguado, 1824), vol. 2, 461. The Spanish people's pride in their religion was evident in many documents of the period. I quote one example from a thousand: in the "Preliminary dissertation" of the first translation into Spanish of the *Biblia Vulgata latina*, the translator, the theologian and pedagogue Felipe Scio de San Miguel, celebrated the fact that "the Catholic faith is so deeply

rooted in our nation and that throughout the Spanish monarchy, reaching all four corners of the earth, shines the purity of religion untainted by any sect whatsoever" (Valencia: Joseph y Thomás de Orga, 1790), xvi.

34. F. de Cabarrús, *Cartas sobre los obstáculos que la naturaleza, la opinión y las leyes oponen a la felicidad pública* (1792) (see note 31 above), 77.

35. *Memorial literario*, Oct. 18, 1797, vol. 1, 23–24 (quoted in E. Conde Naranjo, *El Argos de la Monarquía*, see note 29 above), 443.

36. The newspaper quoted was *El Corresponsal del Censor*, edited by Miguel Rubín de Celis (Madrid, May, 1786, Letter I). The quotation from Livy is from *Ab urbe condita*, 39, 25. The popular verses, are quoted in Lucienne Domergue, *La censure des livres en Espagne à la fin de l'Ancien Régime* (see note 16 above), 290: "[En España] reina ya la libertad/ de opiniones y de conciencia/ y entre tanta turbulencia/ y tan terca obstinación/ se ofende la Religión/ con la mayor insolencia."

37. On the occasion of his visit to Bogota, he evoked, for example, Nariño, imprisoned for the clandestine publication of a translation of the Declaration of Rights of Man and Citizen of 1789. A few years later, the Spaniard Juan B. Picornell, imprisoned in Venezuela in punishment for a republican conspiracy in Madrid (1795), participated in the attempted rebellion of La Guaira, led by Manuel Gual and José María España (July 1797), and translated the French Declaration of Rights of Man and Citizen of 1793. Meanwhile, in Europe some Spanish revolutionaries had sought voluntary exile in France, near the Spanish border, whence they launched campaigns of revolutionary propaganda into the peninsula. One of them, the former Trinitarian friar Luis Gutiérrez, wrote, before fleeing to France in 1799, his epistolary novel *Cornelia Bororquia* or *La victima de la Inquisición* (the first of many editions was published in Paris in 1801). One of the 19th-century's most successful novels about Spain, its tone was strongly anti-clerical: the author stressed the perversity and fanaticism of the clergy: one of the characters claims, along these lines, that "our religion . . . has always reigned by means of terror, intolerance and crime."

127

38. The first printing press in Santiago de Chile was established in 1811. In the case of Portuguese America, there was no authorized printing in Brazil until the court of Lisbon moved to Río de Janeiro (1807). The first printers in the viceroyalties of Nueva Granada or Rio de la Plata date from the 18th century: it appears that printing reached Santafé de Bogotá in 1738 and Buenos Aires in 1780. José Toribio Medina, *Historia de la imprenta en los antiguos dominios españoles de América y Oceania* (Santiago de Chile: Fondo Histórico y Bibliográfico José Toribio Medina, 1958). A chronology of the first printing presses in Spanish America, from 1539 to 1830, is in Rebecca Earle, "The Role of Print in the Spanish American Wars of Independence," in *The Political Power of the Word: Press and Oratory in Nineteenth-Century Latin America*, ed. Iván Jaksic (London: Institute of Latin American Studies–University of London, 2002), 22–25. Some of the first newspapers and gazettes of the period include *La Gaceta de México* (1789–1809); the *Mercurio Peruano* (1791–1795); *Primicias de la cultura de Quito* (1791); *El Telégrafo Mercantil* (Buenos Aires, 1800); the *Semanario del Nuevo Reino de Granada* (Bogota, 1808–1811); and the *Aurora de Chile* (Santiago, 1812–1813). If it is true that the circulation in America of newspapers from the mother country was very intense during these early days of the liberal revolution, the spectacular increase in the number of publications during those years and the first decades of independence bore witness to the growing importance of journalism in the new post-colonial era. François-Xavier Guerra, *Modernidad e independencias. Ensayos sobre las revoluciones hispánicas* (Madrid: Mapfre, 1992; Mexico City: FCE-Mapfre, 2000), chs. 7 and 8. According to Rebecca Earle ("The Role of Print," 31), apparently "45 different newspapers" were published in the whole of Hispanic America "prior to 1810, the earliest in 1679. From 1810 to 1819 some 125 new titles were printed. The subsequent decade saw the publication of nearly 400 new newspapers."

39. Ricardo Levene, *Vida y escritos de Victorián de Villava* (Buenos Aires: Peuser, 1946), xxiii. The passage is included in an appendix to his translation of the *Lezioni di Commercio*, by Antonio Genovesi, the first volume of which was published in Madrid in 1784, by José Collado. Years later, from the court [*audiencia*] of Charcas, where he served as public prosecutor, he wrote the interesting *Apuntes para una reforma de España, sin trastorno del Gobierno Monárquico ni de la Religión* (1797).

40. The figures estimated by Nigel Glendinning indicate that, in total, there was a rise in the number of politically orientated publications, over the years 1730, 1760, and 1816 (*Historia de la literatura española. El siglo XVIII* [Barcelona: Ariel, 1986], appendix D, 235–36), but it was the years from 1808 to 1814, coinciding with the Peninsular War and the beginning of the liberal revolution, that witnessed the real rise of the political press.

41. See also Javier Fernández Sebastián: "De la 'República de las letras' a la 'opinión pública': intelectuales y política en España (1700–1850)," in *Historia, filosofía y política en la Europa moderna y contemporánea*, ed. Salvador Rus Rufino (León: Universidad de León and Max-Planck-Institut für Geschichte, 2004), 13–40; and idem, "The Awakening of Public Opinion in Spain. The Rise of a New Power and the Sociogenesis of a Concept," in *Opinion*, ed. Peter-Eckhard Knabe (Berlin: Berlin Verlag Arno Spitz, 2000), 45–79. See also the collection *L'avènement de l'opinion publique. Europe et Amérique XVIII–XIXe siècles* (see note 7 above).

42. L. Sánchez Agesta, *El pensamiento político del despotismo ilustrado* (see note 3 above), 235–50.

43. Two of the most radical calls were written by Lorenzo Calvo de Rozas and Álvaro Flórez Estrada. By the former, see *Proposición hecha a la Junta Central el 12 de septiembre de 1809 sobre la libertad de imprenta* (included in Juan Francisco Fuentes, ed., *Si no hubiera esclavos no habría tiranos* [Madrid: Ediciones El Museo Universal, 1988], 35–37); by the latter, *Reflexiones sobre la libertad de imprenta* (1809) (in *Obras de Álvaro Flórez Estrada* [Madrid: Atlas, 1958], vol. 2, 345–50). See also the observations of Ignacio Fernández Sarasola, "Opinión pública y 'libertades de expresión' en el constitucionalismo español (1726–1845)," *Historia Constitucional*, no. 7 (2006), § 10–12. There is a rich bibliography regarding this subject; among others, Emilio La Parra, *La libertad de prensa en las Cortes de Cádiz* (Valencia: Nau Llibres, 1984); Miguel Artola, "El camino a la libertad de imprenta," *Homenaje a José Antonio Maravall* (Madrid: CIS, 1985), 211–19; Alicia Fiestas Loza, "La libertad de imprenta en las dos primeras etapas del liberalismo español," *Anuario de Historia del Derecho Español*, 59 (1989): 351–490; Francisco Fernández Segado, "La libertad de imprenta en las Cortes de Cádiz," *Revista de Estudios Políticos*, no. 124 (2004): 29–54.

44. Thus, dogma was excluded from the realm of opinion. In spite of this, the decree met with harsh criticism from traditional sectors, while liberals strove to convince their adversaries that freedom of the press did not involve any threat to religion. On the contrary, they contended, Catholic truth would be reinforced by "free discussion" and "public education," which were the genuine "guardians against impiety." E. La Parra, *La libertad de prensa en las Cortes de Cádiz*; I. Fernández Sarasola, "Opinión pública y 'libertades de expresión,'" § 23–27 (see note 43). An intense debate over freedom of the press accompanied the initial phases of the establishment of representative government throughout the region. While the reformist press viewed this right as the principal safeguard of the liberal system and underlined the prominent role of "writers" in directing public opinion, the absolutist newspapers pointed out that the aim of the liberal journalists was to strip the clergy of spiritual power, establishing instead an entire alternative system of secularized social beliefs: it was basically a case of "spreading with impunity a new gospel, a new morality, a new religion, similar to the Enlightenment of the century in which we live and to the philosophism and reason with which they seek to replace the revelation and faith of our parents" (*El Ciudadano Imparcial*, no. 5 [1813], 40; Orlando Pelayo Galindo, "La libertad de prensa: un debate público en el foro de la prensa madrileña. De mayo a diciembre de 1813," in *La prensa en la Revolución liberal*, ed. Alberto Gil Novales [Madrid: Edit. Universidad Complutense, 1983], 89–90 and 94).

45. José Mor de Fuentes, *La libertad de imprenta* (Cartagena: Impr. de Francisco Juan, 1810). Ignacio García Malo, *La política natural, o Discurso sobre los verdaderos principios del gobierno* (Mallorca: Impr. de Miguel Domingo, 1811), 129.

46. F.-X. Guerra, *Modernidad e independencias* (see note 38), 313–14.

47. *El Patriota*, no. 20 (July 19, 1813), 185–86, quoted in O. Pelayo Galindo, "La libertad de prensa: un debate público en el foto de la prensa madrileña," (see note 44), 89.

48. Hans Blom, John Christian Laursen, and Luisa Simonutti, eds., *Monarchisms in the Age of Enlightenment: Liberty, Patriotism, and the Common Good* (Toronto: University of Toronto Press, 2007).

49. *Semanario Patriótico*, no. 56, May 2, 1811.

50. Jaime E. Rodríguez O., "Introducción," in *Revolución, independencia y las nuevas naciones de América*, ed. Jaime E. Rodríguez O. (Madrid: Fundación Mapfre Tavera, 2005), 16.

51. Carl Ludwig von Haller, *Ueber die Constitution der Spanischen Cortes* ([Winterthur]: [Steiner], 1820), 11–12, quoted in Luis Sánchez Agesta, *Historia del constitucionalismo español* (Madrid: Instituto de Estudios Políticos, 1955; 3rd ed., 1974), 75. Haller's opuscule, which appeared in Vienna, Modena, Paris, Venice, Madrid, and Gerona (within three years, different versions were published in German, French, Italian, and Spanish), is a good example, in a negative sense, of the interest aroused by the Cádiz constitutional code in Europe at that time.

52. This transition appeared to more than fulfill, almost two decades later, Jovellanos's *desideratum*, stated in a letter of May 21, 1794, to his friend Alexander Jardine, British Consul in La Coruña, that the most effective way of eliminating the Inquisition was to deprive that institution of the ability to control printed matter by transferring this responsibility to civil authority—in short, "destroying one authority with another" (Gaspar Melchor de Jovellanos, *Obras publicadas e inéditas*, ed. Cándido Nocedal [Madrid: Rivadeneyra, 1858–59], vol. 2, 366–67).

53. María Teresa Calderón and Clément Thibaud, "De la majestad a la soberanía en la Nueva Granada en tiempos de la Patria Boba (1810–1816)," in *Las revoluciones del mundo atlántico*, ed. M. T. Calderón and C. Thibaud (Bogotá: Taurus, 2006), 366, 373.

54. "The laws which are intended to establish tolerance," claimed the liberal member of parliament Agustín Argüelles during a session of the Cádiz Cortes, "have the opposite effect, cause conflict, shorten tempers, inflame arguments" (quoted in José M. Portillo Valdés, "De la Monarquía católica a la nación de los católicos," *Historia y Política*, no. 17 (2007): 26. A considerably more radical opposition was that voiced by the cleric Francisco de Alvarado: to accept "freedom of conscience" would be tantamount to submerging the monarchy "in an bottomless abyss of evil," as had been demonstrated by the devastating religious wars "throughout northern Europe" since the times of Luther and Calvin (Fray Francisco de Alvarado, *Cartas críticas del Filósofo Rancio* [see note 33], vol. 1, 121).

55. Calderón and Thibaud, "De la majestad a la soberanía en la Nueva Granada en tiempos de la Patria Boba" (see note 53), 387, 390 ff, describe the defense of religious intolerance by a group of South American journalists in response to an earlier apology for tolerance published by Ireland's "William" Burke in the *Gaceta de Caracas* (Feb. 19, 1811). This avalanche of pamphlets was highly symptomatic of the prevailing mentality in the region at the time. See also Marie-Danielle Demélas and Yves Saint-Geours, *Jérusalem et Babylone: politique et religion en Amérique latine* (Paris: Éditions Recherches sur les Civilisations, 1989).

56. Of particular significance was the popularity of works that, beyond their theme or even an author's specific political position, were united by a common religious vision of politics. I refer to such works as *El Evangelio en triunfo [The Gospel Triumphant]*, by the Peruvian Olavide, or *El Triunfo*

129

de la libertad sobre el despotismo [*The Triumph of Freedom over Despotism*], by the Venezuelan Roscio. In *El Evangelio en triunfo*, subtitled *Memorias de un filósofo desengañado* (1797–1798), Pablo de Olavide, former governor of Seville, convicted of heresy by the Inquisition in 1778, reacted against the horrors of the French Revolution, which he attributed to de-Christianization. This lengthy work, the last section of which contains a reformist program of "enlightened Christianity," was a genuine bestseller at the turn of the century. Some years later, the priest Juan Germán Roscio, one of the leaders of Venezuelan independence, submitted to printers in Philadelphia *El Triunfo de la libertad sobre el despotismo* (1817), in which the author sought to demonstrate that the Gospels contained an explicit message of liberty. This influential book has been seen by various present-day Latin American commentators as a precursor of the so-called Theology of Liberation.

57. Pablo Fernández Albaladejo, "El cristianismo cívico de Francisco Martínez Marina," in his *Materia de España. Cultura política e identidad en la España moderna* (Madrid: Marcial Pons Historia, 2007), 323–50.

58. See the works cited at the beginning of note 7.

59. "Once this had been demonstrated," concluded Quintana, "we were convicted of attempting to subvert the fundamental laws of the state and of treason and rebellion against the king" (Manuel José Quintana, *Memoria sobre el proceso y prisión de D. Manuel José Quintana en 1814* [1818] [Madrid: Real Academia Española, 1872], 229).

60. Claude Morange, *Una conspiración fallida y una Constitución non nata (1819)* (Madrid: CEPC, 2006), 409. This was not the first defense of religious freedom by a Spanish liberal. Ten years earlier, Flórez Estrada had presented before the Junta Central (provisional government) a draft constitution, which included an article stipulating that "no citizen will be troubled because of his religion, whatever it may be" (*Constitución para la nación española*, Nov. 1, 1809, art. 102, in *Obras de Álvaro Flórez Estrada* [see n. 43], vol. 2, 335). A Bilbao newspaper of the liberal years 1820–23 asserted that "freedom of thought is the most important constitutional foundation, and the publication of thought its most favorable consequence" (*El Patriota Luminoso*, no. 6, Bilbao, Nov. 17, 1821, quoted in Javier Fernández Sebastián, *La génesis del fuerismo. Prensa e ideas políticas en la crisis del Antiguo Régimen (País Vasco, 1750–1840)* [Madrid: Siglo XXI de España, 1991], 284 and 319).

61. Juan de Olavarría, "*Reflexiones a las Cortes*" *y otros escritos políticos*, ed. Claude Morange (Bilbao: Universidad del País Vasco, 2007), 180.

62. Eugenia Roldán Vera, *The British Book Trade and Spanish American Independence: Education and Knowledge Transmission in Transcontinental Perspective* (Aldershot: Ashgate, 2003), 17. In the case of Río de la Plata (Argentina), the debates regarding the limits and abuses of freedom of the press did not question the very principle of this freedom. The critics of a limitless freedom alleged that Argentine society was too immature and inexperienced to put it into practice. (Noemí Goldman, "Libertad de imprenta, opinión pública y debate constitucional en el Río de la Plata (1810–1827)," *Prismas*, no. 4 [2000]: 9–20). See also Rebecca Earle, "The Role of Print in the Spanish American Wars of Independence" (see note 38 above), 9–33; Paula Alonso, ed., *Construcciones impresas. Panfletos, diarios y revistas en la formación de los estados nacionales en América Latina, 1820–1920* (Mexico City: FCE, 2003); Carlos A. Forment, *Democracy in Latin America, 1760–1900* (Chicago: University of Chicago Press, 2003), 192 ff. In the case of Brazil, the Portuguese revolution of 1820 facilitated the suspension of censorship and afforded a degree of impetus to a limited freedom of the press. See Lúcia Maria Bastos P. Neves, "Ingerência do poder público na produçao das idéias: a censura no Brasil no início dos oitocentos," in *Nuevas perspectivas teóricas y metodológicas de la Historia intelectual de América Latina*, ed. Hugo Cancino Troncoso, Susanne Klengel, and Nanci Leonzo (Madrid: Vervuert-Iberoamericana, 1999), 220. For an analysis of the slow process of secularization in Spanish America during the first half of the 19th century and of the problems arising from the cultural transfer between the

intellectual generation of the Enlightenment and its successors, see Annick Lempérière, "Los hombres de letras hispanoamericanos y el proceso de secularización, 1800–1850," in *Nueva historia de los intelectuales en América Latina*, ed. Jorge Myers (Buenos Aires: Katz Editores, 2008), 242–66.

63. The mere application of the word *opinion* to religious faith was regarded by the Catholics as an unacceptable act of provocation. Indeed this had been one of the reasons cited by the Inquisition for totally rejecting as heretical the work of Hobbes, and it is to be supposed that the immense majority of Spaniards and Hispanic Americans of the age were equally disapproving of those legal texts which—like the French Declaration of the Rights of Man and Citizen of 1789 (article 10)—referred to religion as no more than "opinion."

64. In the 1803 edition of the Spanish Royal Academy's *Diccionario de la lengua* there had appeared for the first time a new acceptance of the old word *tolerance*, in the sense of "civil tolerance" ("Permission granted by a government freely to practise any religious worship"), as well as the new term *toleration* ("Opinion of those who believe that every state should allow the free practice of any religious cult"). Note that, three decades later, in the 1832 edition of this official lexicon, the word *worship* was replaced by *belief*—"[freedom] of all religious belief"—in the definition of these terms. In the case of Spain, however, prior to the constituent Cortes of 1855 there was no significant parliamentary discussion regarding the advisability of incorporating religious freedom into the legislation; full recognition of this right would not appear until the democratic constitution of 1869 (article 21).

65. José María Luis Mora, "Discurso sobre la libertad de pensar, hablar y escribir," *El Observador*, México, June 13, 1827 (included in *Obras sueltas* [Paris, 1837]).

66. Agustín Argüelles, *Examen histórico de la reforma constitucional de España* (London, 1835), ed. Miguel Artola (Oviedo: Junta General del Principado de Asturias, 1999), vol. 2, 54.

Helena Rosenblatt

*R*ousseau, Constant, and the Emergence of the Modern Notion of Freedom of Speech

THE IDEA THAT THE ENLIGHTENMENT PROMOTED FREEDOM OF
thought and expression is so widely accepted that it hardly needs stating. In France, the production of books tripled between 1701 and 1770; the newspaper press went from three titles to several hundred; and the volume of pamphlet literature grew exponentially. Literacy rates doubled; the number of people owning books increased dramatically, as did the average number of books that each person owned. In his *Remonstrances* of 1775, Louis XV's director of book censorship, Chrétien-Guillaume de Lamoignon de Malesherbes, reported that "the age of print" had given the nation "the taste for and the habit of self-instruction through reading."[1] As Reinhart Koselleck and Jürgen Habermas have argued, it was thus that a "public sphere" was created.[2] Print became the primary medium for the creation of a modern critical public.

But the print media was not the only space where the exchange of ideas could occur. Discussion and debate also took place in the many cafés, salons, academies, and masonic lodges that were cropping up all over the country during the eighteenth century. In such places, French men and women learned to formulate opinions and articulate ideas. Often they discussed what they were reading. Some scholars view this growing sphere of debate and exchange as so crucial that they are beginning to define the Enlightenment not so much as a list of shared doctrines or ideals, but rather as a set of communicative practices. Lawrence Klein and Bernadetta Craveri describe the eighteenth century as an age of conversation, and Dena Goodman has also stressed the centrality to the Enlightenment of its "discursive practices."[3] A conversational ideal emerged, so it is argued, and this ideal depended upon the free exchange of ideas. Participants increasingly stressed the close connections between communication and progress.

The political challenges posed by the growing public sphere were not lost on the authorities. By the middle of the eighteenth century, the French crown found its supposed "monopoly on the word,"[4] whether spoken, written, or published, contested everywhere. Individuals continued to be arrested for "*mauvais discours*," a term that referred to a range of criminal offenses from seditious speech and subversive literature to conspiracies against the crown. The perpetrators of such crimes were often severely punished. They could be sent to prison or sentenced to death. However, over the course of the century, it became increasingly clear that the king would never be able to silence the growing number of voices discussing and criticizing his regime. Despite an army of informants and spies, he was losing control.

Although the number of royal censors in France grew from four in 1658 to 178 on the eve of the French Revolution,[5] and more writers than ever were jailed for violating the publishing laws, the authorities could not stem the tide of salacious and seditious print. In reaction to the Damiens Affair of 1757,[6] a royal decree sentenced to death anyone convicted of composing, ordering composed, printing, selling, or distributing writings that attacked religion or royal authority. The decree turned out to be unenforceable, however, and print materials of all types continued to flood the expanding literary marketplace, giving people ever increasing numbers of subjects to discuss.

That French thinkers of the Enlightenment, both "high" and "low," contributed to this expanding public sphere is self-evident. That they complained about the restrictions placed on them by royal censorship and surveillance is also true. Such complaints, however, do not indicate that they unambiguously approved of freedom of expression for all. It has often been assumed that the *philosophes* were committed to full freedom of thought and expression,[7] but it is now becoming clear that this is incorrect. On the one hand, scholars have begun to question how free, egalitarian, and public conversations really were even within the salons.[8] No doubt what was going on within them can only with difficulty be linked with the modern notion of freedom of speech. On the other hand, research has also exposed the elitism of the *philosophes*, who often spoke with disdain of the masses and dismissed their mere "opinions" as inherently irrational and irrelevant. Condorcet said nothing particularly controversial when, in 1776, he defined popular opinion as "that of the stupidest and most miserable section of the population."[9] Few, if any, *philosophes* championed the right to free expression of this "stupid" section of the population. It was even a subject of some debate whether or not, or to what degree, the French masses should be educated.[10]

Voltaire serves as a good example here. His importance to the French Enlightenment is so central that the whole period is often referred to as "the Age of Voltaire." For long he was held up as a champion of freedom of thought and expression,[11] but recent work has shown that he actually favored censorship on various grounds. In *Le Temple du Goût*, for instance, he expressed nostalgia for the seventeenth century, when "polite society" exercised a civilizing control over writing. Elsewhere he displayed an obvious disdain for the decadence of "Grub Street"[12] and the "*canaille de la littérature*" who wrote for it.[13] Personally, Voltaire thrived on Old Regime censorship; not only did he develop coping mechanisms to get around the censor, but he even used censorship positively to create a name for himself and to fashion his literary persona.[14]

Voltaire's *Lettres philosophiques* (1734) contain one of his now famous tributes to the freedom of English writers. The same text, however, also shows that his definition of freedom of expression was quite narrow. On the issue of censorship, Voltaire thought a distinction should be made between *philosophes* and mere Grub Street hacks. One of these distinctions was that *philosophes* "don't write for the people." This was the reason why authorities had little to fear from them.

> *Philosophes* [should not be feared because they] don't write for the people
> and are without enthusiasm. Divide mankind into twenty parts. Nineteen

are composed of those who work with their hands and will never know
that there was a Locke in the world; in the twentieth part that remains,
how few of them read! And, among those who read, there are twenty who
read novels to the one who studies Philosophy. The number of people who
think is excessively small and these people never think about troubling
the world.[15]

By such statements, Voltaire seems to be saying that only he and a few
fellow *philosophes* should be allowed to publish freely because their writings are not dangerous.

In his contribution to the present volume, Jonathan Israel argues
that Voltaire's perspective was common in the so-called moderate
Enlightenment.[16] Few *philosophes* were advocates of freedom of speech
broadly defined. Like Voltaire, they tended to favor a two-tiered policy
of censorship, arguing that the truth was for the few, while, in the
interest of peace and order, censorship was necessary for the masses.
According to Israel, only one part of the Enlightenment—namely, the
"radical Enlightenment"—held that "all men should be enlightened
and that the truth should be told in such a way as to be accessible and
available to all."[17]

I would like to challenge Jonathan Israel's assertions, arguing that
even the so-called radical Enlightenment's commitment to freedom of
speech was weak and fundamentally flawed. The limitations and fatal
contradictions of the Enlightenment's views, whether "moderate" or
"radical," became patently clear during the French Revolution, when
individual liberties—such as freedom of speech—were curtailed in the
name of the public good. Inspired by Enlightenment ideas, a government "by the people" and "for the people" passed more repressive laws
than France had ever seen.

For a broader and more robust theory of free speech, France had
to wait for Benjamin Constant. The tragic paradoxes of the French
Revolution caused Constant to rethink the very nature of "freedom"
and to relate it closely to the protection of individual rights. Only
after the French Revolution did the modern concept of free speech—
in other words, freedom of speech as we know it today—begin to
emerge.

Freedom of Speech According to the "Radical Enlightenment"

Let us begin by examining Paul Henri Thiry d'Holbach's *Ethocratie ou le gouvernement fondé sur la morale* (1776), a text that squarely addresses the issue of freedom of the press. In it, Holbach certainly makes statements strongly approving of "freedom of the press." He states unequivocally that only a tyrannical government would fear freedom of thought and expression. Claiming that a "just and wise" government would always recognize the benefits of "liberty," he argues that

> to hinder and persecute the freedom to think, to write and to publish, are
> undertakings as tyrannical as they are demented, useless and contrary to
> the good of Society.[18]

But it is important not to gloss over the fact that Holbach also believes that limits to this liberty are necessary. First, he places writers into distinct categories. There are those writers who keep in mind "what they owe to virtue, to morals, and to their fellow citizens."[19] They should be left alone to publish freely. So should the authors of books that, because of their complicated and abstruse subject matter, are clearly "beyond the reach of ordinary citizens."[20] Such books will inevitably be judged only by scholars, enabling the "truth" to come out and bestow its benefits on society. However, different rules should apply to the "vile slanderers," "public liars," or "corrupters of innocence," whose "impure writings" are "harmful to good morals."[21] Holbach states unequivocally that the law should "punish" them and their writings. What he means is not that there should be no censorship, but that

> the laws should only condemn libelous writings, [and] licentious works,
> which alone cause real harm to society.[22]

In the end, one gets the distinct impression that he is only asking that he and his *philosophe* friends be allowed to publish, since their works are not for the public anyway. He sounds quite a bit like Voltaire.

Moreover, one should keep in mind that a government's interference with free speech is not only a matter of censorship. Like other members of the "radical Enlightenment," Holbach ascribed an important role

137

to government in the "education," both intellectual and moral, of the public. In practice, this meant government intervention in the realm of ideas. Holbach believed, for example, that government should work with "scholars" to promote the right kind of knowledge.

> Every good administration should, therefore, for the good of the State, excite the activity of minds, divert them from futile objects, and point them toward utility. . . . Sovereigns [who are well intentioned] will encourage knowledge and the research necessary for the people's happiness.[23]

A good government, in other words, one that truly desires the "happiness of its people," will realize that scholars are "useful citizens" who should "cooperate" in the task of government by "preparing minds to receive the good that the Sovereign wishes to do to his people." A wise government will "guide" (*tournera les esprits*) these scholars in the right direction; it will "encourage" useful scholarship and will "reward" it accordingly.[24] An enlightened government, operating in the public's interest, will "divert" men's minds from "frivolous objects" toward "useful" ones. In a similar vein, Holbach recommends that governments play an important role in the management of the arts. "Vigilant legislation" should prevent certain art from "harming the morals of citizens." Legislation should also "direct the taste" of artists so that they produce better, i.e., more useful, work.[25]

Holbach's commitment to spreading "truth" should be seen in the context just described. Jonathan Israel rightly cites Holbach as believing that "truth should be told in such a way as to be accessible and available to all." But whose truth? And how about the freedom to err? Notice, moreover, that Holbach's statement assumes that the "truth" will be made "*accessible* and *available* to all" (emphasis added). In other words, some people (i.e., the *philosophes*) will formulate the truth while others (the people) will imbibe it. This focus on the propagation of the "truth" actually links a "radical" thinker like Holbach to the "moderate" thinkers surveyed by Joris van Eijnatten. Van Eijnatten's "taxonomy" of arguments in favor of freedom of expression repeatedly refers to the "pursuit of truth," the "search for truth," and the "refutation of error."[26] Once again, it must be asked: who decides what the "truth" is?

When we turn to another text of the radical Enlightenment, Louis-Sébastien Mercier's *The Year 2440* (ca.1771), we once again find a less than unequivocal endorsement of free speech. The story is full of contradictions. As before, we find what seems like a strong statement of support for "freedom of the press":

> It has been shown many times over that freedom of the press is the true measure of civil liberty. You cannot attack the one without destroying the other. Thought should be given free rein. To try to curb it or stifle it is a crime against humanity.[27]

As it turns out, however, censorship continues to exist in Mercier's utopia. The authors of "bad books" are still held accountable. What has happened is simply that *prior* censorship, an integral part of the Old Regime censorship system, has been eliminated. We are told, for example, that individuals are now allowed to "write on anything, no matter how shocking,"[28] without obtaining permission before they publish. "Who," asks the imaginary citizen of the year 2440, "would dare to judge a book before the public sees it?"[29] But this does not mean that "bad books"[30] circulate freely and that their authors go unpunished. In some ways the censorship system has become even more severe. For example, authors in the year 2440 may no longer publish anonymously. The purpose of this rule is to force them to answer to "the public" for the principles their books espouse. Anyone who writes a book containing "dangerous principles which are opposed to healthy morals"[31] is subjected to what we in the twenty-first century would not hesitate to term brainwashing. Such an individual would be forced to wear a mask and to submit to daily interrogation by "two virtuous citizens" until he "abjures his errors" and agrees to retract, at which point he is permitted to remove the mask and rejoin the citizenry.[32]

Although there is no pre-publication censorship in Mercier's utopia, and neither the Catholic Church nor a reigning monarch judges the worthiness of printed matter, the "public" now plays a censorship role that Mercier clearly finds crucial.

> Each writer stands personally behind what he writes, and never disguises his name. It is the public who covers him with opprobrium if he

139

> contradicts the sacred principles that serve as a basis for the conduct and
> probity of men. . . . In fact, the voice of the public is the only judge in
> these sorts of cases, and everyone heeds it.[33]

Mercier seems to assume that everybody agrees on what are "the sacred principles that serve as a basis for the conduct and probity of men," and he believes that censorship will be a good thing as long as it is the "public" who plays the role of censor.

Rousseau, the "Abuse of Language," and the Yearning for Unanimity

Some of Mercier's ideas may very well have come from Rousseau, who also offers insight into some of the limitations and contradictions of the Enlightenment when it comes to freedom of the press and speech. Rousseau is rightly seen as a champion of openness and transparency;[34] but he also defended various forms of censorship. In the *First Discourse* (1749), he includes a note admiring the Caliph Omar for having advocated the burning of the library in Alexandria. In the *Letter to d'Alembert* (1758) he supports the censorship of entertainment in Geneva on the grounds that it would protect republican values. In the *Social Contract* (1762), he praises the Roman institution of censors and again claims that censorship is useful for the preservation of morals.

As is well known, Rousseau's pedagogical treatise *Emile* was officially condemned by French authorities when it appeared in 1762. According to standard procedure in such cases, the book was shredded and burned by the public excutioner in Paris. As the author of the "dangerous" book, Rousseau was obliged to leave France or face imprisonment. Soon thereafter, Genevan authorities condemned both *Emile* and *The Social Contract* and issued another warrant for Rousseau's arrest. In 1763, the city's attorney-general, Jean-Robert Tronchin, in *Letters Written from the Country*, explained the Genevan government's position. In 1764, Rousseau replied with *Letters Written from the Mountain*.

Unsurprisingly, given his personal situation, some of Rousseau's strongest and most developed statements on censorship are in *Letters Written from the Mountain*. Even here, however, Rousseau does not actually call into question a government's right to censor; nor does he dispute

140

the necessity of the institution of censorship. Rather, he seems most intent on accusing the Genevan authorities of "irregularity," in other words, of not following the proper procedures as defined by Genevan law.[35] His books having been condemned by civil magistrates on the grounds that they attacked religion, Rousseau questions the right of these magistrates to judge in matters of religion. He argues that they should have taken advice from the Genevan church and that they were not legally entitled to proceed independently of it. Rousseau never questions the idea that "those who dogmatize" and "those who infringe upon good order" should be punished.[36] And while civil magistrates should stay out of religious affairs, they should certainly intervene in the case of "civil offences," since such offences "cause men and the laws a wrong, real harm, for which public security demands necessary reparation and punishment."[37]

Rousseau also expresses the view that censorship laws should distinguish between a man who "dogmatizes, teaches, instructs" and a mere "author," like himself, who simply publishes a book:

> The author of a book, if he teaches, does not gather a crowd, he does not rouse people, he does not force anyone to listen to him, to read him; he does not seek you out, he only comes when you yourself seek him out; he allows you to reflect on what he tells you.

"Dogmatizing," Rousseau insists further on, "is different from writing a book."[38] Yet another reason why the Genevan authorities acted unjustly in their case against him was that his books were "not written for the people"[39]; they were theoretical treatises intended for specialists. Finally, Rousseau argues that the government's actions were illogical and counterproductive: to arrest an author merely served "to increase the publicity for the book, and consequently make the evil worse."[40]

Christopher Kelly has argued convincingly that Rousseau's comportment and writings show that his main goal was never to get rid of censorship, but to eliminate anonymous publication and thereby to promote a writer's responsibility.[41] Indeed, Rousseau distinguished himself among the *philosophes* by refusing to publish anonymously. He signed his name to even his most controversial writings, like *Emile* and the *Social Contract*. Kelly's argument supports what Rousseau writes in the *Letters*, in which he describes himself as "a man of honor who regards publishing things that one does not want to acknowledge as *punishable cowardliness.*" [42] Thus, it seems that what Rousseau really wanted to promote was not freedom of expression, but *self*-censorship and *"responsible* social criticism."[43] He does not explain here who should decide what is "responsible," except that he clearly regarded his own behavior as exemplary. There is a sense, however, in both the *Social Contract* and the *Letters*, that it is "the Sovereign," in other words, the citizen body as a whole, who should be the ultimate judge. In the *Social Contract*, Rousseau describes the act that creates the ideal political state as "the total alienation of each associate, together with all of his rights, to the entire community."[44] One can extrapolate from this that if he considered freedom of speech a natural right,[45] then it was also a right that every individual alienated to the political community through the social contract. We return to Mercier's notion that all is well with censorship as long as the "public" is the judge.

142   Another important element of Rousseau's thought, which relates closely to the notion of freedom of speech, is his well-known mistrust of dissent and disagreement. Such mistrust was also common among the *philosophes*. Others have written about their concept of "public opinion" and the deep-seated anti-pluralism it reflects.[46] They have shown that the *philosophes* never actually sought diversity of opinion as a goal in itself. Moreover, as Sophia Rosenfeld has recently shown, the *philosophes'* suspicion of debate and disagreement is closely related to profound, underlying concerns about language. According to Rosenfeld, the *philosophes* commonly attributed conflicts and disagreements among people to what they referred to as the "abuse of language," by which they tended to mean the effects of faulty communication. Eighteenth-century thinkers often complained about the "linguistic anarchy" that they saw all around them. Thus their dream of restoring a perfect language that would put an end to useless debates and disagreements.[47]

Apprehensions about language pervade Rousseau's writings. In the *Essay on the Origin of Languages* and the *Second Discourse*, he develops a theory about language, elements of which can also be found in his other writings. The two texts tell the story of mankind's gradual estrangement from what Rousseau postulates was an original instinctive language, based not on words, but on gestures and natural cries, and goes on to describe the negative consequences that invariably resulted from this estrangement. It is no accident, for example, that, according to Rousseau's narrative, property was first established by an act of speech: the pronouncement of the words "this is mine"[48] brought property into being by tricking the poor. As Rousseau tells the story, this discursive event paved the way for an ever more oppressive social and political situation that was increasingly founded upon artifice and lies. In modern civilized societies, language had become an effective tool for deception and oppression.

What was the solution to this problem? Simply allowing "free speech" could not possibly heal society. Merely increasing the volume of words, whether verbal or written, would not improve the situation. Something more radical and fundamental was needed, as Rousseau suggests in his novels *Julie, or the New Héloise* (1761) and *Emile* (1762).

The secret to true communication in both books seems to be the avoidance of words. Julie is often silent. The first communication between Julie and Saint-Preux involves no speech at all, and yet—or, rather, *because* of this—they experience transparency of communication. Throughout the novel, instead of speaking, Julie often employs the more effective, and more sincere, language of signs. About Julie's home at Clarens, Saint-Preux recalls affectionately, "How many things were said without opening the lips! How many ardent sentiments were transmitted without the cold agency of speech!"[49] Harmony reigns at Clarens because the people who live there understand each other. And when Saint-Preux leaves Julie to visit Paris, the falseness of the language spoken there is immediately apparent to him. He writes: "I do not understand the language, and no one here understands me."[50] He hears all around him only "babble, jargon, inconsequential talk."[51] In the city, people use words like weapons against each other. They compete relentlessly under the mask of politeness.

In *Emile*, Rousseau again expresses his mistrust of words.[52] Delivering a sweeping indictment of the way children are commonly brought up, he proposes a radically innovative plan for their education. He suggests that, before they learn to speak, children instinctively employ the language of nature—in other words, the language of gestures, facial expressions, and cries described in *Essay on the Origin of Languages*. This natural language is honest and true and should be encouraged, rather than replaced by mere words. Rousseau argues that, in contemporary society, too much time is spent reading books, learning foreign languages, and imbibing words. At a young age, children are bombarded with a "multitude of useless words," nothing but "words, more words, always words." Thus France was being turned into a nation of chatterboxes, people who talk incessantly without communicating.[53] As a remedy, Rousseau proposed what Rosenfeld calls a "radically ascetic linguistic diet."[54] He urged the teachers of children to restrict their students' vocabulary and to spare them long, word-based explanations. Whenever possible, they should instruct not through words, but through actions. They should pay more attention to the language of signs.

In the political solutions Rousseau offers to cure society's ills, one again sees a basic mistrust of speech, because of the disagreements speech supposedly causes. In the *Social Contract*, he states unequivocally that "long debates, dissensions, and tumult betoken the ascendance of private interests and the decline of the state."[55] According to Rousseau, individuals become citizens by surrendering their private interests and opinions to the "general will." This surrender happens in silence, away from debates and dissensions, when people listen not to the opinions of others, but to the "voice of duty." The general will can only emerge from a popular assembly, "provided its members do not have any communication among themselves," which allows each person to "make up his own mind."[56]

An in-depth exploration of the *Social Contract* is beyond my scope here, but one compelling reading sees it as an attempt to create a unanimous general will and to *silence* dissenting voices. The general will, as Rousseau describes it, is something other than majority opinion. He notes, for example, that it is not the same thing as the "deliberations of the people."[57] I will not make a case here for its "totalitarian" aspects; still, it is hard to ignore Rousseau's yearning for unity, consensus, and indivisibility, and his related concerns about the expression of particular opinions and interests. As Caroline Weber has noted, Rousseau saw "the elimination of discursive difference as the necessary precondition of a stable and lasting polity"; the "vocalization of private inclinations must be kept to a minimum."[58]

As noted earlier, state interference with speech concerns more than just censorship or efforts to impose *silence*. It also involves the promotion of the "right" ideas. Holbach ascribed an important role to government in public "education," which he defined broadly. The government should "guide" people's minds. Rousseau also believed that a government had an important role to play in the intellectual and moral life of its subjects. He called public education the "state's most important business." By public education, he clearly meant more than reading or arithmetic. He wanted governments to "make virtue reign."[59] They should inculcate patriotism in the community and thereby "train citizens."[60] Although Rousseau does not spell out how the state will achieve this goal, clearly intervention by the state in the realm of ideas is implied.

Freedom of Speech during the French Revolution

The French Revolution exposed the weaknesses and contradictions in the position of the *philosophes* on freedom of speech and the press. Following an initial loosening of censorship regulations, laws against speech and writings became more severe than ever. In justifying these new laws, revolutionaries explained that free speech and a free press, although crucial under a dictatorship, were unnecessary in a republic, since a government of the people could not possibly oppress the people. Soon a censorship regime was put in place that was more restrictive than France had ever seen.

Article 11 of the Declaration of Rights of Man and Citizen (August 26, 1789) proclaimed:

> The free communication of thoughts and opinions is one of the most precious rights of man. Every citizen may therefore speak, write, and print freely.

So began what Carla Hesse has called a "cultural revolution." She writes that article 11

> brought down the entire literary system of the Old Regime, from the royal administration of the book trade, with its system of literary privileges and its army of censors and inspectors, to the monopoly of the Paris Book Guild on the professions of printing, publishing and bookselling.

> Between 1789 and 1793, the mandate to liberate the Enlightenment
> from censorship and to refound cultural life on enlightened principles
> translated itself into a massive deregulation of the publishing world.[61]

Almost overnight, then, a "free market in the world of ideas" came into being.[62]

Except that it really didn't. Although article 11 did announce that "every citizen may . . . speak, write, and print freely," it also declared that citizens shall accept "responsibility for *any abuse of this liberty* in the cases set by the law" (emphasis added). It is not clear what was meant by "abuse."[63] In any case, it is highly unlikely that the majority of legislators intended to establish a truly laissez-faire regime when it came to the press. Instead, there is every reason to believe that the revolutionaries held the same narrow views on freedom of the press as the *philosophes,* and that what they really meant to abolish overnight was simply *pre-publication* censorship. As Jeremy Popkin has shown, although hundreds of orators, starting in 1789, saluted freedom of the press as one of the main accomplishments of the revolutionary movement, there was never a true consensus in favor of genuine press freedom in France.[64]

From the start of the Revolution, even those who called for the end of censorship simultaneously expressed fears that unrestricted newspaper publication would undermine the construction of a stable political order. Charles Walton's recent book shows that even during the so-called liberal phase of the Revolution, setting limits on speech was seen as a pressing issue, with people holding the contradictory position that the press should be free, but that "calumny" should be punished.[65] Apparently, some initially hoped that a free press would serve to unify public opinion. As Brissot had written in June 1789, newspapers would allow the French to "decide calmly and give their opinion" on political issues,[66] but even he believed that it was necessary for the new government to protect against "license" and "libels."[67] In any case, a free press did not help to "calm" the situation; instead, the revolutionaries found out that a free press helped to divide public opinion into hostile factions. Some people have seen this polemical newspaper press, born during the Revolution, as the beginning of political parties.[68] It helps to account for the fact that demands for press freedom were accompanied by demands for restrictions of it. The majority still believed that injurious speech, or "calumny," should be severely punished. [69]

In fact, what happened overnight was not the establishment of a laissez-faire regime in publishing. Instead, public regulation of the printed word continued. It is telling that as early as January 20, 1790, one of the chief theorists of the Revolution, Emmanuel-Joseph Sieyès, presented a proposal for a law on sedition, libel, and literary property to the National Assembly on behalf of the Committee on the Constitution. [70] In fact, the revolutionaries had no intention of getting rid of laws against seditious libel or "calumny." Rather, the National Assembly took over the royal government's responsibilities and "concern for the public good," [71] and it was now the Assembly's turn to deal with the flood of ideas being unleashed in the literary marketplace. Authors, publishers, and printers would continue to be held legally accountable for "seditious" publications.

In the end, the Penal Code of June 1791 defined seventy-nine crimes against the state, thirty-one of which mandated a death sentence and forty of which carried long prison terms at hard labor. Particularly noteworthy is that capital punishment or long imprisonment did not apply just to those who committed actions deemed criminal, but also to those who committed "verbal incitement to political crimes." Penal laws applied to

> inciting or persuading—by gifts, promises, orders or threats—the authors of crimes to commit them; directly inciting others to commit crimes—by statements in public places, placards, pamphlets, or printed works distributed in public. [72]

According to the Penal Code, even plots and incitements not followed by action were punishable as actions. The result was that, from 1791 on, French legislators treated words as if they were actions, and they treated spoken words as if they were the same thing as written words.

As the liberal phase of the Revolution segued into the Terror, efforts to control the press and speech increased. According to Carla Hesse, laws passed on December 4, 1792, and March 29, 1793, "turned political journalism and pamphleteering into potentially lethal

147

professions"[73]: any call for the dissolution of the government became punishable by death.[74] The first provision of the Law of Suspects (September 17, 1793) once again targeted discourse, condemning "Those who, by conduct, associations, *statements [propos], or writings,* have shown themselves to be partisans of tyranny or of federalism, and enemies of liberty."[75] Not surprisingly, between 1792 and 1793, the number of journals published in Paris dropped by one-half, from 216 to 113. In the year II, the number of periodicals circulating in Paris hit an all-time low of 106 for the revolutionary period.[76] Government censorship was not restricted to newspapers; it extended to any printed material from posters and pamphlets to novels and scientific publications.

As noted above, the Law of Suspects targeted "statements" as well as "writings." Up to one-half of the approximately 8,000 persons in prison in Paris during 1793–1794, on the orders of Parisian authorities or the Committee of General Security, were there for acts of speech.[77] More than one-third of the 2,747 persons executed by judgment of the Revolutionary Tribunal of Paris were condemned for seditious or "counterrevolutionary" opinions stated verbally and publicly.[78] Indeed, by the autumn of 1793, French citizens could be (and were) imprisoned or put to death for uttering statements that were pro-royalist or sympathetic to nonjuror clergy and emigrés or to federalists. They could be punished for expressing views pessimistic about the war, critical of the government, or regarded as "ultra-egalitarian." At one point the Convention voted the death penalty for anyone advocating the agrarian law. Informants were used to spy on people and report back to the authorities. Seen as a despicable activity during the Old Regime, informing now became a virtue, because France had become a republic.[79]

It was not enough to stop bad publications; it was also necessary to encourage good ones. As early as 1791, the National Assembly saw the need to encourage the production of patriotic works for educational and political purposes, a need that intensified as the domestic situation increasingly revealed the disunity of the French nation. During the Terror, the Committee of Public Safety established a corps of official writers whose works would be printed by the government. Their job was to write "useful" works that would instill patriotism in the French nation, thereby binding it together and "republicanizing" it. As Carla Hesse has documented, over the course of the years 1794 to 1799, the commission spent huge sums in the form of government "encouragements" to such authors.[80]

Government intervention in the realm of ideas was not restricted to print; the government also financed art exhibitions and commissioned art for public buildings and paid for cheaper patriotic engravings. Additionally, it designed civic festivals, which involved songs, speeches, and many slogans and symbols, all of which were meant to encourage patriotism and unity.

The French legislators also tried to impose linguistic unity on the nation.[81] They wished to eradicate patois entirely and make the French language uniform everywhere. In this desire for uniformity they were acting upon the ideas also encountered among the French *philosophes*, who, as we have seen, worried about "linguistic anarchy" and tended to attribute differences in opinion to faulty communication due to ineffectual language.

The fall of Robespierre did not fundamentally change matters. The Constitution of 1795, which created the Directory, promised that "no one can be prevented from speaking, writing, printing and publishing his thoughts." The new constitution, however, went on to repeat the 1789 Declaration's reference to legal responsibility for publications. It also included a clause explicitly authorizing "provisional" restrictions on this and other freedoms "when circumstances make it necessary." A law of 27 Germinal IV (April 16, 1797), aimed at both royalists and "anarchists," imposed the death penalty on anyone who advocated changes in the constitution. The Directory also used public funds to support loyal newspapers and distributed free copies of friendly papers to legislative deputies and government officials throughout the country. It established an avowedly official newspaper, the *Rédacteur*, the first of its kind since the fall of the Old Regime.[82] Although they regarded themselves as champions of the ideals of 1789, prominent intellectuals of the period, such as Pierre Claude François Daunou and Madame de Staël, also harbored deep distrust of journalism, and especially of its effect on a highly politicized public.[83] In 1797, even Benjamin Constant admonished journalists for "agitating" the public and threatening the peace.[84] Many progressive individuals during the Directory and Consulate endorsed

149

press restrictions. Napoleon's censorship regime was therefore a continuation of, and not a break from, existing policies.

Constant and the Emergence of the Modern Concept of Freedom of Speech

Most scholars now identify 1806 as a crucial year for Benjamin Constant's development as a political thinker. It was in that year that he made the critical intellectual move that turned him into a true liberal.[85] And it was also this move that turned him into an early proponent of the modern concept of freedom of speech. As will become clear, the crucial distinction regarding freedom of speech is not whether a thinker is of the "radical" or the "moderate" Enlightenment—but how a thinker views state authority in relation to the individual. A modern view of freedom of press, such as Constant would articulate from 1806 on, involves scepticism about state power *no matter who wields it*, combined with a belief in *individual* rights. This attitude is also respectful of diversity of opinion and is the basis of the modern idea that society as a whole benefits when a plurality of views is expressed.

150

To summarize briefly, by 1806 Constant had come to the realization that power itself was a dangerous thing. In *Principles of Politics* of that year, Constant first articulated the tenet that the *form* of government matters less than the *amount* of government. Stated another way, it is significant not *to whom* political authority is granted, but *how much* authority is granted. Throughout *Principles of Politics*, Constant repeatedly argues that political power is dangerous and corrupting; therefore it must be strictly limited. "Entrust [unlimited power] to one man, to several, to all," he writes, and "you will still find that it is equally an evil."[86] Constant was convinced that "[a]ll the ills of the French Revolution"[87] stemmed from the revolutionaries' ignoring this fundamental principle.

Constant argued not only that governments must be strictly limited in the extent of their powers, but also that individual rights must be protected scrupulously. He regretted that Rousseau became the writer who "had the most influence on our Revolution." He specifically refuted Rousseau's contention that in any legitimate state, individuals turn over all their rights to the community. Such a proposition, he maintained, was as "false" as it was "dangerous." On the contrary, the core principle of Constant's liberalism was that "[t]here is a part of human existence which necessarily remains individual and independent, and by right beyond all political jurisdiction. Sovereignty exists only in a limited and relative way."[88] This view of the limited and relative nature of sovereignty involved a fundamental shift concerning freedom of speech.

All of Constant's major political works starting in 1806 include chapters or important sections on freedom of the press and speech, and, by the time of the Restoration, he had become a recognized expert on the issue. Besides speeches on it in the Chamber of Deputies and articles in contemporary newspapers, he was also personally involved in several court cases involving freedom of the press, which helped publicize its centrality to liberal, constitutional government.[89] As Constant once said, a free press was "the boulevard of all rights"[90]; it was the indispensable right that made possible all others. Without this freedom all others became illusory, since it safeguarded the individual from the arbitrary rule of government.

151

Some of Constant's arguments in favor of freedom of the press were not very original, but merely repeated or extended ideas we have encountered before. He claimed, for example, that freedom of expression fostered intellectual improvement. He credited it with "the correcting of all ideas"[91] and "the development of the human mind."[92] He warned that "[w]hen thought is enslaved, everything is silent, everything sinks, everything degenerates and is degraded."[93] Such ideas, expressed in a multitude of ways, were quite common among Enlightenment thinkers. Constant also argued that censorship should be ended because it was impossible to enforce[94] and even counterproductive, as it "encouraged more clandestine, more dangerous texts . . . [and] fed the public greed for anecdotes, personal remarks, and seditious principles."[95] Here he was no doubt only repeating, or building upon, what Charles Walton refers to as the "quasi-libertarian" views of some revolutionaries.

On several occasions, Constant also made it clear that what he was against was only *pre-publication* censorship. What happened *after* publication was another matter. He believed it perfectly legitimate for laws to "deliver sentences against calumny, the provocation of revolts, in a word, against all the abuses that can result from the manifestation of opinions. Such laws do not harm liberty; on the contrary, they guarantee it. Without them, no liberty can exist."[96] Once again, these views do not seem to be very different from what we have encountered before.

Like other liberal thinkers of his time, Constant also made the argument that a free press was in the interest of good government. "Governments do not know the harm they do themselves," he wrote, "in reserving to themselves the exclusive privilege of speaking and writing on their own acts."[97] When the state controlled the press, it caused people to lose faith in their government, for they no longer believed what they read in the papers. In contrast, a genuinely free press was useful to government in that it caused people to have confidence in their constitution and in their leaders.

On the same theme, Constant held that governments would more easily be able to do their job if they were aided by a free and vibrant press. Legislators would then automatically find out "what the majority [of those] who write and speak think about the laws about to be passed." They would "get instructed as to what is suitable to the general disposition" of the nation.[98] Moreover, the "glare of publicity" furnished by newspapers would help governments avoid mistakes and improve themselves. "If there had been freedom of the press under Louis XIV and Louis XV," Constant postulated, "the insane wars of the first and the costly corruption of the second would not have drained the State dry."[99] Again, he was here approaching freedom of the press from the perspective of "governability"; his allies frequently made similar arguments, from the same perspective.[100]

Constant did differ from many of his contemporaries in how far he was willing to extend press freedom. Many who favored freedom of the press wanted it only to apply to certain kinds of publications, namely, to the longer, more expensive works destined for a presumably wealthier and more educated audience. The shorter, cheaper publications that might reach the masses, on the other hand, could be censored. In 1814, for example, only books of a certain length were exempt from pre-publication censorship, and many people, including many liberals, thought that this was as it should be. In contrast, Constant argued that all publications, regardless of length, should be exempt:

All men seem convinced that complete liberty and exemption from censorship should be given to works of a certain length. Since writing them requires time, buying them affluence, and reading them some attention, they cannot produce those popular effects that are feared due to rapidity and violence. But pamphlets, brochures, [and] especially newspapers are written more quickly, one procures them at lower costs, they have a more immediate effect [and] one believes this effect to be more formidable. I propose to prove that it is in the interest of government to grant complete liberty even to writings of this nature.[101]

Elsewhere, Constant accused many among his contemporaries of wanting to "make Enlightenment the monopoly of the rich" and of trying to deprive common people of a means of instruction.[102]

Yet another, and related, argument made by Constant in support of a free press was that it enabled a kind of political participation. He saw it as a good way of drawing more people into the political process: "In countries where the populace does not participate in government in an active way, that is, [where] there is no national representation . . . freedom of the press in some degree replaces political rights."[103] Constant reasoned that this participation was particularly important for citizens of France, who were spread out over a large country or were disenfranchised in one way or another. He further argued that a free national press would help counter the undue political influence of Paris. He believed that the French capital had exerted an exaggerated, and nefarious, influence during the Revolution. Such a thing had never happened in England, and Constant concluded that it was because a free press there had given birth to a truly "*national* opinion." Constant wished for the same thing to happen in France.

A free newspaper press would give France a new existence; it would identify it with its constitution, its government and its public interests. It would engender a confidence that has never before existed. . . . By disseminating enlightenment, it would prevent passing agitations, at the center of the kingdom, from becoming a calamity for everyone, even in the far-away regions.[104]

This view of the press represents a considerable change from the position he held in the late 1790s, when both he and Madame de Staël worried that newspapers were stirring up the political passions of the poor. Now, Constant could say that "freedom spreads calm in the souls and reason in the minds of the men" and that "it was the long *deprivation* of press freedom that . . . made the common people of France credulous, anxious, ignorant and thereby often savage."[105]

So far, we have seen Constant repeating, amending, and expanding arguments that were fairly current in the more enlightened circles of his time. In other words, he argued for freedom of the press on the grounds that it promoted instruction, progress, better government and peace. Where his original and distinctively liberal contribution emerges most clearly is in the link he posits between freedom of the press and the protection of individual rights. The experience of the Revolution and Napoleon had made Constant acutely aware of the problem of *individual* security, and more particularly, of the need to protect individuals from the ever-expanding reach of a "dominating" government.[106]

"The only guarantee against arbitrariness," he declared, "is publicity; and the easiest and most regular form of publicity is the one procured by newspapers."[107] "All defenses," he wrote elsewhere, "become illusory without freedom of the press." "Open publication" was "the only safeguard of our rights" and "the only safeguard of due process."[108] Constant occasionally used even stronger words to make his point: "newspapers are a weapon," he insisted, and "publicity is the resource of the oppressed against the oppressor."[109] A free press was as necessary "as speech is to citizens of all classes. If they need to cry for help when they are attacked . . . if their doors are broken down during the night, they need to be able to protest in the press against [the government's] arbitrary rule.[110] Constant was determined to teach people that "without publicity, authority can do anything," and that "to shackle freedom of the press [was] to put the life, the property and the personhood of the French people in the hands of a couple of ministers."[111]

Constant was not an opponent of all legal restrictions on speech and press. He regarded certain pronouncements, such as, for example, the incitement to murder or civil war, as criminal. Moreover, he never suggested that calumny, in other words slanderous speech, be made legal. His crucial innovation, however, was to argue that it was not up to the government to decide what constituted slander. Nor was it for govern-

154

ment censors to take actions to punish slander. Instead, the initiative to press charges should come from *individuals* who believed that they had been slandered, and it was the role of *juries* to decide whether a crime had been committed. In *Principles of Politics* (1815), Constant explained the crucial provision included in the liberal constitution he had just drafted: "Our present constitution differs from all the previous ones because it establishes the only effective means of repressing the crimes of the press while leaving it its full independence: I mean trial by jury.[112]

According to Constant, lawsuits against calumny would forever be "an inevitable and predictable consequence"[113] of a legally free press, but the remedy was not for government censors to punish journalists or close down newspapers. Such power in the hands of governments only allowed the authorities themselves to engage in slander, while leaving individuals defenseless. Slandered individuals needed recourse to a free newspaper press to restore their damaged reputations before the public.[114] The remedy to calumny was not less freedom, but more.

An equally important distinction between Constant and other thinkers I have discussed can be seen in their attitudes to differences of opinion. Nowhere in his writings does one find that yearning for unanimity we have seen in both the *philosophes* and the revolutionaries. On the contrary, Constant believed that "unanimity always inspires suspicion, and with reason, since there has never been, on important and complicated questions, unanimity without servitude."[115] Elsewhere, he held that "variety is life; uniformity is death."[116] What was so important about newspapers was precisely that they served as the "voice of *diverse* opinions."[117] They thereby helped citizens "to understand each other" and even to "form an intellectual bond between them."[118]

All the same, Constant did share some of Rousseau's apprehensions about language. His novel *Adolphe* shows that language was a deep concern of his, as a major part of this text is devoted to the problem of words.[119] Words, it tells us, can corrupt, oppress, betray, lie. They have a dynamic of their own. They are a crude instrument of self-expression, a medium that is formalistic and conventional. The answer for Constant, however, is not silence, nor is it a unitary politics based on a general will. Again, for Constant, the solution is *more* freedom. A particularly interesting chapter of *Principles of Politics* is entitled "On Discussion in

155

the Representative Assemblies," where he argues that "public discussion in the assemblies" is a good and healthy thing. In fact, he wants to encourage more public discussion by forbidding the delivery of written speeches. Speeches that have been prepared beforehand and are then read out loud in the Chamber "distort . . . the proceedings of our assemblies" by hampering a "proper discussion."

> When orators confine themselves to reading out what they have written in the silence of their study, they no longer discuss. . . . They do not listen, since what they hear must not in any way alter what they are going to say. They wait until the speaker whose place they must take has concluded. They do not examine the opinion he defends. . . . Everyone sets aside whatever he has not anticipated, all that might disrupt a case already completed in advance. In this way there is no discussion. . . . Speakers succeed one another without meeting. . . . They are like two armies, marching in opposite directions.[120]

156 A healthy intellectual and political climate is created by what Constant referred to elsewhere as the "collision of opinions."[121]

This perspective also informs his attitude toward public education. Constant disapproved of any government projects that aimed to "take hold of men's opinions in order to mould them." He devoted long sections of *Principles of Politics* to refute the idea that governments should try to legislate moral virtue. On no account should they try to "direct, improve, and enlighten" the citizen body. The widespread notion that they should "create" or "revive" public opinion was also dangerously flawed. Rather, governments should simply "let things be."[122] A free press would then help engender a nationwide discussion that would sustain a liberal and representative system of government, while also protecting individuals from encroachment on their rights.

Related to this is Constant's view of "the truth." We have seen that members of both the "moderate" and the "radical" Enlightenment placed great emphasis on the propagation of the "truth." For Constant, intellectual and moral improvement were more intimately connected to the *search* for knowledge than to the *possession* of knowledge. "Truth is not just good to know," he wrote, "it is good to search for." Moreover, the search for truth was a human "need," implanted in each human being. When individuals "make their judgment subservient to government," they abandon the "natural road to truth," which involves "reasoning, comparison, [and] analysis." They renounce the responsibility they have to improve themselves intellectually and morally, and permit themselves to become "wretchedly passive creatures." To Constant "everything imposed on opinion by government turns out to be not only useless but harmful, *truths as much as error*." An explanation of his thinking illustrates well this point of view:

> The adoption of an error on our own accord, because it seems true to us, is an operation more favorable to the improvement [*perfectionnement*] of the mind than the adoption of a truth on the say-so of any government whatever. In the former case, analysis is formative. If this analysis in the particular circumstance does not lead us to happy results, we are on the right track even so. Persevering in our scrupulous independent investigation, we will get there sooner or later. Under the latter supposition we are reduced to a plaything of the government before which we have humbled our own judgment. Not only will this result in our adopting errors if the dominating government gets things wrong or finds it useful to deceive us, but we will not even know how to derive from such truths as this government has given us the consequences that must flow from them. The abnegation of our intelligence will have rendered us wretchedly passive creatures. Our mental resilience will be broken.[123]

157

Once again, we see that Constant's perspective is that of the individual who faces a "dominating government." He wants to "shelter . . . individuals from government."[124] It is not through government intervention in the realm of ideas, but through "public opinion,"[125] as expressed by a free press and by healthy debate, that there can be a "free, gradual, and peaceful"[126] improvement of the intellectual and moral capacities of the entire population. The greatest service governments can do to further enlightenment is therefore "not to bother with it."[127] In the matter of morals and intellectual improvement, "laissez-faire" should be their policy.[128] In all this Constant marks a decisive turn and complicates our view of what constitutes "Enlightenment."

Notes

1. As quoted by Roger Chartier, *The Cultural Origins of the French Revolution*, trans. Lydia Cochrane (Durham, NC: Duke University Press, 1995), 44.

2. Reinhart Koselleck, *Critique and Crisis: Enlightenment and the Pathogenesis of Modern Society* (New York: Berg, 1988); and Jürgen Habermas, *The Structural Transformations of the Public Sphere: An Inquiry into a Category of Bourgeois Society* (Cambridge: MIT Press, 1991).

3. Dena Goodman, "Difference: An Enlightenment Concept," in *What's Left of Enlightenment: A Postmodern Question*, ed. Keith Michael Baker and Peter Hanns Reill (Stanford, CA: Stanford University Press, 2001), 129–47; and idem, *The Republic of Letters: A Cultural History of the French Enlightenment* (Ithaca, NY: Cornell University Press, 1994).

4. Lisa Jane Graham, *If the King Only Knew: Seditious Speech in the Reign of Louis XV* (Charlottesville: University Press of Virginia, 2000).

5. On the growing numbers of royal censors, see Anne Goldgar, "The Absolutism of Taste: Journalists as Censors in Eighteenth-Century Paris," in *Censorship and the Control of Print in England and France 1600–1910*, ed. Robin Myers and Michael Harris (Winchester: St. Paul's Bibliographies, 1992), 88; Raymond Birn, "Book Censorship in Eighteenth-Century France and Rousseau's Response," paper delivered at the Oxford-Princeton Partnership Conference: The History of Censorship, September 26–27, 2003, at Princeton University (available online at http://web.princeton.edu/ sites/english/csbm); and idem, *La Censure royale des livres dans la France des Lumières* (Paris: Odile Jacob, 2007), 47, 159.

6. In 1757, a half-demented domestic servant named Robert-François Damiens tried to assassinate Louis XV with a dagger. He had apparently overheard his masters discussing their religious and political disagreements with the king. Damiens was tried, convicted, and tortured to death. The affair sparked widespread controversy and debate in France and is said to have helped to bring about the Revolution. See Dale Van Kley, *The Damiens Affair and the Unraveling of the Ancien Régime, 1750–1770* (Princeton: Princeton University Press, 1984).

7. Nicholas Cronk surveys common misperceptions in his paper, "Voltaire and the Benefits of Censorship: The Example of the *Lettres philosophiques*," delivered at the Oxford-Princeton Partnership Conference: The History of Censorship, September 26-27, 2003, at Princeton University (available online at http://web.princeton.edu/sites/english/csbm), in *An American Voltaire: Essays in Memory of J. Patrick Lee*, ed. E. Joe Johnson and Byron Wells (Newcastle upon Tyne, U.K.: Cambridge Scholars Publishing, 2009).

8. Antoine Lilti, *Le monde des salons: sociabilité et mondanité à Paris au XVIIIe siècle* (Paris: Fayard, 2005); Benedetta Craveri, *The Age of Conversation*, trans. Teresa Waugh (New York: New York Review Books, 2005); Steven Kale, *French Salon: High Society and Political Sociability from the Old Regime to the Revolution of 1848* (Baltimore: Johns Hopkins University Press, 2004).

9. As quoted by Arlette Farge, *Subversive Words: Public Opinion in Eighteenth-Century France*, trans. Rosemary Morris (Cambridge, UK: Polity Press, 1994), 2.

10. Harvey Chisick, *The Limits of Reform in the Enlightenment: Attitudes Toward the Education of the Lower Classes in Eighteenth-Century France* (Princeton: Princeton University Press, 1981); Harry Payne, *The Philosophes and the People* (New Haven: Yale University Press, 1976).

11. This is particularly true of Peter Gay's *Voltaire's Politics: The Poet as Realist* (New Haven: Yale University Press, 1988), as noted by Sophia Rosenfeld, "Writing the History of Censorship in the Age of Enlightenment," in *Postmodernism and the Enlightenment: New Perspectives in Eighteenth-Century French Intellectual History*, ed. Daniel Gordon (New York: Routledge, 2001), 119. See also Albert

Bachman, *Censorship in France from 1715 to 1750: Voltaire's Opposition* (New York: Institute of French Studies, Columbia University, 1934).

12. This, of course, is Robert Darnton's expression in *The Literary Underground of the Old Regime* (Cambridge: Harvard University Press, 1982).

13. Cited by Roger Chartier, "The Man of Letters," in *Enlightenment Portraits*, trans. Lydia Cochrane, ed. Michel Vovelle (Chicago: University of Chicago Press, 1997), 146.

14. Nicholas Cronk describes this as "creative dynamic of censorship" (see note 7). Recent work on eighteenth-century censorship has noted that it "depended above all upon collusion between two supposedly opposing sides" (Rosenfeld, "Writing the History," 121.) See William Hanley, "The Policing of Thought: Censorship in Eighteenth-Century France," *Studies on Voltaire and the Eighteenth Century* 183 (1980): 265–95; Daniel Roche, "Censorship and the Publishing Industry," in *Revolution in Print: The Press in France, 1775–1800*, ed. Daniel Roche and Robert Darnton (Berkeley: University of California Press, 1989), 326; Barbara de Negroni, *Lectures interdites: le travail des censeurs au XVIIIème siècle, 1723–1774* (Paris: A Michel, 1995); Nicole Herann-Mascard, *La Censure des livres à la fin de l'Ancien régime, 1750–1789* (Paris: PUF, 1986); and Raymond Birn, *Forging Rousseau: Print, Commerce and Cultural Manipulation in the Late Enlightenment* (Oxford: Voltaire Foundation, 2001).

15. My translation from the Thirteenth Letter of *Lettres philosophiques*.

16. See also Jonathan Israel, *Radical Enlightenment: Philosophy and the Making of Modernity, 1650–1750* (New York: Oxford University Press, 2001); idem, *Enlightenment Contested: Philosophy, Modernity and the Emancipation of Man, 1670–1752* (New York: Oxford University Press, 2006).

17. See the essay in this volume by Jonathan Israel.

18. Paul Henri Thiry d'Holbach, *Ethocratie ou le gouvernement fondé sur la morale* (Amsterdam: March-Michel Rey, 1776), 24. All translations from this text are my own.

19. Ibid, 161.

20. Ibid.

21. Ibid.

22. Ibid., 24.

23. Ibid., 165.

24. Ibid., 158.

25. Ibid., 167.

26. These quotations are taken from the paper Joris van Eijnatten distributed before his talk at the Columbia University Seminar on Eighteenth-Century European Culture.

27. Louis-Sébastien Mercier, "The Year 2440: A Dream If Ever There Was One," in Robert Darnton, *The Forbidden Best-Sellers of Pre-Revolutionary France* (New York: W.W. Norton, 1996), 312.

28. Ibid.

29. Ibid., 312

30. Ibid., 311

31. Ibid.

32. Ibid., 312.

33. Ibid.

34. Jean Starobinski, *Jean-Jacques Rousseau, Transparency and Obstruction*, trans. Arthur Goldhammer (Chicago: University of Chicago Press, 1988).

35. Jean-Jacques Rousseau, *Lettres écrites de la montagne*, in *Œuvres complètes*, ed. Jean-Daniel Candaux (Paris: Gallimard, 1964), vol. 3, 777. Translations from this text are my own.

36. Ibid., 776.

37. Ibid., 780.

38. Ibid., 782.

39. Ibid., p. 783.

40. Ibid., pp. 781–83.

41. Christopher Kelly, "Rousseau and the Case for (and against) Censorship," *The Journal of Politics* 59, 4 (Nov. 1997): 1232–51.

42. Rousseau, *Lettres écrites de la montagne*, 793 (emphasis added).

43. Kelly, "Rousseau and the Case for (and against) Censorship" (emphasis added).

44. Jean-Jacques Rousseau, *On the Social Contract, or Principles of Political Right*, in *The Basic Political Writings*, trans. Donald Cress (Indianapolis: Hackett Publishing Company, 1987), 148.

45. Rousseau's position is complicated by his view that speech does not exist in the pure state of nature; it is acquired through socialization.

46. Keith Michael Baker, "Politics and Public Opinion Under the Old Regime: Some Reflections," in *Press and Politics in Pre-Revolutionary France*, ed. Jack Censer and Jeremy Popkin (Berkeley: University of California Press, 1987), 205–46; and Mona Ozouf, "L'opinion publique," in *The Political Culture of the Old Regime*, ed. Keith Michael Baker, vol. 1 of *The French Revolution and the Creation of Modern Political Culture* (Oxford: Pergamon Press, 1987), 419-34; Jeremy Popkin, "The Concept of Public Opinion in the Historiography of the French Revolution: A Critique," *Storia della Storiografia* 20 (1991): 77–92; Collette Ganochaud, "L'Opinion publique chez Jean-Jacques Rousseau (Paris: Honoré Champion, 1980); Jon Cowan, *To Speak for the People: Public Opinion and the Problem of Legitimacy In the French Revolution* (New York: Routledge, 2001); and John A. Gunn, *Queen of the World: Opinion in the Public Life of France from the Renaissance to the Revolution* (Oxford, U.K.: Voltaire Foundation, 1995).

47. Sophia Rosenfeld, *A Revolution in Language: The Problem of Signs in Late Eighteenth-Century France* (Stanford, CA: Stanford University Press, 2001).

48. Jean-Jacques Rousseau, *Discourse on the Origin and Foundations of Inequality Among Men*, in *The Basic Political Writings*, 60.

49. *Julie, or the New Heloise*, Part V, Letter III, my translation.

50. Ibid., Part Two, Letter XIV.

51. Ibid., Part Two, Letter XVII.

52. I rely heavily here on the work of Rosenfeld, *A Revolution in Language*.

53. Jean-Jacques Rousseau, *Emile or On Education*, trans. Allan Bloom (New York: Basic Books, 1979), 70, 108.

54. Rosenfeld, *A Revolution in Language*, 89.

55. *On the Social Contract*, 205.

56. Ibid., p. 156. An insightful and relevant argument about Rousseau's mistrust of rhetoric is found in Bryan Garsten, *Saving Persuasion: A Defense of Rhetoric and Judgment* (Cambridge, MA: Harvard University Press, 2006).

57. *On the Social Contract*,155.

58. Caroline Weber, *Terror and Its Discontents: Suspect Words in Revolutionary France* (Minneapolis: University of Minnesota Press, 2003), 20, 8.

59. Jean-Jacques Rousseau, *Discourse on Political Economy*, in *The Basic Political Writings*, 119.

60. Ibid., 124.

61. Carla Hesse, *Publishing and Cultural Politics in Revolutionary Paris 1789–1810* (Berkeley: University of California Press, 1991), 3

62. Ibid.

63. The more general problem of compromises in and conceptual ambiguities of the Declaration of Rights is insightfully explored by Keith Michael Baker, "The Idea of a Declaration of Rights," in *The French Idea of Freedom: The Old Regime and the Declaration of Rights of 1789*, ed. Dale Van Kley (Stanford: Stanford University Press, 1994), 154–96.

64. Jeremy Popkin, *Revolutionary News: The Press in France, 1789–1799* (Durham, NC: Duke University Press, 1990), 169.

65. Charles Walton, *Policing Public Opinion in the French Revolution: The Culture of Calumny and the Problem of Free Speech* (New York: Oxford University Press, 2009).

66. As quoted by Popkin in *Revolutionary News*, 181

67. Ibid., 169.

68. See, for example, Raymond Huard, *La naissance du parti politique en France* (Paris: Presses de la Fondation nationale des sciences politiques, 1996), 56.

69. Walton, *Policing Public Opinion*.

70. Alma Söderhjelm, *Le régime de la presse pendant la Révolution française* (Helsingfors: Hufvudstadsbladet, 1900–1901), vol. 1, 118–27; Claude Bellanger et al., eds., *Histoire générale de la presse française* (Paris: Presses universitaires de France, 1969–76), vol. 1, 432; and Hesse, *Publishing and Cultural Politics*.

71. Hesse, *Publishing and Cultural Politics*, 121.

72. Part II, Title III, articles 1–2, as cited by Richard Mowery Andrews, "Boundaries of Citizenship: The Penal Regulation of Speech in Revolutionary France," *French Politics and Society* 7, 3 (Summer 1989): 90–109.

73. Hesse, *Publishing and Cultural Politics*, 128.

74. Jacques Godechot, "La Presse française sous la Révolution et l'Empire," in Bellanger et al., *Histoire générale de la presse française*, vol. 1, 504

75. As quoted by Andrews, "Boundaries of Citizenship" (emphasis added).

76. Godechot, "La Presse française," 436, 504.

77. Andrews, "Boundaries of Citizenship."

78. Donald Greer, *The Incidence of the Terror during the French Revolution: A Statistical Interpretation* (Cambridge: Harvard University Press, 1966), 74–85.

79. François Furet and Denis Richet, *La Révolution française* (Paris: Hachette, 1973), 211. On the issue of denunciations, see Colin Lucas, "The Theory and Practise of Denunciation in the French Revolution," *Journal of Modern History* 68, 4 (December 1996): 768-85. On Constant's response to the practice of denunciation, see Stephen Holmes, "The Liberty to Denounce: Ancient and Modern," in *The Cambridge Companion to Constant*, ed. Helena Rosenblatt (Cambridge: Cambridge University Press, 2009), 47–68.

80. Hesse, *Publishing and Cultural Politics*, 161.

81. David Bell, "Lingua Populi, Lingua Dei: Language, Religion and the Origins of French Revolutionary Nationalism," *American Historical Review* 100 (1995): 1403–37.

82. Popkin, *Revolutionary News*, 173. On the Directory's restrictions on, and use of, the press, see pp. 173–77. On the Directory-era debate about the press, see Jeremy Popkin, "The Newspaper Press in French Political Thought, 1789-99," *Studies in Eighteenth-Century Culture* 10 (1981): 113–33.

83. Popkin, *Revolutionary News*, 176.

84. *Des réactions politiques*, ed. Philippe Raynaud (Paris: Flammarion, 1988), 119.

85. This understanding is supported by Etienne Hofmann's groundbreaking work, *Les "Principes de politique" de Benjamin Constant: la genèse d'une œuvre et l'évolution de la pensée de leur auteur, 1789–1806* (Geneva: Droz, 1980).

86. Benjamin Constant, *Principles of Politics Applicable to All Governments*, trans. Dennis O'Keeffe, ed. Etienne Hofmann (Indianapolis: Liberty Fund), 20.

87. Ibid., 5.

88. Ibid., 31.

89. Most notably, the case of Wilfrid Regnaud, involving a man unjustly convicted of murder. On this, see Etienne Hofmann, *Une erreur judiciaire oubliée: l'Affaire Wilfrid Regnaud* (Geneva: Slatkine, 2009).

90. "Observation sur le discours prononcé de S. E. le ministre de l'intérieur en faveur du projet de loi sur la liberté de la presse," in Benjamin Constant, *Œuvres*, ed. Alfred Roulin (Paris: Gallimard, 1957), 1265.

91. *Principles of Politics*, 107.

92. Ibid., 112

93. *The Spirit of Conquest and Usurpation and Their Relation to European Civilization*, in Benjamin Constant, *Political Writings*, ed. Biancamaria Fontana (Cambridge: Cambridge University Press,1988), 125.

94. This is a main point in "De la liberté des brochures, des pamphlets et des journaux considérée sous le rapport de l'intéret du gouvernement," in *Œuvres*, 1219–43.

95. *Principles of Politics*, 106.

96. "De la liberté des brochures," 1219.

97. *Principles of Politics*, 109.

98. "De la liberté des brochures," 1223.

99. *Principles of Politics*, 108.

100. See Lucien Jaume, "La conception doctrinaire de la liberté de la presse," in *Guizot, les Doctrinaires et la presse*, ed. Dario Roldán (Le Val Richter: Fondation Guizot-Val Richer, 1994), 111–23. See also Lucien Jaume, *L'individu effacé ou le paradoxe du libéralisme français* (Paris: Fayard, 1997), pt. 2, ch. 3.

101. "De la liberté des brochures," 1219.

102. "Sur le projet de loi relatif à la police de la presse," in *Œuvres*, 1355.

103. *Principles of Politics*, 112.

104. "De la liberté des brochures," 1231, 1233.

105. *Principles of Politics*, 109.

106. Ibid., 302.

107. "De la liberté des brochures," 1240.

108. *Principles of Politics*, 111.

109. "Sur la censure des journaux," in *Œuvres*, 1296.

110. "Sur le projet de loi relatif à la police de la presse" in *Œuvres*, 1348.

111. Benjamin Constant, *Collection des ouvrages sur le gouvernement représentatif et la constitution actuelle de la France formant une espèce de Cours de politique constitutionnelle* (Paris: P. Plancher, 1818), vol. 1, xviii.

112. *Principles of Politics Applicable to all Representative Governments*, in *Political Writings* (see note 93 above), 272; henceforth, *Principles of Politics* (1815).

113. "Questions sur la législation actuelle de la presse en France et sur la doctrine du ministère public," in *Collection des ouvrages*, vol. 2, 404.

114. Frank Puaux, "Benjamin Constant et la calomnie," *La Revue*, no. 122 (Feb. 1918): 541–44.

115. "De la liberté des brochures," 1228.

116. *The Spirit of Conquest*, 77.

117. "Sur le projet de loi relatif à la police de la presse" (note 90 above), 1352 (emphasis added).

118. Ibid.

119. Tzvetan Todorov, "The Discovery of Language: *Les Liasons dangereuses* and *Adolphe*," trans. Frances Chew, *Yale French Studies* 45 (1970): 113–26; idem, "La parole selon Constant," in *Critique* 26, no. 255–56 (Aug.–Sept. 1968): 756–71; and David Baguley, "The Role of Letters in Constant's *Adolphe*," *Forum for Modern Language Studies* 11, 1 (Jan. 1975): 29–35.

120. *Principles of Politics* (1815) (note 112 above), 222.

121. *Réflexions sur les constitutions et les garanties* in *Cours de politique*, 321.

122. *Principles of Politics* (1815), book IV, chapters 1–7.

123. Ibid., 302 (emphasis added).

124. Ibid., 178.

125. Ibid., 371.

126. Ibid., 304.

127. Ibid., 116.

128. Ibid.

163

$\mathcal{T}$oward an
Archaeology of the
First Amendment's
Free Speech
Protections

DESPITE THE SCHOLARLY NECESSITY OF AVOIDING ANACHRONIS-   165
tic presentist approaches to the past, there is no avoiding the fact that
the Enlightenment has been a hot topic over the last decade. The turn of
the twenty-first century has been difficult for anyone who values what
is usually associated with the political dimension of the Enlightenment:
the persuasive power of reason against faith, the effectiveness of a free
press debating policy issues in the public sphere, and the expansive hos-
pitality of toleration—all have been under extreme and highly visible
stresses. The internationally prominent events that highlighted these
stresses are too numerous and often too painful to list here; unfortunately, they are also so familiar that no introductory review is necessary.
But as Elizabeth Powers has described in the introduction to this volume, the violent reaction to a Danish newspaper's decision to publish
figurative cartoon representations of the Prophet Mohammed inspired
her to put together a seminar series, and subsequently this collection, on
the eighteenth-century defense and development of freedom of speech.
My talk in that series focused on what I see as a later seventeenth- and
then eighteenth-century reaction against the relative freedom of the
press in England during the 1640s. I was asked, then, to contribute
a conceptual prologue to the Enlightenment discussion of freedom of

expression. At the time, the stresses and strains on familiar Enlightenment ideals were associated in the metropolitan press with Islam. In parts of the United States, however, there are also palpable, albeit less visible, pressures toward a shared and public Christianity, what we might call a confessional state of mind, unfairly characterized in the national press—through the lens of the Enlightenment—as ignorance or a lack of education. It is important, then, not to overstate how diffused or ingrained the Enlightenment is in the so-called Western and/or modern world.

This essay, then, attempts to tread a fine line: valuing the secular Enlightenment and its commitment to freedom of expression and inquiry; pointing out its paradoxically Christian history; implying that this history is affecting the so-called Islamic reaction to European and American press freedoms; and arguing that the European and American press reactions to Islam are also being affected by this now relatively obscured Christian history of Enlightenment freedoms. During the summer of 2010, the virulent controversy over the so-called Ground Zero Mosque proposed for a site near the base of the World Trade Center towers has made visible the tensions implicit in the decade's debate over what can be recognized as Enlightenment terms—e.g., freedom of expression, the separation of church and state, and tolerance. It would seem that the legacy—and the future—of the Enlightenment is at stake in these debates, with a loss to the Enlightenment if the so-called mosque were to be blocked or even moved. At the same time, some have argued that the fact there has been a debate in the United States about the location of the mosque speaks to the continued vitality of the public sphere, and how the First Amendment's separation of Church and State can be sustaining for the variety of religious traditions practicing in the United States. My point, though, in this case, like so many others, shows that the Enlightenment is not what we thought it was—neither a historical period that has come and gone nor an ideal to be achieved in the future. Rather, it is a particular way of living in history, a way that has its own history.

No document better captures the focus of this collection than the First Amendment to the U.S. Constitution, as it codifies the emerging eighteenth-century commitment to freedom of expression. But familiarity and habit have made it easy to overlook that the First Amendment is actually quite a strange paragraph. It brings together what is known as the Establishment Clause (more properly an anti-establishment clause: "no law respecting an establishment of religion"); a religious freedom clause ("or prohibiting the free exercise thereof"); a defense of what it initially calls "freedom of speech" and, then, expands to include the press as well, an articulation of a "right of the people peaceably to assemble"; and, echoing the earlier shift from speech to print, "to petition the Government." That is, this crucial paragraph brings together a series of rights each of which could just as well merit its own entry in the Bill of Rights or could represent its own amendment to the Constitution. It is possible, for example, to imagine these same rights enumerated as a list or a series of distinct paragraphs—one for a refusal by the government to establish a religion, another for the right of citizens to free exercise of religious preference, a third for protections of speech, another for printing, and so on. Even if only as an exercise, such an enumeration highlights the differences characterizing religion, speech, print, assembly, and petitioning. Their proximity in the First Amendment, however, can serve to show how the various rights could also be oppositional, as for example when a free exercise of religion also represents an establishment of religion, or, alternatively, when the right of free expression contravenes the free exercise of religion.

167

These tensions, both between the various rights and their encapsulation in the same paragraph are related to the fact that the U.S. Constitution is an eighteenth-century document. Or, to put it in other terms, the combination of what seem to be conflicting rights in the same document reflects an entanglement in history that is at odds with what are now viewed as universalizing claims made for free speech and for the Enlightenment. The focus of this essay is to describe both the internal tensions between speech and religion that characterize the First Amendment and the pre-history of those tensions. I will include, then, first, some conceptual issues relating to the freedoms of religion and speech, and, second, the issues as they were set forth in the works of a few major figures: John Milton, John Locke, and, to a lesser extent, Jean-Jacques Rousseau, all of whom wrote prior to the constitutional codification in the United States of the joint rights of religion, speech, print, and assembly. There are familiar as well as more abstruse objections to overstating the possibility of *free* speech. In Stanley Fish's pithy formulation, "there's no such thing as free speech."[1] Some point out the *de jure* limitations: e.g., no yelling "fire" in a crowded theater; community and decency standards; national security restrictions, and so on. Others have explored *de facto* limitations on freedom of speech. For instance, poststructuralists point out that, even if speaking freely is allowed, it is not conceptually possible to say all; others have wondered whether it is even desirable to say all. As Wittgenstein put it, "What we cannot speak about we must pass over in silence."[2]

Such explorations of the conceptual limits of free speech, however, share a common interest in speech, whether in pushing against its limit or in celebrating a mystical potential to exceed it. Overlooked, and particularly difficult to recover, is the possibility that religion itself is at issue in the defense of freedom of speech and the separation of church and state so strangely entangled in the First Amendment. While the First Amendment would seem to point toward a secularizing modernity, it also preserves an ancient argument within a particular religious tradition. In other words, the First Amendment, too, makes possible a curious mixture of the ancient and the modern. Or, as Bruno Latour put it, we have never been modern.[3] I contend that this mixture is a result of the eighteenth-century context of the First Amendment; the paragraph, in bringing together a defense of speech with a defense of religion, has an *in medias res* quality. In part, the document reflects a process whereby religion is being turned into its own separate category. Where earlier it would have been an overarching set of practices that organized daily life (e.g., daily matins and vespers and weekly mass, etc., to take admittedly parochial examples), after the Enlightenment religion emerges as something presumed to be distinct, in a word, separate. At the same time, though, some debates concerning the First Amendment are also debates *within* the complicated paragraph of the First Amendment, as freedom of expression plays off ideas about religion.

I will review three figures from seventeenth- and eighteenth-century Europe, whose writings on freedom of expression, full of religious implications, point toward the complexities that would later manifest themselves in the complicated paragraph of the First Amendment. I begin with a sketch of the seventeenth- and eighteenth-century European context of religious turmoil and the Enlightenment response to it, and then turn to John Milton's *Areopagitica*. This essay is considered particularly important in the history of the articulation of a right to freedom of expression, but his argument derives from a specifically Protestant understanding of the right. Later in the seventeenth century, John Locke's *A Letter Concerning Toleration* was published. Besides representing another important development in the defense of freedom of speech, it is also commonly interpreted as marking a decisive development in the domestic English argument for a separation of church and state (something for which the young Milton does not press), in the process articulating an important development in political theory. Finally, I will review Rousseau's *On the Social Contract* (1762). Influenced by the natural state arguments that both Milton and Locke pursue, Rousseau radicalizes the so-called moderate enlightenment, precisely because of what he sees as its implicit Christianity. As a result, the separation of church and state emerges from Rousseau's argument as a specific Christian contribution to political philosophy. After Rousseau, the political problem with which we are left, less than two decades before the drafting of the U.S. Constitution, is whether the separation of church and state is already a Christian political position. Recent discussions focus instead on whether the gap between the church and the state is too small or too great, not on whether such debates are a consequence of Christianity. That at least, is the sense one has in discussions in countries with free speech protections. It may be, however, that it has been difficult to hear a very different question, a religious one, about what might be seen as a religious trace embedded in this secular political philosophy.

We are familiar with the long-standing narrative of how the Founding Fathers drafted a constitution and, with a performative speech act, called a new nation into being. The First Amendment, we have been told, was in part a response to and an attempt to overcome the dissension and political upheaval associated, especially in the seventeenth century, with having an established religion in the British Isles. Thus, it protects open expression of conscientious differences (or differences of conscience). In this larger sense, then, the First Amendment is

one of the many shifts attendant to the Protestant Reformation, including the central question of whether reforming and protesting would
mean separation from Rome (but not from the concept of an established
church) or freedom of individuals to believe and practice as their
conscience saw fit, apart from any particular denomination or church.
Those larger shifts cannot be separated from Gutenberg's invention and
the subsequent spread and decreasing price of moveable type (as three
decades of debates over "print culture" have recently emphasized). In
this larger picture, then, the First Amendment is thus often considered
one of the culminating achievements of the Enlightenment, at least in
its Anglo-American form. In this triumphalist reading, we have a document facilitating a powerful secularism, one that separates church and
state, and that opposes openness, reason, and tolerance to violence, faith,
and superstition. This document, and others like it, from what Thomas
Paine taught us to call the Age of Reason, are thus said to offer a universal model for freedom of conscience.

170   There is, however, another possible reading, one that does not
emphasize the separation of speech and religion. In this reading, if
freedom of conscience and freedom of speech are inextricably tied to
developments in western Europe, those larger historical currents are
not overcome by the First Amendment. Rather, those currents come
together in its complicated paragraph. That is to say, the First Amendment combines speech, press, assembly, *and* religion because they were
seen as acutely related, especially when the eighteenth century looked
back on the wars of the sixteenth and seventeenth centuries. Thus, the
First Amendment offers not a model of conscience, toleration, freethinking, and so on, but instead has very much to do with a European
context, one in which the residents of half a continental land mass had
been at war with each other over religious differences for centuries. In
this reading the First Amendment is a document, arising from tensions
within Christianity, that gives different religions and differences among
religions a protected space in which to disagree agreeably or to live with
their differences. Important questions follow from the First Amendment
thus read as an intervention in western European history of religious
conflict. To begin with, there is the question of whether this western
European development can then be transferred universally. Further, in

order to separate church and state, is it necessary to know and accept at least something of that European religious history and to have grown up with the practices that have been altered by the Enlightenment? There is also the related question of whether the separation of church and state is itself a religious decision. While some might argue that the anti-establishment clause reflects a preference for, say, Protestant individualism, there is also in the eighteenth century a related and larger question of whether the anti-establishment clause is recuperating a sense of Christianity lost when Constantine brought church and state together.

In recent decades, two readings of the First Amendment's "Enlightenment" protections of speech and conscience, and the related separation of church and state, have become at times violently opposed: defenders of the secularizing vision of the Enlightenment have aligned themselves with reason, science, to some extent atheism, and the universal, which they oppose to the irrational, the faith-based, the fundamentalist, and to a lesser extent the local. Within this universalist defense of speech there is also usually the presumption that we have entered a period that has put debates over free speech behind it, in no small part thanks to the hard-fought struggles of the major and many minor figures of the seventeenth and eighteenth centuries. The breach that the Enlightenment is said to represent, the victory of reason over unreason, makes it tempting to read the recent rise of religion "chronologically," more specifically as an anachronism—an eruption of the Middle Ages long after the theology associated with that period has passed. Indeed, the very terms for understanding historical development that were developed during the Enlightenment contribute to this sense of a contemporary clash of historical periods, the result of uneven historical development. This argument has its partisans in the academy as well. To take only two prominent examples, historian Gertrude Himmelfarb with *The Roads to Modernity* and philosopher Jürgen Habermas with *The Structural Transformation of the Public Sphere* tell different versions of an eighteenth-century struggle for a universal freedom. In their reading, Ayatolleh Khomeini's *fatwa* against Salman Rushdie's *Satanic Verses*, the subsequent attacks on several of its translators, and, nearly two decades later, the violent reaction to publishing the so-called Mohammed cartoons are an eruption of anti-modern irrationalism that would restrict a modern, universal right to freedom of expression. Recently, Martin Amis is among the most well known of those who have publicly made precisely this case, but there are others making similarly large claims for secularism, reason, and science. Richard Dawkins and Christopher Hitchens come to mind.[4]

The opposing position, one that argues for restrictions on speech, has of late been broadly associated in the popular imagination with Islam. There are reasons for this association. The Iranian Revolution, for example, reconnected religion and state, pointedly rejecting a modernizer in the person of the Shah. The rise of such groups as the Muslim Brotherhood in Egypt and the Taliban in Afghanistan (and now Pakistan), and of course the violence following the publication of the Mohammed cartoons, seem to represent an objection to the universalist understanding of the Enlightenment (and the related entanglements in the First Amendment). However, religiously inspired political movements are not restricted to Islam, but are instead part of a worldwide "rise of religion" over the last few decades, a phenomenon with many overlapping causes and explanations—and not confined to any particular religious tradition. For some, this phenomenon indicates a "return of the repressed," as in those communist countries in which religious practice was suppressed during the middle decades of the twentieth century. For Samuel Huntington, this rise lends support to his view of a global "clash of civilizations," according to which the collapse of the Soviet Union unleashed ancient rivalries along what Huntington sees as tectonic civilizational boundaries.[5] From Huntington's argument one might conclude that it is only *Others* who are returning to putatively ancient religious patterns, only *Others* who will need to be addressed in some future form of what during the Cold War the foreign policy establishment called "containment."

The concept of a "clash of fundamentalisms"[6] has also figured in response to Huntington's argument, with the so-called rise of religion seen as part of a dialectic produced by modernity. Representing neither Huntington's clash of civilizations, nor an Enlightenment clash of historical epochs, this clash-of-fundamentalisms model contends that religious traditions have emerged as a preferred alternative to a perceived modernity; in this model, the rise of religion, tied to a reaction against mo-

dernity, offers the narrowest visions of the different religious traditions, widens differences among religions, and, unfortunately, monopolizes the contemporary discussion about religion. That is to say, science, technology, and increasing global interconnectedness are rejected in favor of a return to a partially imagined past of purity, imagined in part by contrast to what is received as modernity. Evangelical Christian movements, for instance, during this period that has witnessed a rise of religion, have pushed back against what they see as the creeping and invasive secular humanism of the latter half of the twentieth century. In the United States, one result has been the so-called culture wars, which, though associated with the early 1990s, continue to resonate. The writings of the influential evangelical Presbyterian Francis Schaeffer are instructive in this regard. One of his early titles, *Escape from Reason*, encapsulates what might be thought of as an anti-modern, anti-Enlightenment strain represented by what would later come to be called the Moral Majority and the Christian Coalition.[7]

By distinguishing between moderate and radical Enlightenments, 173 Jonathan Israel offers a seventeenth- and eighteenth-century version of these contemporary tensions.[8] For Israel, the moderate, Anglophone Enlightenment, influenced by and associated with Locke, does not pursue the positive implications of the rise of reason as much as does a radical Enlightenment influenced and represented by the Dutch philosopher Spinoza. This helpful distinction highlights differences within the Enlightenment itself, differences that are often overlooked at least in the universalist narrative concerning the freedoms achieved in the eighteenth century. For Israel, unless we break with the Anglophone tradition, we will misunderstand both eighteenth-century intellectual history (which is not as Anglophone as its historiography would suggest) and the continuing potential of a radical Enlightenment. In Rebecca Goldstein's terms, we would be "betraying Spinoza" yet again not to pursue what Israel calls the radical enlightenment.[9] Consequently, it is important to be careful about the differences between what Israel has called the moderate and the radical Enlightenment. The pre-history of our protection of freedom of speech, as set down in the First Amendment, is dominated by figures more associated with the "moderate" side. In their seventeenth- and eighteenth-century manifestations, these two versions of Enlightenment play out as a "Christian" and a "non-Christian" Enlightenment. It seems to me that an Enlightenment whose definition of toleration is specified as Christian is not necessarily moderate. Nor, of course, would it be considered particularly radical, either. This aspect of the Enlightenment archaeology recorded in the First Amendment runs counter to the full universalist potential of the Enlightenment project.

The focus here on a few canonical works by major figures in literature and philosophy (or intellectual history) from the seventeenth and eighteenth centuries should not obscure the lengthy history of attempts to separate the exercise of religion and freedom of expression from the control of civil authorities, a history that extends backward for centuries prior to the First Amendment. This history takes place across a wide variety of what are today many different fields: religion, literature, law, and politics, to name just a few. In England, such a history would include the theologian and reformer John Wycliffe (d. 1384), one of England's earliest antagonists of papal encroachment on civil power, who produced the first English translation of the Bible in the fourteenth century. It might also include the Oxford martyrs, who for reasons of conscience dissented from the Roman Catholic doctrine of transubstantiation in the middle of the sixteenth century. It has even been argued that the Star Chamber decree that centralized censorship in 1586, in what would come to be a notorious secret royal tribunal, was nonetheless an important development in the protection of the right to publish.[10]

In July 1641, the English Parliament dissolved the Star Chamber. Not surprisingly, the following year saw a dramatic increase in the number of titles published. Thanks to an avid seventeenth-century collector, we know that at least 2,000 titles were published in England in 1642 alone, more than would be published again in a single year until 1695. Between 1640 and 1660, more titles were published than had been printed in the preceding 150 years.[11] The sheer quantity of such publication is an important development, but the contents of the works also contributed to the general social and political ferment occurring in the mid-seventeenth century: petitions, statements of political philosophy, and adventuresome theology conveyed a sense of what Christopher Hill has described as a "world turned upside down."[12] In 1643, Parliament, despite disbanding the Star Chamber only two years earlier, passed a Licensing Order that reinstated prepublication requirements of the older Star Chamber laws, such as licensing and the registration of the names of the author, printer, and publisher of each title. But the order also marked a slight shift of focus, from the stationer, who would print, to the author who had written the book in question. This shift has come to be seen as an important development in articulating (and thus later protecting) authors' rights.[13]

In the following year, 1644, with *Areopagitica: A Speech for the Liberty of Unlicensed Printing*, John Milton responded both to these brief conditions of openness and to the Parliament's instituting of new licensing requirements. With its title referring to a rocky outcropping on the path up to the Acropolis, a site overlooking the Agora and seat of the Athenian upper council, Milton's essay from the outset aims to take the high ground, staking a claim to ancient democracy and famously making a pioneering argument for freedom of the press. Apparently acting as if the Licensing Order did not exist, *Areopagitica* was published "unlicensed, unregistered, and issued without the print of publisher or printer."[14] In other words, Milton's publication enacted its own claim, evading the licensing to which it is opposed. At the same time, by including the name of the author, *Areopagitica* contributed to the slow emergence of the modern idea of the author as originator of a text. In one of the most familiar claims from the essay, Milton demands, "Give me the liberty to know, to utter, and to argue freely according to conscience above all liberties" (CPW, II.560). This ringing statement encapsulates what will come to be associated with a secularist Enlightenment ideal of freedom of expression. Milton invokes a freedom of publication that would later be associated with the press during the eighteenth century and with the First Amendment, though such press freedom did not exist at the time *Areopagitica* appeared. Not having been given the liberty to publish, Milton goes one step further, and simply takes it. Consequently, *Areopagitica* has been described as the "the foundational essay of the free speech tradition."[15] Whether appealing to an ancient model of democracy or presciently describing a later modern democratic ideal, he envisions a public sphere in which citizens can petition a responsive government: "when complaints are freely heard, deeply consider'd, and speedily reform'd, then is the utmost bound of civill liberty attain'd" (CPW II.487).

Milton's defense of the political and social value of a free press in *Areopagitica*, even of a press that might publish evil, is linked to his understanding of reason. Early in the essay, casting censorship and licensing as violence, Milton describes books as "not absolutely dead things" that are capable of being brought to life (CPW, II.492). That is, books "preserve as in a viol the purest efficacie and extraction of that living intellect that bred them" (CPW, II.492). If, then, there are those who would suppress books, "a kinde of homicide may be thus committed" (CPW, II.493). Specifically, what would be killed in any suppression of printing is reason: "hee who destroys a good Booke, kills reason it self" (CPW, II. 492). Milton makes several related points in defending his belief that books are the living preservative of reason itself. First, in the Renaissance humanist model, books are a means to immortality, both

because they can survive over time and also because they offer some access to truth understood in the Platonic sense as unchanging and eternal. Second, Milton has a very distinct sense of "the labour of book-writing," of what authors do (CPW, II.532). In a sentence that is nearly two hundred words long, Milton contends that authors deliberate, search, meditate, consult, confer, and summon, to list just a few of the verbs. In short, the author "summons up all his reason" and offers to the world "the most consummate act of his fidelity and ripenesse" (CPW, II.532). According to this demanding and optimistic vision of the work of writing, authors provide the most informed and skilled use of their reason possible. And in those cases where authors fail to display their reason, then it is up to the reader to respond with an informed act of reasonable reading as well. Readers, that is, can exercise their reason, too. For Milton, "reason is but choosing" (CPW, II.527).

This connection between the value of a free press and the active exercise of reason, of choosing, would become important for the Enlightenment generally and for its subsequent universalizing vision in particular: publishing, say, cartoons that some might find offensive would thus become both the measure of and the condition for the strength of a political entity. Indeed, Milton makes a claim in *Areopagitica* that could almost stand for the late eighteenth-century sense of the knowledge-forming function of an active public sphere: "where there is much desire to learn, there of necessity will be much arguing, much writing, many opinions; for opinion in good men is but knowledge in the making" (CPW, II.554). We can hear in this claim the seventeenth-century scientific method applied to publication, a process of trial and error in the public square or in the court of informed public opinion; but we also hear Thomas Paine's use of the press in the early United States or Kant's later defense of scholar-citizens addressing public matters in "An Answer to the Question 'What is Enlightenment?'" (1784). And long before the Danish cartoons, we can also hear Milton's idea of the role and volubility of publication.

It should be noted that Milton himself does not make a case for voluble, opinionated public reasoning in universal terms. Threaded throughout *Areopagitica* are a series of overlapping and sometimes contradictory images—analogies—that situate Milton's claim, important as it was for the later Enlightenment, in a debate over English Protestantism. While Milton casts the Licensing Order of 1643 as a new form of the recently expired Star Chamber, more importantly he portrays it as almost an extension of the Roman Catholic Church, with its "imprimaturs" (CPW, II.504) and Inquisition: "this project of licencing crept out of the Inquisition" (CPW, II.493). Milton reminds Parliament, which was then debating whether Charles the First was sufficiently Protestant, that it was "the Popes of Rome" who had "extended their dominion over mens eyes," so much so that "Wicklef and Husse" provoked even stricter control of publishing by the Church (CPW, II. 502). Milton also reminds his readers of the nearly contemporary example of Galileo, "a prisoner to the Inquisition, for thinking in Astronomy otherwise than the Franciscan and Dominican licencers thought" (CPW, II.538). In case there are any lingering questions about the heliocentric universe (which as it turns out there were), Milton adds "we all know the Bible it selfe [was] put into the first rank of prohibited books" (CPW, II.517). Lest the finer implications of this point might have been lost on less engaged readers, Milton accuses "Lambeth house," the London home of the Archbishop of Canterbury, of "apishly Romanizing" (CPW, II.504). For good measure, Milton goes on to connect the Licensing Order to "that policie wherewith the Turk upholds his Alcoran, by

177

the prohibition of Printing" (CPW, II.548). Although this reference to Islam is greatly outnumbered by analogies to Roman Catholicism, it is now a particularly suggestive shard in the archaeology of the religious implications that inhere in the First Amendment's strange paragraph.

It is easy to overlook how much the understanding of "reason" had to change before there could be a First Amendment. In short, reason itself had to be secularized, a lesson that Habermas, among others, has sought to impart since the early 1960s. As such it is a much larger story than can be told in this sketch of the historical entanglements embedded in the eighteenth-century discussion of speech, print, and religion. This "age of reason" was accompanied by the rise and popularization of scientific enquiry, of empiricism. But John Milton is certainly an early figure in this transition. Nonetheless, we see again a religious entanglement, one with a distinctly Protestant cast. In the early 1640s, with *Areopagitica*, Milton defends reason as choosing, as a means, that is, of reaching different conclusions. By contrast, in the earlier Aquinas model, for example, reason was a means of reaching the same conclusions—the truth (and/or God). By *Paradise Lost* (1667), Milton narrates the prospective positive consequences of choosing the very thing that God had prohibited, consequences that involve both the revelation of differences and the *felix culpa* through which we can now know the good. Nonetheless, even this "reason" of difference and confrontation remains connected for Milton to the God of nature and truth to which Aquinas thought reason led. After all, "God gave him reason," Milton says of Adam (CPW, II.527).

At the end of the 1640s, at what turned out to be the end of both the reign and the life of Charles the First, Milton published *The Tenure of Kings and Magistrates*, in which he ventured into the realm of civil authority, basing his argument for executing the monarch on his understanding of reason:

> If men within themselves would be govern'd by reason, and not generally
> give up thir understanding to a double tyrannie, of Custom from without,
> and blind affections within, they would discerne better, what it is to
> favour and uphold the Tyrant of a Nation (CPW III.190).

In this, the first sentence of the essay, Milton sets up another opposition that will go on to become familiar in the Enlightenment: reason versus the ties of custom and affection. Hume will invoke similar oppositions in his essay "Of Superstition and Enthusiasm" a century later. For Milton, if people were able to follow reason, tyranny would end; people not only get the government that they deserve, but, to Milton's way of thinking, that they also desire. Milton goes on to argue that a reasonable citizenry would see that monarchy tends to tyranny and is, therefore, unreasonable. A republican form of government allows for the full range of differences that follow from the conjunction of reason and choosing that Milton has earlier described. Later in the essay, Milton contends "all men naturally were born free, being the image and resemblance of God" (CPW III.198). Before customs adhere and affections develop, when reason can predominate, we are free. In this natural, reasonable state Milton is positing, there is no need, then, for government. Or, conversely, governments are already an indication of what we might call a fallen and unreasonable state. Of course, Rousseau will go on to make a similar claim more than a century later: "Men are born free but are everywhere in chains."[16] But what makes Milton's claim as influential as it is transitional has to do with how Milton ties this natural state to God.

Milton casts his own discussion of reason as an English extension, a fulfillment even, of the Protestant Reformation. "Why else was this Nation chos'n before any other, that out of her as out of *Sion* should be proclaim'd and sounded forth the first tidings and trumpet of Reformation to all *Europ*," he asks (CPW, II.552). Here, England becomes a chosen nation, made elect, to spread to Europe the benefits, first, of breaking from Rome and, relatedly, of the freedom of expression that follows from this break. London becomes a new Jerusalem: "Behold now this vast City; a City of refuge, the mansion house of liberty, encompast and surrounded with his protection" (CPW, II.553–54). That is, special safety flows to London and those who seek refuge there because it has been chosen, and it has been chosen, according to Milton, because it is the capital of the country that broke with Rome more than a century earlier. Consequently, as a mansion house of liberty, it offers its residents—refugees—freedom of expression. In the process, England has been called "to the reforming of the Reformation it self," Milton contends, in that God "reveal[s] Himself to his servants, and as his manner is, first to the English-men" (CPW, II.553). While, as we have seen, Milton defends freedom of expression, it is a limited freedom: "I mean not tolerated Popery," as he points out toward the end of *Areopagitica* (CPW, II.565). Thus not only is freedom of expression not extended to Catholics; Milton quite specifically refuses it to them.

Areopagitica's defense of unlicensed publication does not make an argument for separation of religion and politics. Certainly Milton advocates a separation between a particular state, England, and a particular religion, Roman Catholicism. But freedom of expression is a possibility available only in a state conforming to what he sees as Reformation principles. In other words, freedom of expression depends on the right state being connected to the right religion, a reformed Reformation, clear of any association with, say, the intolerance of the Roman Catholic Inquisition. True, the images in *Areopagitica* occasionally conflict. For example, invoking an image from Arthurian romance, he argues "I cannot praise a fugitive and cloister'd vertue, unexercis'd & unbreath'd, that never sallies out and sees her adversary" (CPW, II.515). In this analogy, every good reader becomes something like the Green Knight at the beginning of the tale, convinced of his or her purity and ready to take on the adversary by reading the ethically demanding text. But Milton thereby also aligns his argument, and his readers, with the knights of the Crusades. While this phase in European and Christian history preceded the Inquisition, the Imprimatur, and the execution of earlier translators of the Bible, it does not defend a freedom of expression that is without or separated from religion.

After the restoration of the Stuart monarchy in 1660, there was a retreat from the press and religious freedoms of the 1640s and 1650s. There were many proposals for limiting press freedom, while in 1662 the Licensing of the Press Act restored censorship. The following year, Roger L'Estrange was appointed Surveyor of the Press and was effectively charged with implementing the 1662 act. At the same time, there were important countervailing pressures, principally in the theater, also restored in London upon the new monarch's return from exile in, among other places, neo-classical France. The Restoration theater held up a mirror to a range of socialite types in a newly consumerist London, and it also featured actresses performing on the London stage for the first time. Some of them went on to become the most famous actresses in English theatrical history, such as Nell Gwynn. Drama's negative associations generally, and the fact that women were being paid to perform, put the theater in a complicated position with regard to freedom of expression. By the turn of the eighteenth century, in the *Short View of the Immorality and Profaneness of the English Stage* (1698), Dissenting minister Jeremy Collier called for a kind of censorship of theater, arguing that "the business of plays is to recommend virtue and discountenance vice."[17] During the early decades of the eighteenth century the political commentary occurring in contemporary theatrical productions—the freedom of expression we have been told to expect from eighteenth-century England—also led, by 1737, to the Lord Chamberlain being given censorship powers over the stage.

It was in this environment, especially amid late-seventeenth-century fears of the rising influence of Catholicism, that the most influential of all English philosophers, John Locke, responded to the problem of religion and government by making an argument for a new understanding of the two. Locke, a sophisticated philosopher, and well connected socially through early patronage of Anthony Ashley Cooper, First Earl of Shaftesbury, also had good timing: the 1685 revocation in France of the Edict of Nantes and the Glorious Revolution in England in 1688. After England had experienced the Exclusion Crisis of 1679–81, prompted by fears of a Catholic monarch again on the throne, France provided evidence of the problem of enforcing religious conformity and, in effect, of disallowing toleration. The Exclusion Crisis would ultimately be more or less resolved with a peaceful abdication by James II and the commitment to a Bill of Rights from the incoming Protestant king William. Thus, Locke defended religious toleration without a perception that he was deranged (which is how some of the radicals from the 1640s had been received), or that he was more interested in leveling up than in leveling down, to invoke Johnson's phrase.[18] Much of what Locke proposes in *A Letter Concerning Toleration* (1689) is not only consistent with classical liberalism; it also helps to create it.[19] The influence of Locke's treatise on the U.S. Constitution is well known. While in Paris, for example, Thomas Jefferson sought out a portrait of John Locke that he later hung in the parlor of his home in Monticello. In the Declaration of Independence, Jefferson reworked a phrase that in Locke's *Letter* reads, "life, liberty, health, and indolency of body; and the possession of outward things" (393). The fact that Jefferson would revise Locke's terms in the Declaration of Independence testifies to the influence that Locke's idea of civil government had on classical liberalism and on the universalizing vision of the Enlightenment. Yet much of the frame of Locke's *Letter* is at odds with the universalizing defense of the church and state separation with which we are familiar in recent years.

In what might be considered the classical liberal aspect of *A Letter*, Locke argues it is "above all things necessary to distinguish exactly the business of civil government from that of religion" (393). He thus describes a clear separation between the state's interest in the citizens' material welfare and the individual's interest in the spiritual. He argues even more emphatically that "the Church itself is a thing absolutely separate and distinct from the commonwealth. The boundaries on both sides are fixed and immoveable" (403). Here Locke appears as clear as he is emphatic. The commonwealth, concerned solely with civil matters, has the material and the physical as its domain: "The care of souls is not committed to the civil magistrate" (394). Of course there are many who would argue that it would be better for the individual, even materially, if the state were to insist on the individual's spiritual life. They might argue, for example, that locally most of the citizens agree on and are committed to the importance of a particular religion. This can still be a controversial point today; in the United States there have been several movements over the last few decades trying to retake the country for Christianity. The Ten Commandments, for example, have been placed in courthouses (and also traveled the country on flatbed trucks) to make the case that the United States is insufficiently Christian because Church and State have been separated. In response to those who would argue that life, liberty, and health depend on the state certifying that citizens be a particular type of Christian—or, perhaps more specifically, on *someone else*'s becoming a particular type of Christian—Locke makes a very important proviso: "nor can any such power be vested in the magistrate by the consent of the people, because no man can so far abandon the care of his own salvation as blindly to leave it to the choice of any other" (394). For Locke, "the care . . . of every man's soul belongs unto himself, and is to be left unto himself" (405–6).

Locke casts his defense of the toleration of individual conscience against the background of the wars of religion that would have been fresh in people's memory across Europe in the seventeenth and eighteenth centuries: "How pernicious a seed of discord and war, how powerful a provocation to endless hatred, rapines, and slaughters they thereby furnish unto mankind" (402). We seem to see here a defense of the Enlightenment as part of a long, slow, progressive change limiting government power over the individual, diffusing information, and decreasing the likelihood of religiously inspired violence. Moreover, the aim is what Locke calls "mutual toleration," which applies both to "private persons" and to "particular Churches" (400) and indeed extends to those whom he calls heathens—"if a heathen doubt of both Testaments, he is not therefore to be punished" (420). The notion of what constitutes toleration would seem to have been universalized: if religion is responsible for so much violence, and if there is to be mutual toleration extended even to the unbeliever, well then surely moving beyond religion itself would be the most "enlightened" prospect. In other words, and as Richard Dawkins and Christopher Hitchens have argued recently, atheism is the next logical step in this progression. But on this point, too, Locke is not an "enlightened secularist." The presumption extended to heathens does not apply to atheists. "Those are not to be tolerated who deny the being of a God. Promises, covenants, and oaths, which are the bonds of human society, can have no hold upon an atheist" (426). The atheist emerges in Locke's polity as a figure something like the poet in Plato's *Republic*: neither can be trusted, because in both cases there is nothing to ground the truth of what is being claimed.

Thus, while Locke is quite specifically advocating religious toleration, it is understood to be toleration for those of other religions, not toleration of all ideas or toleration without regard to religion. An argument for a government whose task is not to supervise the spiritual life of its citizens becomes, paradoxically, an argument on behalf of religion itself. In prose works such as *Areopagitica*, Milton did not separate the spheres of church and state. On the contrary, a complete break from the Roman Catholic Church would make a more perfect religious state in England, a state that would fulfill the Reformation's potential. And while Locke distinguishes the realms of the church and state, he does not make what we might call a secularist argument. His portrait of religious toleration is instead part of a larger portrait of "tolerant religion." And, for Locke, Christianity is a religion of tolerance. As he puts it, "I esteem that toleration to be the chief characteristical mark of the true Church" (390). It is likely that Locke's "true Church," like Milton's, is not Roman Catholic, and there is much to be said for re-reading the history of Christianity as intrinsically tolerant—looking past, say, the Crusades, the Inquisitions, or the sixteenth- and seventeenth-century wars of religion among Christians. Toleration is greatly to be preferred. There is the hope that saying it might make it so. It plays to an English-language audience's best sense of the religion, broadly understood, that most of the audience practices.

Locke seems to be suggesting that Christianity has unique access to toleration. As part of his description of Christianity as a voluntary society different from civil society, Locke claims "nobody is born a member of any Church" (396). This, too, is another important universalist claim made about the Enlightenment, a defense of freedom of belief and the freedom to choose one's religion. At the same time, however, there are religions into which the congregants are born. Judaism comes to mind, conversions notwithstanding. It may be that Locke meant the word "church" quite precisely, i.e., Christian and different from, say, temple or mosque. Although Anabaptists of the sixteenth century (and more contemporarily for Locke, Dissenters and Non-Jurors) acted on their belief that a religion is something that an individual chooses, their very name—re-baptize—points to a long history of infant baptism during which time it was not the case that Christians chose their religion. Locke contends that "toleration . . . is so agreeable to the Gospel of Jesus Christ, and to the genuine reason of mankind" (393). Again we have that implication that toleration is Christian. But what is added here is a change in the definition of "reason." As we have seen, while for Milton reason is given to all humans, and a gift that makes choosing possible, for Locke there is a distinction between "the Gospel" and "reason." That is, the single possibility that toleration might be acceptable to the Gospel does not suffice; toleration is also, according to Locke, consistent with reason, a capacity that is thereby cast as something separate, from

184

the Gospel in this case. In other words, this *Letter*, while it appeals to the Gospel, also represents another step in an ongoing secularization of reason.

By 1762, when *On the Social Contract* appeared, Rousseau could draw on more than a century of debates on these issues. Perhaps as a consequence, some of the formulations are pithier in Rousseau's prose than in Milton's or Locke's. The famous first sentence of Rousseau's book, "Man is born free, and everywhere he is in chains," for example, encapsulates similar points made by Milton and Locke. In the *Tenure of Kings and Magistrates*, as we have seen, Milton made a similar point, that men are naturally born free and, instead of chains, become subject to customs and affections. In the decision of Adam and Eve to eat the forbidden fruit, *Paradise Lost* narrates a change from a Godly and natural state in Eden to a subsequent fallen one, with a review of human history hinting at the effects of what Blake in "London" would later call "mind-forged manacles." Across many of his works, Locke, too, invokes this distinction between a prior state of nature and the present societal one. In *A Letter Concerning Toleration*, for example, he reminds us that "princes indeed are born superior unto other men in power, but in nature equal" (*Letter*, 407). In their natural condition, men are equal; it is "power" that makes distinctions. In Rousseau's terms, it is this princely power that forges chains for everyone. At the same time, in Rousseau's formulation, paralleling Locke's, no man is born into a religion.

185

Rousseau, however, makes claims that seem the logical outcome of these prior discussions, particularly concerning the relationship between Christianity and toleration. In the less-read later sections of *On the Social Contract* he writes, regarding Jesus, "in separating the theological system from the political system, this made the state to cease being united and caused internal divisions that never ceased to agitate Christian peoples" (97). Think, for example, of "render unto Caesar the things which are Caesar's." Whereas Milton at the time of *Areopagitica* wanted England to separate fully from the Roman Catholic church as a sign of the use of reason (without, at least at that point in his career, separating the church from the state) and whereas Locke saw the separation of the civil and the spiritual as an aspect of Christian toleration, Rousseau went one step further and claimed that it was Christ himself who separated theology from politics. In this dramatic formulation, either Christ is the first figure of the Enlightenment, or our sense of the Enlightenment profoundly underestimates the degree to which what is regarded as one of the Enlightenment's key contributions—the separation of church and state and the consequent freedom of expression—is at root Christian, going all the way back to Christ himself. Rousseau points to a quite important reading of the geo-political stakes in Jesus's life and death. The Roman empire, under which Jesus lived and died, not only adopted polytheism as its official religion but also demanded of its citizens allegiance to the state's gods. But the Romans also governed, among others, monotheists who kept alive a monarchical lineage—Judaism—that likewise combined religion and government in shared rituals and legal codes. This combination Jesus is seen to upset, by pointing to a higher law.

Rousseau's invocation of Christ, unlike Locke's reference to the Gospels, is not made for the persuasive effect on a largely Christian audience. Indeed, Rousseau *dislikes* the consequences of what he sees as Christ's separation of church and state: "perpetual jurisdictional conflict ... has made all good polity impossible in Christian states" (98). While Locke and others regarded the separation of the spheres of church and state as a contribution to political stability, since toleration would allow the peaceful coexistence of different denominations, Rousseau inverts that claim. How, he asks, can a state be peaceful when the believer can always appeal to a higher law and violate civil laws accordingly? If the church and state are separate, there will be no way to adjudicate differences in belief. Rather than a progressive Enlightenment, Rousseau sees what is known idiomatically as a free-for-all, a Hobbesian state of nature, a war of each against each, because of the variety of religions. Rousseau regrets that "the spirit of Christianity has won everything" (98). In other words, the separation of church and state has become the rule, and the model, if not the law. In light of recent conflicts concerning speech and religion, it is interesting to note that Rousseau argued that "Mohammed had very sound opinions. He tied the political system together very well" (98). Rousseau went so far as to praise Islam's combination of mosque and government: with "the caliphs, this government was utterly unified, and for that reason it was good" (98). This praise is not inconsistent with Rousseau's desire for rule by the "General Will," in which (as Helena Rosenblatt mentions in her contribution to this volume) dissent ceases and all voices merge in unanimity.

Rousseau dealt in paradoxes. This makes him an unusual figure in the Enlightenment, which, as we have learned to view it, was about the triumph of reason. But he is a figure in the Enlightenment, and his argument concerning the separation of religion and society highlights a recurring correlation in the seventeenth and eighteenth centuries between Christianity and the legal separation of church and state. In our connection, he asserts two paradoxes. The first concerns the Christian origins of the separation of church and state. The second asserts that the separation of the two does not effect a true separation. Such a seeming separation may very well combine church and state in a way that is associated with one of the religions of the book, Christianity. Rousseau thereby profoundly challenges our understanding of tolerance, freedom of expression, and the "establishment" clause of the First Amendment. In essence, the question is how to dis-establish the establishment clause: is it possible to make a defense of speech and of limited government involvement in the spiritual lives of the citizens that is not Christian involvement in the spiritual lives of fellow citizens? Rousseau hopes so (as would Kant later), and he proposed "a purely civil profession of faith . . . not exactly as dogmas of religion, but as sentiments of sociability" (102). As Lynn Hunt and others have argued, these often-novelistic sentiments of sociability were central to inventing human rights in the second half of the eighteenth century.[20] It is not clear, however, whether even such purely civil professions of faith, or professions of faith in the purely civil, would be able to leave this religious history behind. Nor is it clear that they necessarily ought to. But there are a series of risks if we were to forget this history, not the least of them being an unfortunate tendency to assign the religious only to the other, and to other traditions.

The universal, and often radical, Enlightenment—one of rational, open, skeptical, secular, and even anti-clerical transparent debate—is quite attractive. But there are many lessons to be drawn from such a prologue of historical entanglements that characterize both the Enlightenment and the late-eighteenth-century protections afforded by the First Amendment to speech, print, assembly, and religion. Not the least

187

of these lessons is the danger in overstating the extent to which such skeptical openness characterized the Enlightenment or the eighteenth century. It has been argued that if the First Amendment had not this implicit archaeology, the United States would lose a sustaining tension: how some free speech acts contravene religious prohibitions. This tension, it is claimed, is lacking in much of western Europe (read France, Germany, and urban England), which now finds itself too secular to notice religious implications. As Roger Scruton, writing from Hobbes' hometown, Malmesbury, England, puts it, "Western civilization has left behind its religious belief and sacred text."[21] By contrast, as is often pointed out, the Establishment (or, the anti-establishment) Clause allows religions to flourish in the United States. If (as is claimed in the United States), much of western Europe (again, read France, Germany, and urban England) has become so secularized, then there is also a tendency to associate religion only with some demographic Other, presently often immigrants from Islamic societies (which, in dialectic theory at least, can only increase the religiosity of the Other). Somewhere between the universal secularist and the rise of religion, there is the forgotten possibility of an Enlightenment that is also Christian. At the same time, though, Christianity's paradoxical commitment to secularity has also been forgotten. Also discounted, therefore, is the possibility that the universal secularist vision of the Enlightenment might strike other traditions as a religion.

Notes

1. Stanley Fish, *There's No Such Thing as Free Speech: And It's a Good Thing, Too* (New York: Oxford University Press, 1994).

2. Ludwig Wittgenstein, *Tractatus Logico-Philosophicus*, trans. D. F. Pears and B. F. McGuinness, intro. Bertrand Russell (London: Routledge & Kegan Paul, 1961), 74.

3. Bruno Latour, *We Have Never Been Modern*, trans. Catherine Porter (Cambridge: Harvard University Press, 1993).

4. See Richard Dawkins, *The God Delusion* (Boston: Houghton Mifflin, 2006), and Christopher Hitchens, *God Is Not Great: How Religion Poisons Everything* (New York: Warner Books, 2007).

5. Samuel Huntington, *The Clash of Civilizations and the Remaking of World Order* (New York: Simon & Schuster, 1996).

6. Tariq Ali, *The Clash of Fundamentalisms: Crusades, Jihads and Modernity* (New York: Verso, 2003).

7. Francis A. Schaeffer, *Escape from Reason: A Penetrating Analysis of Trends in Modern Thought* (Downers Grove, Ill.: InterVarsity Press, 1968).

8. See Jonathan Israel, *Radical Enlightenment: Philosophy and the Making of Modernity, 1650–1750* (New York: Oxford University Press, 2001), and *Enlightenment Contested: Philosophy, Modernity, and the Emancipation of Man, 1670–1752* (New York: Oxford University Press, 2006). See also his chapter in this volume.

9. Rebecca Goldstein, *Betraying Spinoza: The Renegade Jew Who Gave Us Modernity* (New York: Nextbook, 2006).

10. Joseph Lowenstein, *The Author's Due: Printing and the Prehistory of Copyright* (Chicago: University of Chicago Press, 2002), 37–39.

11. Lee Morrissey, *The Constitution of Literature: Literacy, Democracy, and Early English Literary Criticism* (Stanford: Stanford University Press, 2008), 26, 61–62.

12. Christopher Hill, *The World Turned Upside Down: Radical Ideas During the English Revolution* (New York: Viking, 1972).

13. Lowenstein, *The Author's Due*, 39.

14. John Milton, *Complete Prose Works*, ed. Douglas Bush et al. (New Haven: Yale University Press, 1959), II.480–570, here 480. Hereafter cited parenthetically in the text as CPW, with volume and page number.

15. Vincent Blasi, "Milton's *Areopagitica* and the Modern First Amendment," *Ideas* 4.2 (1996). http://nationalhumanitiescenter.org/ideasv42/blasi4tp.htm: accessed September 19, 2010.

16. Jean-Jacques Rousseau, *On the Social Contract*, trans. Donald A. Cress, intro. Peter Gay (Indianapolis: Hackett, 1987), 17. Hereafter cited parenthetically with page number.

17. Jeremy Collier, *A Short View of the Immorality and Profaneness of the English Stage* (1698), in *Restoration and Eighteenth-Century Comedy*, ed. Scott McMillan (New York: Norton, 1973) 391–404, here 391.

18. James Boswell, *The Life of Samuel Johnson, L.L.D.* (New York: Everyman, 1949), I, 277.

19. John Locke, *A Letter Concerning Toleration* (1685), in *John Locke: Political Writings*, ed. David Wootton (Indianapolis: Hackett, 1993), 390–436. Hereafter cited parenthetically with page number.

20. Lynn Hunt, *Inventing Human Rights: A History* (New York: Norton, 2007).

21. Roger Scruton, *The West and the Rest: Globalization and the Terrorist Threat* (Wilmington, DE: Intercollegiate Studies Institute, 2002), ix.

Conclusion:
A Way Forward?

"I do not believe that it can be too often repeated that the freedoms of
speech, press, petition and assembly guaranteed by the First Amendment
must be accorded to the ideas we hate or sooner or later they will be denied to the ideas we cherish. The first banning of an association because
it advocates hated ideas—whether that association be called a political
party or not—marks a fateful moment in the history of a free country."

(Justice Hugo Black, 1961)[1]

IN THE INTRODUCTION IT WAS MENTIONED THAT THERE WAS NO
inevitability about the institutionalization of the right of freedom of
speech in the West. "Progress" has not been narrated here. Certainly
the *philosophes*, in their demands for the right to discuss the philosophic
and scientific issues of the day, could scarcely have conceived of a society of individuals who would be free to pursue their own self-interest,
regardless of the larger claims of "truth," and in the process produce the
profusion of competing claims and viewpoints that characterizes the
public square today—all the while managing to live together amidst
the clash of conflicting opinions, without the social order descending
into the Hobbesian chaos that many *philosophes* feared.

In the eighteenth century crown and church in most of Europe still enjoyed a virtual monopoly on "the word," printed or spoken, that is unfathomable today. Peter the Great of Russia, as we learn in the essay by Douglas Smith, forbade everyone in his realm, except for religious teachers, from writing behind locked doors, while anyone who failed to report such an offense would face a charge of sedition. In Spain, the Inquisition still played a role, while in Vienna even the gestures of actors on the popular stage were subject to scrutiny. The regulation of the book trade in France, as Helena Rosenblatt writes, monitored by the crown, was assisted by an army of censors and inspectors. Only Britain escaped such extensive and intrusive regulation.

Such prohibitions, however, could not restrain the veritable tide of scientific and technical knowledge, the spread of the findings of "natural science" through discussion and writing, that began to sweep across Europe. So it was that, before it became a legal right, freedom of speech, and with it the toleration of competing ideas, was a reality on the ground. Moreover, unfettered proliferation of theories and opinions, even of crackpot ideas—and many inventions must have appeared as such to contemporaries—unleashed individual risk-taking, ingenuity, invention, and a historically unprecedented march of wealth creation.[2]

This emphasis on the benefits of unfettered speech to material progress is not meant to minimize the political transformation that also began to occur in the eighteenth century. While some sovereigns wished to "modernize"—Peter the Great wanted good roads and efficient ca-nals—the new knowledge and the possibilities it allowed for individual enterprise also undermined the veneration for traditional sources of power. Thus, a reconception of the rights of individuals vi-à-vis author-ity, which now finds expression in modern liberal constitutions, was a by-product of the material transformation of the West. "Liberal" thus stands in contrast not only to the material austerity but also to the perva-sive regimentation of all aspects of life in the premodern period. Today, the more liberal a nation, the more advanced is its economy. The linch-pin of this system, what keeps it in motion and differentiates it from all earlier political models, are individual rights, in particular freedom of speech and all that speech has come to encompass.

Over the past three centuries this combination of freedom of individual enterprise and freedom of speech has created a true "cultural product": the West. Europe and its offshoots now share both a standard of living that is historically unprecedented and similar legal instruments protecting individual rights.[3]

This cultural product seems in crisis today. A defense of freedom of speech is challenged in the non-Western world and even rejected in places within the West itself. The West now stands accused, like European monarchs of old, of monopolistic behavior in the matter of rights.

The current challenges regarding the extent of permissible speech, however, have purchase, as in the eighteenth century, only on the high plane of elite discourse and also tend to replicate eighteenth-century anxieties. The Mohammed cartoons protests in 2006, as was mentioned in the introduction, were the inspiration, so to speak, for this volume. In a remarkable turn of events, as this conclusion is being written, Americans are protesting the construction of an Islamic cultural center near the site of "Ground Zero" in Manhattan; others have been burning Korans. The protests on either side of the Atlantic have drawn strikingly different reactions. The Danish events did more to elevate the notion of "hate speech" (and to strengthen arguments for limiting speech) than had two decades of academic writing on that subject. The American protesters, meanwhile, have been characterized as "bigoted," "intolerant," "xenophobic," and so on. These terms betray their eighteenth-century origins, as do two others that deserve attention.

193

The first is "divisive," again usually applied to those accused of hate speech. As Helena Rosenblatt reminds us in her essay, even supposedly radical thinkers were uncomfortable with free debate and dissent, precisely because it was divisive. Thus, Rousseau advocated in his novel *Julie* the avoidance of words. "Divisive," however, suggests that all arguments have been settled, after which unanimity should reign. But, as Benjamin Constant wrote, "unanimity always inspires suspicion, and with reason, since there has never been, on important and complicated questions, unanimity without servitude." Indeed, Mercier's utopian novel, *The Year 2440*, described draconian punishments for people whose views were out of line.

A second term, "Islamophobic," is advanced on the theory that harm may be suffered by affected groups, in this case Muslims. Harm also has precedents in views of eighteenth-century thinkers concerning the immaturity or ignorance of the masses and the harmful effects of unlimited speech. Herder, for instance, in claiming that "blasphemous, voluptuous, and scandalous writings" would not harm the "thinking man," worried about "society's weakest, most defenseless members." (See Douglas Smith's essay.) Eighteenth-century writers were troubled by the prospect of the harm resulting from what they called "linguistic anarchy." Harm of course has always been a handy tool for governments wishing to stifle opposition to unpopular mandates. Between 1917 and 1918, over 2,000 people, protesting the entry of the United States in World War I, were convicted under the Espionage Act on the basis of the "clear and present danger" test formulated by Justice Oliver Wendell Holmes.[4] One suspects that contemporary Western governments find the notion of harm useful in getting a handle on the inevitable and unsettling consequences of social change produced by the immigration of large numbers of people to the West since the fall of the Berlin Wall in 1989.

"Islamophobia" also converts a religion into an organic culture, in a Herderian sense, one that has to be respected and protected from change. At a minimum, it indicates the application of the same yardstick to large numbers of people who, in truth, have many differences and divisions among them. Sunni, Shia, and Sufi Muslims, for instance, incorporate practices and traditions that, historically, have divided adherents from one another,[5] much as were Christians in the Middle Ages by (today) seemingly inconsequential but deeply felt practices (tonsure controversy, infant baptism).[6] Muslim immigrants to the West come from Pakistan and Bangladesh, as well as from Turkey, Morocco, Syria, Iran, and so on. The same can be said for other immigrant groups, e.g., Hindus and Sikhs, who are likewise pigeonholed as embodying ethnic constants. Thus, multiculturalists and government policy, especially in Europe, have for decades treated minority groups as "uniform, single-minded, conflict-free and defined by ethnicity, faith, and culture."[7]

In this connection, there is a similar inclination to view the West as an undifferentiated block. What is overlooked, especially by those who insist on universal rights, is that the peoples of the West did not set out to become "Westerners." They have "grown" into that status over time, and no amount of market integration can disguise the fact that the West—like "the Muslim world—has been fashioned from strikingly different cultures and histories. While trade and commerce contributed to the spread of emancipatory ideas in the West in the eighteenth century, the advocates of these ideas represented different national traditions, and the pace at which these ideas have been legislated has been uneven. The essays in this volume have sought to recall these national differences and thereby "excavate" the tensions underlying the abstract language of Western laws. Thus, Lee Morrissey's "archaeological" approach to the First Amendment problematizes the triumphalist Enlightenment narrative—one of progress toward universal tolerance—a narrative that effaces the historical entanglements of religion and speech, not only in the First Amendment but also in European laws.[8] Likewise the case of Spain, as Javier Fernández Sebastián writes, where religious and secular tensions persisted into the twentieth century. The language of Western rights (e.g., "We hold these truths to be self-evident") represents a post hoc facto consensus masking such historical differences.

195

It also bears saying that most people migrating to the United States or Europe wish to participate in the cultural product I have described. Despite criticism of the West's economic and political values during the era of U.S.–U.S.S.R. rivalry, many peoples around the world continued to be inspired by the West's "values," finding an appeal in the words of Benjamin Constant, even if they had never heard or read them: "There is a part of human existence which necessarily remains individual and independent, and by right beyond all political jurisdiction." Today, however, as people living under dictatorships have begun dramatically to test the limits of speech and assembly,[9] the West shrinks from defending its own cultural product, thereby fueling the animus of those who are antipathetic to it.[10]

Benjamin Constant's words express a precious insight, yet one that only finds its full flowering when individuals have the means with which to craft their own way of life, which returns me to my earlier contention concerning the cultural product I have described. The issue of whether certain words are divisive may have less to do with speech itself than it appears: ultimately, the solution to the present conflicts over speech is not a special protected status for newcomers but, instead, their integration in the economic marketplace—in other words, their participation in the engine that created the West's liberal values. The unemployment rate of non-European residents of Europe is shockingly high today. Many are unemployed and dependent on welfare, and it is no surprise that they feel alienated from the predominant Western culture. The United States has historically benefitted from immigration, but, since 2008, Americans have been acutely susceptible to the pocketbook anxieties that have affected Muslim immigrants in Europe for decades already. Thus, the current tensions in the United States concerning immigrants, Hispanic, Muslim, or otherwise, reflect an inchoate awareness on the part of the public that, should the new arrivals not integrate economically (but instead continue functioning as low-paid, unprotected labor), not only will the edifice of rights be overthrown but also that the material plenty that has supported the West's way of life—and its tolerance for differing points of view and for different religions—will be endangered.

The absorption of immigrants will involve negotiating identities, assumptions, and experiences of groups and individuals, all of which are mixed up in complex ways, not reducible to a common yardstick. In view of the history of the past three centuries and especially of the uneven development that characterizes the emergence of the modern West, there is no reason to assume that this process of absorption will—or should—be conflict-free (or that the West's "cultural product" can be transplanted elsewhere).[11] Ideological clashes cannot be avoided when different cultures come together, which returns me to the anxieties of eighteenth-century thinkers and of contemporary commentary on freedom of speech.

Despite all we owe to the thinkers of the eighteenth century, who first articulated the arguments, they were indebted to intellectual traditions that valorized the pursuit of truth and thus, ultimately, agreement. But, as Helena Rosenblatt writes concerning baron d'Holbach: *whose truth?* Truth is not the standard of liberal democracies, which function not by imposing a few grand ideas handed down from on high, but by encouraging a marketplace of diverse, competing, rapidly changing, and unrestrained opinions. I would suggest that only by giving up our attachment to Truth—which is what universal and absolute standards represent—will we begin to understand what freedom of speech is about. If this freedom is in trouble today, the threat is not from outside, but from within, and is due to our failure to reflect on the enabling conditions of this freedom. Let us not forget that, in the past, the pursuit of truth involved the assiduous refutation of error. It has been trial and error, however, not dogma, in whatever form, that created the West. Freedom of speech, if we are serious about it, must allow for unpopular, even "wrong," opinions.

Notes

1. *Communist Party of the United States v. Subversive Activities Control Board No. 12*, dissenting opinion. See http://www.law.cornell.edu/supct/html/historics/USSC_CR_0367_0001_ZD1.html.

2. As in the title of Joyce Appleby's recent book, *The Relentless Revolution: The History of Capitalism* (New York: W.W. Norton, 2010).

3. That the West now represents a culture is evidenced by its ability, more or less, to pick up after every disaster during the past two centuries and to move on as such. The strength of this model is indicated by the average increase in GDP of 2 percent over the entire twentieth century, even in the countries devastated by the two world wars. That the United States has believed that its fate is bound up with Europe's is clear from its participation in those wars and its role as guarantor of western Europe's security during the Cold War. See William J. Bernstein, *The Birth of Plenty: How the Prosperity of the Modern World Was Created* (New York: McGraw-Hill, 2004), 23–27.

4. *Schenck v. US* 249 47, 52 (1919) was "the first significant free speech decision rendered by the Supreme Court. Among other restrictions, the Espionage Act made it a crime to cause refusal of duty in the armed forces or willfully to obstruct the recruitment or enlistment service of the United States" (James Weinstein, "Extreme Speech, Public Order, and Democracy: *Lessons from the Masses*," in *Extreme Speech and Democracy*, ed. Ivan Hare and James Weinsein [New York: Oxford University Press, 2010], 23-61, here 40 n. 57). Among those convicted was Eugene Debs, who ran for president of the United States from prison in 1920. Justice Holmes' standard has since been abandoned. As Weinstein points out, juries were required to make guesses about "the likely consequences of speech." Since *Brandenburg v. Ohio* in 1969, it has been held that an actual incitement to lawlessness must obtain.

5. Not to forget, as Oliver Roy points out (*Secularism Confronts Islam* [New York: Columbia University Press, 2007], 10), that "many people defined sociologically as Muslim have no religious practices."

6. The Church of Rome and the Eastern Orthodox church have still not settled their differences, nor have Catholics and Lutherans managed to unite despite centuries of attempts to do so.

7. Kenan Malik, *From Fatwa to Jihad: The Rushdie Affair and Its Aftermath (How a Group of British Extremists Attacked a Novel and Ignited Radical Islam)* (Brooklyn, NY: Melville House, 2009), 67.

8. It is beyond the scope of this conclusion to discuss the "return of religion" in Europe, but it certainly plays a role in the current conflicts. Since the 18th century, religion has been regarded by elite opinion as something to be overcome, in the name of "progress." As Oliver Roy writes (xiii), "The redefinition of the relations between religion and politics is a new challenge for the West, and not only because of Islam. Islam is a mirror in which the West projects its own identity crisis."

9. It is likewise evident that the scientific and technological expertise developed in the West can coexist—North Korea and Iran come to mind—in regimes in which there is scarcely any political freedom.

10. Recently several writers have suggested political motivations behind the protests of Islamic fundamentalists, and, further, that their activities and the Middle East conflict represent—indeed they may be a continuation of—the kind of ideological struggle that characterized the Cold War. In the opinion of these writers, the West's "free press" has elevated religious radicals to undeserved prominence as spokesmen. See, for instance, Malik (*From Fatwa to Jihad*, 67), according to whom the press reflects government policies that have empowered "community leaders" who, with no electoral mandate, have become "the surrogate voice for their own ethnically defined fiefdoms." Oliver Roy (*Secularism Confronts Islam*) and Gilles Kepel (*Jihad: The Trail of Political Islam* [London: I.B. Taurus, 2004]) have also contributed similarly lucid analyses.

11. Oliver Roy asks (*Secularism Confronts Islam*, 41): "Does the fact that a given [political] model arose in a precise religious or historical context make it thereby specific and not exportable to other cultural realms?"

Milestones in the History of
Freedom of Speech

Appendix I: Freedom of Expression in the Netherlands and Britain[1]

A. Texts

Phase 1: Freedom of expression and religious toleration					
THE NETHERLANDS			**BRITAIN**		
date	*author*	*text*	*date*	*author*	*text*
1582	Dirk Volckertsz Coornhert (1522–1590)	Synod, or on the freedom of conscience	1644	John Milton	*Areopagitica*
1670	Baruch Spinoza (1632-1677)	*Tractatus* Theologico-Politicus	1679	Philopatris [= Charles Blount] (1654–1693)	A just vindication of learning

Phase 2: Freedom of expression and preventive / repressive censorship					
THE NETHERLANDS			**BRITAIN**		
date	*author*	*text*	*date*	*author*	*text*
			1704	Matthew Tindal (1655–1733)	Reasons against restraining the press
			1704	Daniel Defoe (1660–1731)	Essay on the regulation of the press
			1712	Joseph Addison (1672–1719)	The thoughts of a Tory author, concerning the press
			1720-1723	Thomas Gordon (?–1750) and John Trenchard (1662–1723)	Cato's letters
1733	Justus van Effen (1684–1735)	Hollandsche Spectator, essay 220	1731	Henry St. John, 1st Viscount Bolingbroke (1678–1751)	The doctrine of innuendo's discuss'd
1749	Élie Luzac (1721–1796)	Essai sur la liberté de produire ses sentimens	1741	David Hume (1711–1776)	"Of the liberty of the press," in Essays, moral and political
			1742	Anonymous	Independent Briton
1764	Anonymous	The Thinker, essays 24 and 30	1763	John Wilkes (1725–1797)	North Briton no. 45
1769	Anonymous	Letter to a gentleman in the government of Holland on limiting press freedom	1766	William Bollan (1710?–1776)	The freedom of speech and writing upon public affairs, considered
1769	Élie Luzac	Memorandum of considerations regarding an edict concerning blasphemous books and writings	1765–69	William Blackstone (1723–1780)	Commentaries on the laws of England
			1775	James Burgh (1714–1775)	Political disquisitions

Phase 3: Freedom of expression and the rights of man					
THE NETHERLANDS			**BRITAIN**		
date	*author*	*text*	*date*	*author*	*text*
1781	Joan Derk van der Capellen tot den Pol (1741–1784)	An address to the people of the Netherlands			
1782	Anonymous	The liberty of the press, indivisibly connected with the liberty of the Republic			
1782	Johannes Allart (1754–1816)	Freedom			
1784	Diligence, the Mother of Sciences [private society]	Prize essays on the freedom of the press	1791- 1792	Thomas Paine	The Rights of Man
1786	Jacob van Dijk (no dates)	The freedom of the press	1792	Thomas Erskine (1750– 1823)	Celebrated speech [in the case against Thomas Paine]
1793	Johan Meerman (1753–1815)	The beneficial consequences of civil freedom and the adverse consequences of popular freedom, particularly in relation to this commonwealth	1793	Robert Hall (1764– 1831)	An apology for the freedom of the press, and for general liberty
1793	Adriaan Kluit (1735–1807)	The rights of man in France are no imagined rights in the Netherlands	1794	Archibald Bruce (1746– 1816)	Reflections on freedom of writing; and the impropriety of attempting to suppress it by penal laws

B. Institutional Events[2]

Phase 1: Freedom of expression and religious toleration					
THE NETHERLANDS			**BRITAIN**		
date	*event*	*effect*	*date*	*event*	*effect*
			1538	Henry VIII requires Privy Council to approve all writings prior to publication	Formalized system of preventive censorship
			1557	Mary Tudor grants printing charter to Worshipful Company of Stationers	Better control over print production
1579	Union of Utrecht	Article 13 guarantees freedom of conscience	1566	Star Chamber uses prerogative of granting printing privileges to control the Stationers' Company	Regulation of all printing in the realm; the Star Chamber reinforces the decree of 1566 in 1586, 1623, and 1637
1651	Grand Meeting	Union of Utrecht is ratified by the Seven United Provinces	1641	Abolition of Star Chamber	Parliament passes new licensing and printing acts; Court of King's Bench (a superior court of common law) inherits jurisdiction regarding libel
			1662	Licensing act is passed	Censorship "for preventing abuses in printing seditious, treasonable, and unlicensed books and pamphlets, and for regulating printing and printing-presses"

Phase 2: Freedom of expression and preventive / repressive censorship					
THE NETHERLANDS			**BRITAIN**		
date	*event*	*effect*	*date*	*event*	*effect*
			1695	Parliament refuses to renew licensing act	Abolition of prior restraint
			1712	Imposition of stamp tax	Press regulated through taxation; similar legislation passed in 1725 and 1757
			1738	Stage licensing act	Publicly staged plays need to be approved by the Lord Chamberlain
1769	Draft "plan" for system of preventive censorship submitted to States of Holland	Much public debate, but plan is not passed			

Phase 3: Freedom of expression and the rights of man					
THE NETHERLANDS			**BRITAIN**		
date	*event*	*effect*	*date*	*event*	*effect*
			1784	Classic formulation of the role of truth in cases of criminal libel (by Chief justice William Murray, 1st Earl of Mansfield, in the case against William Shipley, Dean of St. Asaph)	It is not in the province of the jury to inquire or decide on the intent of the defendant, or whether the disputed publication is true, false, or malicious
1795	Publication of the *Rights of Man and of the Citizen*	First written guarantee for freedom of expression	1792	Fox's Libel Act	Juries have the right to pronounce general verdicts in criminal libels (i.e., to determine whether a libel is or is not seditious)
1798	Article 16 of the first Dutch constitution	Constitutional guarantee for freedom of expression ('every citizen may express and disseminate his sentiments as he thinks fit...')			
			1843	Campbell's Libel Act	Truth is admitted as a defense in court

Notes

1. The events and texts here are those discussed in the essay by Joris van Eijnatten, who also prepared these tables. The orriginal tites of Dutch works appear in the essay.

2. Because the Dutch Republic had a highly fragmented, federal political structure, many individual laws were enacted on the provincial and/or urban level.

Appendix II: Freedom of Expression in Northern Europe, Habsburg Lands, and Russian Empire

Northern Europe

1741   Johann Lorenz Schmidt defends freedom of speech and press in introduction to his German translation of Matthew Tyndal's *Christianity as Old as Creation*

1749   Dutch lawyer Elie Luzac's *Essay on Freedom of Expression* appears in French

1759   Swedish naturalist Peter Forsskål publishes *Tankar om borgerliche friheten*

1763   Johann Struensee's articles in praise of Diogenes and dogs published in a German periodical

1766   Swedish government declares freedom of the press, except in matters of religion

1770   Johann Struensee, as Danish prime minister, issues rescript granting freedom of the press in Denmark, Norway, and Danish territories in northern Germany, the Caribbean, and India

1771   Johann Struensee executed and 1770 rescript withdrawn

1776   George Mason's Virginia Declaration of Rights grants freedom of the press

1784   Ernst Ferdinand Klein publishes *Über Denk-und Druckfreiheit*

1788   Christoph Martin Wieland publishes "Gedanken von der Freiheit über Gegenstände des Glaubens zu philosophieren"

1793   Johann Gottlieb Fichte publishes *Zurückforderung der Denkfreiheit von den Fürsten Europas*

Habsburg Lands

1655   First appearance in high drama of a peasant group using Viennese dialect

1708   Theater at the Carinthian Gate, the first fully enclosed commedia dell'arte theater in German-speaking lands, is built and opens to general audiences

1710   Josef Anton Stranitzky assumes direction of Vienna Theater at the Carinthian Gate to great public acclaim

1736   First edition of Johann Christoph Gottsched's *Ausführliche Redekunst* (The Complete Art of Rhetoric)

1755   Vienna publisher Johann Thomas Trattner dominates German book market with fifteen printing presses

1761   Joseph von Sonnenfels becomes president of the German Society, a literary circle in Vienna

1765   Periodical *Der Mann ohne Vorurtheil* (The Unprejudiced Man) launched by Joseph von Sonnenfels

1770   Joseph von Sonnenfels made censor for Austrian theater

1774   Maria Theresa issues Decree on General Schooling calling for mandatory elementary education for all

1776   Joseph II changes name of the Court Theater to the German National Theater and declares "Freedom of the Theater" (*Spektakelfreiheit*) to be the norm in his lands

1781   Joseph II's Patent of Toleration and Censorship Decree

1781–88   Intense public discussion, both spoken and written, of Joseph II's reform programs

1789   Appointment of Count Anton von Pergen as Joseph II's police minister is followed by growing surveillance of printed as well as spoken word

1795   Freemasonry forbidden in Austrian lands and intensification of censorship of speech and press

Russia

1700   Emperor Peter I grants charter to Dutchman Jan Tessing to print books and drawings "for the greater glory of the Great Sovereign amongst European Monarchs and for the general benefit and profit of the Nation, but nothing that detracts from the Supreme Honor of Our Majesty or the Glory of Our Realm"

1718   Emperor Peter I issues decree prohibiting anyone, except religious instructors, from writing behind locked doors

1762   "The Sovereign's Word and Deed" (*slovo i delo Gosudarevo*)—
        any unauthorized discussion of the ruler's person or of
        the state's policies and actions—is no longer consid-
        ered a treasonable offense punishable by death

1767   Empress Catherine II publishes her *Great Instruction* (*Velikii
        Nakaz*) addressed to the Legislative Commission that
        argues, among other things, that freedom of expression
        is a natural right of all citizens which it is the state's
        duty to protect

1783   Empress Catherine II issues decree sanctioning private
        presses

1790   Radishchev publishes *Journey from St. Petersburg to Moscow*;
        though he is later arrested and sentenced to death,
        the sentence is subsequently commuted; copies of the
        Journey are seized and destroyed; Empress Catherine II
        bans *Journey*

1794   Empress Catherine II orders all copies of Shakespeare's
        Julius Caesar seized from booksellers

1796   Empress Catherine II revokes right of private citizens to
        own and operate presses; introduces censorship com-
        mittees in all major cities of the Russian Empire

1800   Emperor Paul I bans import of all foreign publications,
        including musical scores

1858   Radishchev's *Journey* published by Alexander Herzen in
        London

1868   Emperor Alexander II lifts the 1790 imperial ban against
        Radishchev's *Journey*

1905   Freedom of the press established in Russia; first full edition
        of Radishchev's *Journey* published in Russia

Appendix III: Freedom of Expression in Spain[1]

A. Texts

DATE	AUTHOR	ORIGINAL TITLE	ENGLISH TRANS.
1687	Juan de Cabriada	*Carta filosófica, medico-chymica*	*Philosophical, Medical-Chemical Letter*
1736	Benito Jerónimo Feijoo	*Teatro Crítico Universal,* vol. 7, discurso 13, § 11	*Universal Critical Theater,* vol. 7, discourse 13, § 11
1745	Benito Jerónimo Feijoo	"De la crítica," Cartas Eruditas y Curiosas, vol. II, Carta 18	"On Criticism," in *Erudite and Curious Letters,* vol. 2, letter 18
1752–56	Juan Enrique de Graef	Discursos Mercuriales Económico-Políticos (Seville)	Mercurial Economic-Political Discourses
1759	Miguel Antonio de la Gándara (1719–1783)	Apuntes sobre el bien y el mal de España	Notes on good and evil in Spain
1768	Francisco Romá y Rosell	*Señales de la felicidad de España, y medios de hacerlas eficaces*	*Signs of Spain's happiness and the means of achieving these with efficacy*
1780	Valentín de Foronda (1751–1821)	Sobre la libertad de escribir	Speech on the freedom to write
ca. 1780	Gaspar Melchor de Jovellanos (1744–1811)	Reflexiones sobre la opinion pública	Reflections concerning public opinion
1786	Pedro Montengón (1745–1824)	Eusebio (novel)	
1785–86	Duque de Almodóvar (Duke of Almodóvar)	*Historia politica de los establecimientos ultramarinos de las naciones europeas* (Madrid) (Spanish adaptation of *Histoire des deux Indes* by Raynal: vol. 2, appendix to book 3, and vol.3, appendix to book 4)	*Political History of the Overseas Settlement of European Nations*

DATE	AUTHOR	ORIGINAL TITLE	ENGLISH TRANS.
1788	León de Arroyal (1755–1813)	Cartas económico-políticas (Carta tercera de la parte segunda)	Economic-political letters (3rd letter of the second part)
1788	Manuel de Aguirre	Sobre el tolerantismo	On toleration
1792	Francisco Cabarrús (1752–1810)	Cartas sobre los obstáculos que la naturaleza, la opinión y las leyes oponen a la felicidad pública	Letters on the obstacles to happiness posed by nature, opinion, and the laws
1793	Antonio Nariño	Declaración de Derechos del Hombre y del Ciudadano (Bogotá)	Translation of the French Declaration of Rights of Man and Citizen (1789)
1793	Leandro Fernández de Moratín	Apuntaciones sueltas de Inglaterra	Notes on England
1795	Antonio Nariño	*Papel periódico de la Ciudad de Santafé de Bogotá*	
1800	Manuel José Quintana (1772–1857)	*Oda a la invención de la imprenta*	Ode on the invention of printing
1808	José M. Blanco White (1775–1841)	Prospecto-editorial del *Semanario Patriótico*	Prospectus editorial of journal *Semanario Patriótico*
1809	Lorenzo Calvo de Rozas (1773–1850)	Proposición hecha a la Junta Central sobre la libertad de imprenta	Proposal to the Junta Central of the Regency concerning freedom of printing
1809	Álvaro Flórez Estrada (1765–1853)	Reflexiones sobre la libertad de imprenta	Reflections on freedom of printing
1809	Gaspar Melchor de Jovellanos (1744–1811)	*Bases para la formación de un plan general de Instrucción Pública* (Sevilea)	*Basis for the Formation of a General Plan of Public Education*
1809	José Isidoro Álvarez	Memoria sobre la libertad política de la imprenta	Memorial on the political freedom of printing
1809	Alberto Lista	"Ensayo sobre la Opinión Pública," in El *Espectador Sevillano* (republished often during the first half of the 19th century in several Spanish- and Portuguese-language newspapers in Europe and the Americas)	"Essay on Public Opinion," in El *Espectador Sevillano* (Seville)

DATE	AUTHOR	ORIGINAL TITLE	ENGLISH TRANS.
1810	Manuel Jiménez Carreño	Reflexiones sobre la libertad de la prensa	Reflections on freedom of the press
1810	José Mor de Fuentes (1762–1848)	La libertad de la imprenta	The freedom of the press
1811	Valentín de Foronda (1751–1821)	Cartas sobre varias materias políticas	Letters on several political subjects
1811	Manuel Freire del Castillo	Nuevas ocurrencias contra la libertad de imprenta	New ideas against freedom of printing
1811	William Burke (pseudonym)	Apology for toleration published in the *Gaceta de Caracas* and subsequent polemic (Venezuela and New Granada)	
1813	Anonymous	*Derechos del hombre y del ciudadano; con varias máximas republicanas y un discurso preliminar dirigido a los americanos* (Bogotá)	*Rights of Man and Citizen*; with several republican maxims and a discourse addressed to Americans
1814	Anonymous	El Maldicente: sátira contra el abuso de la libertad de imprenta	The Damning: satire on abuse of the freedom of printing
1818	Álvaro Flórez Estrada	Carta a Fernando VII, en su *Representación en defensa de las Cortes* (El Español Constitucional, London)	Letter to Ferdinand VII, in *Discourse in Defense of the Cortes*
1820	El Amigo de la Libertad y de las Ciencias	A la libertad de imprenta: romance heroico	Heroic poem: To the freedom of printing
1820	Manuel N. Pérez del Camino	*La Opinión* (Bordeaux)	The Opinion
1820–22	Alberto Lista, Sebastián Miñano, Félix J. Reinoso, José M. Gómez Hermosilla	*El Censor* (Madrid)	Several articles and essays advocating freedom of the press and the crucial role of an enlightened public opinion
1821	Anonymous	*Quaes os bens e os males que podem resultar da liberdade da Imprensa; e qual era a influencia que elles podem ter no momento em que os representantes da nação portugueza se vão congregar?* (Rio de Janeiro)	Goods and evils that could result from freedom of the press

211

DATE	AUTHOR	ORIGINAL TITLE	ENGLISH TRANS.
1825	Juan Egaña	*Memoria política sobre si conviene a Chile la libertad de culto* (Santiago de Chile)	Political report on the advisability of freedom of worship in Chile
1827	José María Luis Mora	Discurso sobre la libertad de pensar, hablar y escribir (Mexico)	Discourse on the freedom of thought, speech, and writing
1830	Vicente Rocafuerte	Ensayo sobre la tolerancia religiosa (Mexico)	Essay on religious toleration
1838	Antonio Alcalá Galiano (1789–1865)	Lecciones de derecho político	Lessons of political law
1840	Joaquín María López (1798–1855)	Lecciones de política constitucional	Lessons of constitutional law
1849	José Baralt	Libertad de imprenta	Freedom of printing
1876	Nicolás Salmerón (1838–1908)	La prensa y la dictadura	The press and dictatorship

B. Legislation²

DATE	EVENT	EFFECT
1480	Royal decree on book imports	No taxes on foreign publications
1502	Decree on book licensing	All publications require royal stamp and license, under penalty of burning and a fine
1554	Decree on licensing	Royal Council is given publication licensing power
1558	General regulation for licensing and import of books	Prohibits books banned or censored by the Inquisition
1598	Decree on taxes for books	Special tax on all books
1610	Regulation of books by Spanish authors	Censors works of Spanish authors abroad
1682	Decree on books about state affairs	Censors publications on political issues
1692	Derogation of privileges for editors and printers	Editors fall under judicial control
1705	Renovation of decree on imported books	
1716	Decree on publications in former kingdoms of Aragón, Valencia, and Catalonia	Derogates specific laws concerning printing and unifies procedures with those of Castile
1745	Decree on books about state affairs	King reserves right to license books on political issues
1749	Decree on libels and banned printings	A copy of all published leaflets is to be delivered to the Royal Council
1752	Legislation on printing	Details procedures for printing

DATE	EVENT	EFFECT
1762	Decree on taxation of books	Suppresses taxes on many kinds of books for Spanish printers
1764	Decree on property rights	Rights are extended to heirs of authors
1768	Decree on censorship	Regulates Inquisition's censorship procedures
1785	Royal decree on newspapers	Publication of newspapers is encouraged
1792	Decree on imported books	Bans all publications on issues relating to French Revolution
1805	Legislation on judicial treatment of printing crimes	Creation of a special tribunal and regulations
1810	Decree by the Regency on freedom of printing	Freedom of publishing for books and newspapers, with certain restrictions
1811	Decrees of freedom of the press (Rio de la Plata)	
1811	Federal Constitution (Venezuela), arts. 1 and 181	Upholds Catholicism and freedom of printing and the press and aims at their protection
1811	Constitution of Cundinamarca (Colombia), tit. I, arts. 3 and 16, tit. II and tit. XII, art. 11	Upholds Catholicism and freedom of printing and the press and aims at their protection
1812	Constitution of Cádiz, arts.12 and 371	Upholds Catholicism and freedom of printing and the press and aims at their protection
1812	Reglamento Constitucional Provisorio (Chile), art. 23	
1813	Decree on procedures for freedom of printing	Regulates censorship
1813	Decree abolishing the Spanish Inquisition (Cortes of Cádiz)	
1814	Constitución de Azpatzingán (Mexico), arts. 1 and 40	Upholds Catholicism and freedom of printing and the press and aims at their protection
1819	Project of a Constitutional Act of Spaniards of Both Hemispheres	Upholds religious freedom and freedom of the press and aims at their protection
1820	Special law on freedom of the press	Restricts right to print subversive texts
1823	Constitution (Peru), arts. 8, 9, 60.26, 60.27, and 193.7	Upholds Catholicism and freedom of printing and the press and aims at their protection
1823	Constitution (Chile), arts. 10 and 262-8	Upholds Catholicism and freedom of printing and the press and aims at their protection

DATE	EVENT	EFFECT
1824	Federal Republican Constitution (Mexico), arts. 3 and 50.3	Upholds Catholicism and freedom of printing and the press and aims at their protection
1825	Decree on imported books	Bans importation of foreign books, with retroactive effect
1830	Special legislation on print	Reenacts former legislation repressing printing rights and creates special bureaucratic office to supervise licenses and censorship
1834	Royal decree on freedom of the press	Maintains previous censorship
1837	New Spanish constitution, arts. 2 and 11	Upholds Catholicism and recognition of freedom of printing and press
1837	Law on freedom of printing	Establishes juries for determining abuses of freedom of printing
1845	Decree of reform of law for printing	Suppresses juries for printing crimes
1846	Restrictive legislation concerning freedom of printing	Creation of a special tribunal for censorship
1854	Reenactment of 1837 legislation	Expands freedom of printing and reestablishes juries
1856	Reenactment of 1846 legislation	Return to restriction on print and press freedoms
1864	Law on print and press	Further restrictions
1868	Decree of freedom of printing and press	Total freedom of printing and press
1869	New constitution, arts. 17.1 and 21	Upholds freedom of religion and wide definition of freedom of the press

Notes

1. These tables were prepared by Javier Fernández Sebastián. Unless otherwise indicated (in parentheses), the reference is to peninsular Spain.

2. Unless otherwise indicated (in parentheses), the reference is to peninsular Spain.

Bibliography

Alonso, Paula, ed. *Construcciones impresas. Panfletos, diarios y revistas en la formación de los estados nacionales en América Latina, 1820–1920*. Mexico City: FCE, 2003.

Andrews, Richard Mowery. "Boundaries of Citizenship: The Penal Regulation of Speech in Revolutionary France." *French Politics and Society* 7, 3 (1989): 90–109.

Baker, Keith Michael. "Politics and Public Opinion Under the Old Regime: Some Reflections." In *Press and Politics in Pre-Revolutionary France*, edited by Jack Censer and Jeremy Popkin, 205–46. Berkeley: University of California Press, 1987.

——. "The Idea of a Declaration of Rights." In *The French Idea of Freedom: The Old Regime and the Declaration of Rights of 1789*, edited by Dale Van Kley, 154–96. Stanford: Stanford University Press, 1994.

Bell, David. "Lingua Populi, Lingua Dei: Language, Religion and the Origins of French Revolutionary Nationalism." *American Historical Review* 100 (1995): 1403–37.

Blasi, Vincent. "Milton's *Areopagitica* and the Modern First Amendment." *Ideas* 4.2 (1996): accessed September 19, 2010, http://nationalhumanitiescenter.org/ideasv42/blasi4tp.htm

Bodi, Leslie. *Tauwetter in Wien. Zur Prosa der österreichischen Aufklärung 1781–1795*. Frankfurt am Main: S. Fischer, 1977.

Butler, Judith. *Excitable Speech: A Politics of the Performative*. New York: Routledge, 1997.

Chiaramonte, José Carlos. *La Ilustración en el Río de la Plata. Cultura eclesiástica y cultura laica durante el Virreinato*. Buenos Aires: Editorial Sudamericana, 2007.

Chisick, Harvey. *The Limits of Reform in the Enlightenment: Attitudes Toward the Education of the Lower Classes in Eighteenth-Century France*. Princeton: Princeton University Press, 1981.

Choldin, Marina Tax. *A Fence Around the Empire: Russian Censorship of Western Ideas under the Tsars*. Durham: Duke University Press, 1985.

Cowan, Jon. *To Speak for the People: Public Opinion and the Problem of Legitimacy in the French Revolution*. New York: Routledge, 2001.

Cushman, Robert E. *Civil Liberties in the United States: A Guide to Current Problems and Experience*. Ithaca: Cornell University Press, 1956.

Davis, R.W., ed. *The Origins of Modern Freedom in the West*. Stanford: Stanford University Press, 1995.

Earle, Rebecca. "The Role of Print in the Spanish American Wars of Independence." In *The Political Power of the Word: Press and Oratory in Nineteenth-Century Latin America*, edited by Iván Jaksic, 9–33. London: Institute of Latin American Studies–University of London, 2002.

Elliott, John H. *Empires of the Atlantic World: Britain and Spain in America, 1492–1830*. New Haven and London: Yale University Press, 2006.

Farge, Arlette. *Subversive Words: Public Opinion in Eighteenth-Century France*. Cambridge, UK: Polity Press, 1994.

Fernández Sarasola, Ignacio. "Opinión pública y 'libertades de expresión' en el constitucionalismo español (1726–1845)." *Historia Constitucional*, no. 7 (2006) [electronic journal].

215

Fernández Sebastián, Javier. "The Awakening of Public Opinion in Spain: The Rise of a New Power and the Sociogenesis of a Concept." In *Opinion*, edited by Peter-Eckhard Knabe, 45–79. Berlin: Spitz, 2000.

———. "Opinión pública." In *Diccionario político y social del siglo XIX español*, edited by Javier Fernández Sebastián and Juan Francisco Fuentes, 477–86. Madrid: Alianza Editorial, 2002.

———. "De la 'República de las letras' a la 'opinión pública': intelectuales y política en España (1700–1814)." In *Historia, filosofía y política en la Europa moderna y contemporánea*, edited by Salvador Rus Rufino, 13–40. León: Universidad de León, and Max-Planck-Institut für Geschichte, 2004.

———, and Joëlle Chassin, eds. *L'avènement de l'opinion publique. Europe et Amérique XVIII–XIXe siècles*. Paris: L'Harmattan, 2004.

Fish, Stanley. *There's No Such Thing as Free Speech: And It's a Good Thing, Too*. New York: Oxford University Press, 1994.

Fontana, Biancamaria, ed. *The Invention of the Modern Republic*. New York: Cambridge University Press, 1994.

Forment, Carlos A. *Democracy in Latin America, 1760–1900*. Chicago: University of Chicago Press, 2003.

Foucault, Michel. *Fearless Speech*. Los Angeles: Semiotexte, 2001.

Ganochaud, Collette. *L'Opinion publique chez Jean-Jacques Rousseau*. Paris: Honoré Champion, 1980.

Glossy, Carl. "Zur Geschichte der Wiener Theatercensur, " pt. 1. *Jahrbuch der Grillparzer Gesellschaft* 7 (1897): 238–340.

Goldman, Noemí. "Libertad de imprenta, opinión pública y debate constitucional en el Río de la Plata (1810–1827)." *Prismas* 4 (2000): 9–20.

———. "Legitimidad y deliberación. El concepto de opinión pública en Ibero-américa, 1750–1850." In *Diccionario político y social del mundo iberoamericano. La era de las revoluciones, 1750–1850*, edited by Javier Fernández Sebastián, 979–1113. Madrid: Centro de Estudios Políticos y Constitucionales, 2009.

Graham, Lisa Jane. *If the King Only Knew: Seditious Speech in the Reign of Louis XV*. Charlottesville: University Press of Virginia, 2000.

Guerra, François-Xavier, Annick Lempérière et al. *Los espacios públicos en Iberoamérica. Ambigüedades y problemas. Siglos XVIII–XIX*. Mexico City: Fondo de Cultura Económica, 1998.

Gunn, John A. *Queen of the World: Opinion in the Public Life of France from the Renaissance to the Revolution*. Oxford, U.K.: Voltaire Foundation, 1995.

Hare, Ivan, and James Weinstein, eds. *Extreme Speech and Democracy*. New York: Oxford University Press, 2009.

Hunt, Lynn. *Inventing Human Rights: A History*. New York: Norton, 2007.

Israel, Jonathan. *Radical Enlightenment: Philosophy and the Making of Modernity, 1650–1750*. New York: Oxford University Press, 2001.

———. *Enlightenment Contested: Philosophy, Modernity and the Emancipation of Man, 1670–1752*. New York: Oxford University Press, 2006.

———. *A Revolution of the Mind: Radical Enlightenment and the Intellectual Origins of Modern Democracy*. New York: Oxford University Press, 2009.

Jaksic, Iván, ed. *The Political Power of the Word: Press and Oratory in Nineteenth-Century Latin America*. London: Institute of Latin American Studies–University of London, 2002.

Klausen, Jytte. *The Cartoons That Shook the World*. New Haven: Yale University Press, 2009.

Lang, Davd M. *The First Russian Radical: Alexander Radishchev (1749–1802)*. London: Allen & Unwin, 1959.

La Parra, Emilio. *La libertad de prensa en las Cortes de Cádiz*. Valencia: Nau Llibres, 1984.

Laursen, John Christian. "David Hume and the Danish Debate about Freedom of the Press in the 1770's." *Journal of the History of Ideas* 59 (1998): 167–73.

———. "Spinoza in Denmark and the Fall of Struensee, 1770–1772." *Journal of the History of Ideas* 61 (2000): 189–202.

———. "Denmark, 1750–1848." In *Censorship: An Encyclopedia*, edited by Derek Jones, 663–64. London: Fitzroy Dearborn, 2001.

———. "Luxdorph's Press Freedom Writings Before the Fall of Struensee in Early 1770's Denmark-Norway." *The European Legacy* 7 (2002): 61–77.

———. "Voltaire, Christian VII of Denmark, and Freedom of the Press." *SVEC [Studies on Voltaire and the Eighteenth Century]* 2002 (06): 331–48.

———. "Censorship in the Nordic Countries, ca. 1750–1890: Transformations in Law, Theory, and Practice." *Journal of Modern European History* 3 (2005): 110–16.

———, and Johann Van der Zande, eds. *Early French and German Defenses of Freedom of the Press: Elie Luzac's "Essay on Freedom of Expression" (1749) and Carl Friedrich Bahrdt's "On Freedom of the Press and Its Limits" (1787) in English Translation*. Leiden: Brill, 2003.

Lempérière, Annick. "Los hombres de letras hispanoamericanos y el proceso de secularización, 1800–1850." In *Historia de los intelectuales en América Latina*, edited by Jorge Myers, 242–66. Buenos Aires: Katz Editores, 2008.

Levy, Leonard W., ed. *Freedom of the Press from Zenger to Jefferson: Early American Theories*. Indianapolis: Bobbs-Merrill, 1966.

Lohenstein, Joseph. *The Author's Due: Printing and the Prehistory of Copyright*. Chicago: University of Chicago Press, 2002.

López-Vidriero, María Luisa. "Censura civil e integración nacional: el censor ilustrado." In *El mundo hispánico en el siglo de las Luces*, vol. 2, 855–67. Madrid: Editorial Complutense, 1996.

Malik, Kenan. *From Fatwa to Jihad: The Rushdie Affair and Its Aftermath*. Brooklyn, NY: Melville House, 2010.

Maravall, José Antonio. "Notas sobre la libertad de pensamiento en España durante el siglo de la Ilustración." *Nueva Revista de Filología Hispánica* (Mexico), 33, no. 1 (1980): 34–58 (also in José Antonio Maravall, *Estudios de la historia del pensamiento español. Siglo XVIII* [Madrid, Mondadori, 1991], 423–42).

Marker, Gary. *Publishing, Printing, and the Origins of Intellectual Life in Russia, 1700–1800*. Princeton: Princeton University Press, 1985.

Mazella, David. *The Making of Modern Cynicism*. Charlottesville: University of Virginia Press, 2007.

McConnell Allen. *A Russian Philosophe: Alexander Radishchev, 1749–1802*. The Hague: M. Nijhof, 1964.

McCoy, Ralph E. *Freedom of the Press: An Annotated Bibliography*. Carbondale: Southern Illinois University Press, 1968.

217

Aperçus

——. *Freedom of the Press: A Bibliocyclopedia: Ten-year Supplement (1967–1977)*. Carbondale: Southern Illinois University Press, 1979.

Melton, James Van Horn. *The Rise of the Public in Enlightenment Europe*. Cambridge: Cambridge University Press, 2001.

Morange, Claude. "Teoría y práctica de la libertad de prensa durante el trienio constitucional: el caso de El Censor (1820–1822)." In *La prensa en la revolución liberal: España, Portugal y América Latina*, edited by Alberto Gil Novales, 203–19. Madrid: Edit. Universidad Complutense 1983.

——. (2001): "Opinión pública: cara y cruz del concepto en el primer liberalism español." In *Sociabilidad y liberalismo en la España del siglo XIX. Homenaje al profesor Alberto Gil Novales*, edited by Juan Francisco Fuentes and Lluis Roura, pp. 117–45. Lérida: Milenio, 2001.

Morrissey, Lee. *The Constitution of Literature: Literacy, Democracy, and Early English Literary Criticism*. Stanford: Stanford University Press, 2008.

Moyn, Samuel. *The Last Utopia: Human Rights in History*. Cambridge: Belknap Press, 2010.

Nash, David. "Analyzing the History of Religious Crime: Models of 'Passive' and 'Active' Blasphemy since the Medieval Period." *Journal of Social History* 41 (2007): 5–29.

Oehler, Joseph. *Geschichte des gesamten Theaterwesens zu Wien*. Vienna: Oehler, 1803.

Ozouf, Mona. "L'opinion publique." In *The Political Culture of the Old Regime*, edited by Keith Michael Baker, 419–34. Oxford: Pergamon Press, 1987.

Papmehl, K. A. *Freedom of Expression in Eighteenth-Century Russia*. The Hague: Nijhof, 1971.

Parthe, Kathleen. *Russia's Dangerous Texts: Politics Between the Lines*. New Haven: Yale University Press, 2004.

Payne, Harry. *The Philosophes and the People*. New Haven: Yale University Press, 1976.

Pipes, Daniel. *The Rushdie Affair: The Novel, the Ayatollah, and the West*. New York: Carol Publishing Corp., 1990; rev. Piscataway, NJ: Transaction Publishers, 2003.

Popkin, Jeremy. "The Concept of Public Opinion in the Historiography of the French Revolution: A Critique." *Storia della Storiografia* 20 (1991): 77–92.

Rosenblatt, Helena, ed. *The Cambridge Companion to Constant*. Cambridge: Cambridge University Press, 2009.

Rosenfeld, Sophia. *A Revolution in Language: The Problem of Signs in Late Eighteenth-Century France*. Stanford: Stanford University Press, 2001.

Ruud, Charles A. *Fighting Words: Imperial Censorship and the Russian Press, 1804–1906*. Toronto: University of Toronto Press, 1982.

Sáiz, María Dolores. *Historia del periodismo en España. Los orígenes. El siglo XVIII*. Madrid, Alianza, 1983.

Schauer, Frederick. "Free Speech and Its Philosophical Roots." In *The First Amendment: The Legacy of George Mason*, edited by T. Daniel Shumate, 132–55. Fairfax, VA: George Mason University Press, 1987.

Schwartz, Bernard. *The Roots of the Bill of Rights*. New York: Chelsea House, 1980 [orig. *The Bill of Rights* (1971)].

Seoane, María Cruz. *Historia del periodismo en España. El siglo XIX*. Madrid, Alianza, 1983.

Sloterdijk, Peter. *Critique of Cynical Reason*. Minneapolis: University of Minnesota Press, 1987.

Smith, Stephen A. "The Origins of the Free Speech Clause." *Free Speech Yearbook* 29 (1991): 48–82.

Stauffer, Hermann. *Erfindung und Kritik. Rhetorik im Zeichen der Frühaufklärung bei Gottsched und seinen Zeitgenossen.* Frankfurt a.M.: Lang, 1997.

Todorov, Tzvetan. "La parole selon Constant." *Critique* 26, no. 255–56 (1968): 756–71.

———. "The Discovery of Language: *Les Liasons dangereuses* and *Adolphe.*" *Yale French Studies* 45 (1970): 113–26.

Walton, Charles. *Policing Public Opinion in the French Revolution: The Culture of Calumny and the Problem of Free Speech.* New York: Oxford University Press, 2009.

Wangermann, Ernst. *Die Waffen der Publizität. Zum Funktionswandel der politischen Literatur unter Joseph II.* Vienna: Verlag für Geschichte und Politik/Munich: R. Oldenbourg, 2004.

Weber, Caroline. *Terror and Its Discontents: Suspect Words in Revolutionary France.* Minneapolis: University of Minnesota Press, 2003.

Winkle, Stefan. *Johann Friedrich Struensee: Arzt, Aufklärer, Staatsmann.* Stuttgart: G. Fischer, 1983, 1989.

———. *Struensee und die Publizistik.* Hamburg: Christians, 1992.

Yates, W.E. *Theatre in Vienna: A Critical History, 1776–1995.* Cambridge: Cambridge University Press, 1996.

Contributors

JORIS VAN EIJNATTEN is professor of cultural history, Utrecht University, the Netherlands. He has written on both early modern and modern intellectual and religious history, including such topics as liberty and toleration, freedom of the press, irenicism, and the Dutch poet and thinker Willem Bilderdijk (1756–1831).

JAVIER FERNÁNDEZ SEBASTIÁN is professor of the history of political thought at the Universidad del País Vasco (Bilbao). His publications include *L'avènement de l'opinion publique. Europe et Amérique XVIIIe–XIXe siècles* and *Diccionario político y social del siglo XX español*. He currently coordinates two projects: a collection of classical texts on political thought in the Basque country; and *Iberconceptos*, a conceptual comparative history of the Ibero-American world.

221

PAULA SUTTER FICHTNER is professor emerita of history, Brooklyn College, the City University of New York. She is a specialist in the history of the Habsburg monarchy and early modern Europe. Most recently she is the author of *Terror and Toleration: The Habsburg Empire Confronts Islam, 1526–1850*. A revised edition of her *Historical Dictionary of Austria* appeared in 2009.

JONATHAN I. ISRAEL is professor of modern history, Institute for Advanced Study, Princeton. He has worked extensively on the Dutch Golden Age and is currently working on an outline survey of the European Enlightenment.

JOHN CHRISTIAN LAURSEN is professor of political science, University of California, Riverside. He is the author or editor of more than a dozen books and scores of articles and chapters, mostly on the implications of skepticism and cynicism for political thought, and on issues concerning toleration, cosmopolitanism, and freedom of the press.

LEE MORRISSEY is professor and chair of the Department of English, Clemson University. He is the author of *The Constitution of Literature:*

Literacy, Democracy, and Early English Literary Criticism and *From the Temple to the Castle: An Architectural History of British Literature, 1660–1760*. His work focuses on relationships between literature and intellectual history, political philosophy, and the arts in the seventeenth and eighteenth centuries.

ELIZABETH POWERS was chair of the Columbia University Seminar on Eighteenth-Century European Culture from 2003 to 2010. She is a scholar of German literature and is currently writing a study of Goethe's concept of world literature.

HELENA ROSENBLATT is professor of history at Hunter College and the Graduate Center, the City University of New York. Her field of interest is eighteenth- and nineteenth-century European intellectual history. The author of *Rousseau and Geneva* and *Liberal Values: Benjamin Constant and the Politics of Religion*, she is also the editor of the *Cambridge Companion to Constant*.

222

DOUGLAS SMITH is a resident scholar at the University of Washington's Jackson School of International Studies. He is the author of three books on eighteenth-century Russia, including *The Pearl: A True Tale of Forbidden Love in Catherine the Great's Russia*.

Index

Addison, Joseph, 33; *The thoughts of a Tory author, concerning the press* (1712), 24, 201; on censorship, 26
Aguirre, Manuel: on religious tolerance, 109–10, 210
Alvarado, Francisco de: on freedom of conscience, 129n54
Álvarez de Cienfuegos, Nicasio, 114
anonymous publication, 24, 42n21, 52, 70; Rousseau on, 141
Antisthenes. *See* cynic philosophy
Areopagitica (1644). *See* Milton, John
Argüelles, Augustín: on religious tolerance, 121, 129n54
Arroyal, León de: on freedom of expression, 112, 113, 210

Bahrdt, Carl Friedrich, *On Freedom of the Press and Its Limits* (1787), 55
Bayle, Pierre, 50, 53
Beaufort, Lieven de, 32
Beckmann, Johann, *Beiträge zur Geschichte der Erfindungen* (1786–1805): influence of, on Radishchev, 66
Berlin Wall: effect of fall of, xii
Bill of Rights (U.S.), xxi, 55, 167; influence of, on Struensee, 46
Blackstone, William, *Commentaries on the laws of England*, on libels, 36, 54, 201
Blount, Charles, *A just vindication of learning, and of the liberty of the press* (1679), 24–25, 201; as translator of Spinoza, 53
Boétie, Étienne de La, *Discourse on Voluntary Servitude* (1548), 48
Bollan William, *The freedom of speech and writing upon public affairs, considered* (1766), 20, 22, 201
Bonnet, Charles, 2, 3, 13
Boulanger, Nicholas Antoine, *L'Antiquité devoilée par ses usages* (1766), influence of, on Struensee, 13–14
Briefe über die wienerische Schaubühne. See Joseph von Sonnenfels
Brouwer, Jan, 25
Brown, Wendy: on moralism in politics, 57
Burgh, James, *Political disquisitions* (1775), 36–37
Burke, Edmund, 37

Cabarrús, Francisco de: advocacy of freedom of opinion by, 112, 113, 126n31, 210
Catherine the Great: *Great Instruction* of, xviii, 72, 73; reaction of, to *Journey from St. Petersburg to Moscow*, xviii, 75–77; reforms under, xviii, 207; establishment of private presses by, 65, 74; publication of *Encyclopédie* by, 71; policies of toleration under, 71–72; on freedom of expression, 72; censorship under, 73–74, 77

Cato's letters (1720–1723), 31, 201
censorship, 22, 23, 26, 27, 28, 53, 178, 196; "two-tier," 1–4, 135, 136; Struensee's revocation of, 10; preventive, 21, 22, 28, 33; John Locke on, 29; David Hume on, 33–34; Blackstone on, 35, 54; prepublication, 54, 55, 145, 150, 175; post-publication, 54; in Russia, 65, 66, 72–73, 76, 77, 207; of Viennese theater, 83–96, 196; in Spain, 108–13, 212, 213, 214; Mercier on, 138, 139; Rousseau on, 140–41; during French Revolution, 145–48; under Napoleon, 148; Constant on, 150, 151; in England, 175–80
Chatterjee, Kumkum, xii
clandestine publication, 3, 4, 6, 10, 54, 127n37, 150
clear and present danger test, xxiiin2, 194
Collier, Jeremy, *Short View of the Immorality and Profaneness of the English Stage* (1698), on theater censorship, 181
Collins, Anthony, *A Discourse on Freethinking* (1713), 53
Commonwealthmen ideology, 37
Condorcet, marquis de: criticism of Voltaire of, 6; on popular opinion, 135
Constant, Benjamin: on government power, xxi, 136, 152–53, 154, 155–56; on nature of freedom, 136, 198; arguments of, for freedom of speech and press, 150–55; on prepublication censorship, 150; on publicity as preserver of liberty, 150–56; *Principles of Politics* (1815), 155; on calumny, 155; on unanimity of opinion, 155–56, 196; *Adolphe* (1816), 155; on government legislation of morals, 155–56; on "truth," 156, 196; on public opinion, 156–57
Coornhert, Dirk Volckertsz, 20, 28; *Synod, or on the freedom of conscience*, 23, 35, 201
cosmopolitanism, 46, 48, 51, 54, 58n7
Crates. *See* cynic philosophy
cynic philosophy: among ancients, 46, 47–49; in eighteenth century, 49; effect of, on Struensee, 50–53, 55–56

Damiens affair, 134, 158n6
Daunou Pierre Claude François: and distrust of journalism, 149
Dawkins, Richard, 172, 183
Declaration of the Rights of Man and Citizen (France, 1789), 33, 75, 81, 131n63, 161n63; link between freedoms of press and speech in, 55; limits on speech under, 70, 72; Spanish translations of, 127n37, 211; Article 11 of, 144
Defoe, Daniel, *Essay on the regulation of the press* (1704), 30, 201
Der Mann ohne Voururteil. *See* Joseph von Sonnenfels

223

d'Holbach, Paul Henri Thiry, xvi, 7, 8, 10, 15, 116, 196; preliberal character of, xxi; *Essai sur les préjugés* (1770), 3, 4, 5; on freedom of publication, 15; reaction of Frederick the Great to, 4–5; on censorship of the press, 136–37; on role of scholars and government in promoting virtue, 137, 138, 144; on truth as standard for freedom of expression, 137, 138, 196

Diderot, Denis, xvi, 5, 6, 8, 10; defense of Holbach by, 5

Dijk, Jacob van, 26, 201

Dio Chrysostom, 48

Diogenes Laertius. *See* cynic philosophy

Diogenes of Sinope: philosophy of, 50–52; and libertinism, 52; influence of, on Struensee, 53–55

Dworkin, Ronald, ix

Enlightenment: on publication of philosophic truths, 1–4, 8, 135, 136; in Spanish context, 105, 106–7, 122n2, 122n3, 123n8, 123n9; and promotion of freedom of expression, 133, 167; conversational ideal of, 134; as "Age of Voltaire," 135; complications of concept of, 139, 156, 166, 167, 168, 174, 181, 183, 184, 185, 186, 194; and reason, 185, 190–91; and religion, 167, 169; secularizing narrative of, 171, 194. *See also* moderate Enlightenment; *philosophes*; radical Enlightenment

Epictetus. *See* cynic philosophy

Erskine, Thomas: defense of Thomas Paine by, 37, 201

Establishment Clause, 167. *See also* First Amendment

Ethocratie ou le gouvernement fondé sur la morale (1776). *See* d'Holbach, Paul Henri Thiry

Europe: ambiguity of designation of, xii, xxivn18; evolution of, xx

Feijoo, Friar Benito Jerónimo, 106, 124n11

Fernández Moratín, Leandro: advocacy of religious tolerance by, 110, 210

First Amendment, xv, xxii, xxiiin2, 55, 70, 81, 174, 191, 194; contemporary debates concerning, xii, 171–72; historical tensions in, xxii, 168, 171, 195; inseparability of press and speech in, 55; tensions between religion and speech in, 167, 172, 185, 186; and development of secularism, 166, 167, 168, 178

Fish, Stanley: on free speech, xxivn13, 168

Floridablanca, count of: and French Revolution, 111

Fontana, Biancamaria: on Western liberal politics, xiii, xxvn20

Foronda, Valentín de: on freedom to write, 108, 124n19, 209, 211

Foucault, Michel, 45, 57

France: book production in, 133; public sphere in, 133–34; censorship in, 134; growth of anti-monarchical literature in, 134; and repression of speech during French Revolution, 136, 144–48; religious conformity in, 180

Frederick the Great: on censorship, xv, 1; reaction of, to Holbach's writings, 4–5; attitude of *philosophes* to, 5, 6; on truth, 6; and Voltaire, 7; criticism of, in *Journey from St. Petersburg to Moscow*, 67

Frederick VII (Spain): persecution of liberals by, 119

freedom of speech: historical differences in, between U.S. and Europe, ix–xi; and Holocaust denial, x; dissent from expansive readings of, xi; as Western cultural product, xii, 192–93; constitutional protections of, xxiiin3; and access to "truth," xvi, 22, 23, 27, 67, 120, 137, 138, 155; under Struensee, xvii; and spread of knowledge, xvii, xviii, 111; under Catherine the Great, xviii; justification for, in sacred texts, 22; classical authors on, 22; cultural arguments for, 24–25; role of, in combatting ignorance, 24–26; arguments for, from political liberty, 24; and progress, 24; as promoting enlightenment, 24; arguments for, from history, 26; effects of politics on, 26; arguments for, from reason, 27, 175–78; arguments for, from practicality, 28; arguments for, from trade and commerce, 29; good government arguments for, 29–31, 126n29; natural law arguments for, 32–33; arguments for, from national security, 33; arguments for, from social peace, 34; and libel and sedition, 34–37; effect of French Revolution on, 36, 144–48; growth of legal protections for, 38–39; and blasphemy, 44n66; and religion, 44n66, 167, 172, 182–83; link of, with freedom of the press, 55, 97; under Peter the Great, 71; under Catherine the Great, 71, 72, 73; and the theater, 89, 95; difference of, from print, 97; and religious tolerance, 106–21, 167, 168–86; exclusion of dogma from, in Spain, 119, 124n13, 128n44; Constant on, 149–53, 155; conceptual limitations of, 168–69; contemporary debates concerning, 171–72; and toleration of competing opinions, 192

freedom of the press: and Struensee's reforms, 10–12, 45, 52–53, 205; as human right, 56–57; effect of French Revolution on, 73, 115, 136, 144–48; Constant's arguments in favor of, 149–53; and Mohammed cartoons, 167; in England, 175–79

French Revolution, effect of, on speech and press: in England, 36; in Russia, 73–74; in Habsburg realms, 95; in Spain, 111–12; in Spanish colonies, 114; in France, 136, 144–48

Gándara, Miguel Antonio de la: on freedom to write, 108

Garton Ash, Timothy, xxivn15
Gerson, Hartog: influence of, on Struensee, 13, 49
Goldstein, Rebecca, 173
Góngora, Mario: and concept of Catholic Enlightenment, 122n2
Gordon, Thomas, *Cato's letters* (1720–1723), 31, 201
Gottsched, Johann Christoph, 89, 90, 206; and reform of theater discourse, 86–87
Graef, Juan Enrique de: on freedom to write, 108, 124n18, 209
Gutiérrez, Luis, *Cornelia Bororquia* (1799), 127n37

Habermas, Jürgen: and public square, xx, 105, 133; critiques of, xxvn29; on eighteenth-century establishment of freedoms, 172; on secularization of reason, 177
Habsburgs: censorship under, xviii–xix, 54, 82, 86–97, 205–6
Hägelin, Franz Karl: and censorship of Viennese stage, 92, 94–96
Hall, Robert, *An apology for the freedom of the press, and for general liberty* (1793), 25, 201
Hamilton, Alexander, 46, 55
Hanswurst: on Viennese stage, 82, 84, 85, 89
hate speech, xxivn12, 193
Hawes, Clement, xii
Hayter, Thomas (bishop), 32–33
Helvétius, Claude-Adrien, 5; on publication, xvi; on liberty of the press, 14–15
Herder, Johann Gottfried: influence of, on Radishchev, xviii, 67–70; on censorship, 194
Himmelfarb, Gertrude, 171
Hirsi Ali, Ayaan, xxivn15
Hitchens, Christopher, 172, 183
Holland: and development of rights in the West, xiv, xxvn22; debates in, concerning freedom of expression, 22–39, 201; republican traditions of, 31; periodicals in, 32; declaration of rights of man and the citizen in (1795), 32–33, 204; constitution of (1797), 33
Holmes, Oliver Wendell, 194
Huber, Christiana, Viennese actress, 90
Humboldt, Alexander von: on Spanish colonies, 114
Hume, David, 54, 201; on freedom of the press, 33–34; on dangers of speech, 34; influence of, on Struensee, 53; on custom and affection, 177–78
Hunt, Lynn, 187
Huntington, Samuel: on clash of civilizations, 72

Illustración. *See* Spain
Independant Briton (1742), 28, 201
Inquisition, 51, 67, 87, 109, 110, 111, 117, 125n28, 129n52, 131n63, 176, 182, 192, 213; and Enlightenment, 107; and

censorship of foreign publications, 108, 112, 125, 212
Islam, x, xi, xiii, 166, 171, 177, 183, 185, 193, 194
Islamophobia, 194

Johnson, Samuel: on censorship, 28
Joseph II, emperor, 67: attempts to reform Viennese stage under, 86, 91–96, 97, 206
Journey from St. Petersburg to Moscow (1790): publication of, 61, 74, 207; as defense of freedom of speech, 61–62, 67, 70; description of, 65; as indictment of Russia, 65; critique of censorship in, 65–67; intellectual sources of, 67–70; Catherine the Great's reaction to, 74–76; ban of, 207. *See also* Radishchev, Alexander
Jovellanos, Gaspar Melchior de, 114, 125n21, 129n52, 209, 210
Julian, emperor: on cynicism, 48

Kant, Immanuel, 177
Klemm, Christian Gottlob: attempts of, to regulate Viennese theater, 90
Kurz, Josef, Viennese comic actor, 90

language: attempts to purify, 86–87, 148; fears of abuse of, by philosophes, 141, 142, 154, 193
La Mettrie, Julien Offray de, *Man as Machine* (1748), 13, 54
Law of Suspects (1793): and targeting of speech, 148
lèse majesté, xviii, 72
A Letter Concerning Toleration (1689), 169, 180–83; influence of, on U.S. Constitution, 181; liberal character of, 181–82; defense of toleration in, 182–84; on natural state of men, 184–85. *See also* Locke, John
libel, 20, 25, 70, 72, 137; English arguments concerning, 34–37; charges of, against Thomas Paine, 36; charges of, against John Wilkes, 37–38; during French Revolution, 145–46; legislation concerning, 203, 204, 212
libertas philosophandi, 1, 8, 30, 53
libertinism, 118; effect of cynic philosophy on, 49
Licensing Order (England, 1643): and prepublication censorship, 175–78
Locke, John, 7, 24, 136, 167, 169, 173; on censorship, 30; and defense of religious toleration, 180–84; understanding of reason of, 184
Luzac, Elie, 29–30, 54, 201, 205

Malesherbes, Chrétien-Guillaume de, 2–3, 133
Mansvelt Regnerus van: refutation of Spinoza by, 9
Maria Theresa, empress: attempts to reform Viennese stage under, 85–90, 98
Marmontel, Jean François (*Bélisaire*), 29, 71

225

Martínez Marina, Francisco: on "civic Christianity," 119

Mason, George, 46

Mayans, Gregorio, 106

Meinppus. *See* cynic philosophy

Mercier, Louis-Sébastian, *The Year 2440* (1771): censorship in, xxi, 139–40, 142, 193

Mill, John Stuart, xi

Milton, John, xxii, 20, 21, 23, 24, 26, 27; defenses of freedom of the press of, 53, 169, 175–80, 201; objections of, to Roman Catholicism, 176, 178; on the effects of custom, 183

moderate Enlightenment, 1, 136, 172, 186; and freedom of expression, xv, xvii, 15–39

Mohammed cartoons, x, xiii, xxiiin8, xxiiin11, 165

Montague, Lady Mary: on Viennese popular theater, 84

Montengón, Pedro, *Eusebio* (1786): advocacy of religious tolerance in, 110, 125n26, 209

Mor de Fuentes, José: on freedom of the press, 115, 209

Mora, José María Luis (*Discourse on Freedom of Thought*), 121

Münter, Balthasar, 13

Murray, William (1st Earl of Mansfield): on criminal libel, 36, 202

Musaeus, Johann: refutation of Spinoza by, 9–10

Naigeon, Jacques-André 28; *Discours préliminaire*, 11

Nestroy, Johann, 97

North Briton, 38, 39, 201

Oakeshott, Michael: on moralism in politics, 56–57

Ofili, Chris, ix

Paine, Thomas, 40, 170, 177, 201; libel trial of, 37–38

parrhesia, 22, 45, 47, 49, 57

Peter the Great: curbs on writing and publication under, 70–71, 192

philosophes: on two-tier censorship, xvi, 1–4, 135, 136; influence of cynical tradition on, xvii; allegiance of, to republic of letters, xx, 53; discomfort of, with dissent, xx, 141, 143, 153; on access to truth, 1, 5–6, 137, 138, 191, 196; and *libertas philosophandi*, 1–16, 30; opposition of, to Frederick the Great, 4–6; elitism of, 134–135; on public opinion, 135, 141; contradictions of, on freedom of speech and the press, 134–44; mistrust of language of, 148, 193

Ponz, Antonio: on tolerance and economic growth, 110

Prehauser, Gottfried, Viennese comic actor, 83, 90, 93

public opinion, xix, 28, 72, 125n28, 145, 154, 176; Spinoza on, 9, 10; advent of, in Spain, 106, 112, 115, 123n6, 123n7, 209, 210–12; Constant on, 155–56

Quintana, Manuel José, 114

radical Enlightenment, xvi, 1, 137, 173, 186: and freedom of expression, xv, 1–16, 136–48

Radishchev, Alexander: education and career of, 62; and publication of *Journey from St. Petersburg to Moscow*, 63, 74; intellectual influences on, 63–70; arrest and trial of, 75–76. See also *Journey from St. Petersburg to Moscow* (1790)

Raimund, Ferdinand, 97

Raynal, Guillaume, 11, 63, 209; *L'Histoire philosophique . . .* (1770), 6

Reformation, xiii, xxii, 23, 24, 68, 179, 180, 184; England, and development of rights in the West, xiii–xiv; arguments in, on freedom of expression, 21–40; seventeenth-century rise in publication in, 175; press censorship in, 175–80

Reitz, Johann Friedrich, *On the censors of books* (1751), 29

religious tolerance, 12, 210, 211–12; John Locke on, xxii, 180, 181–83; arguments concerning, in Spain, 109–11, 113, 117, 118, 119, 129n54 129n55; Rousseau on, 184; secular character of, 182, 192. *See also* tolerance

rights: claims for universal nature of, xi–xii, xv–xvi, 6, 194; cultural nature of, xii, 185, 195; development of, in West, xiii–xiv; in natural law, 21, 32, 38; limitations on, 70; in Rousseau, 141, 149; connection of, with freedom of the press, 152; economic basis of, 192; legislation of, 205, 212, 213

Roselli, Salvador María, 108

Rousseau, Jean-Jacques, 13, 51, 62, 94; and apprehensions about language, xxi, 141–43, 193; on separation of church and state, xxii, 169, 184, 185; *First Discourse* (1749), 139; *Letter to d'Alembert* (1758), 139; advocacy of censorship by, 139–41; *Letters Written from the Mountain* (1764), 140; *Emile* (1762), 140, 141, 142, 143; *On the Social Contract* (1762), 140, 141, 143, 169; on anonymous publication, 141; on the ideal political state, 141; *Essay on the Origin of Languages* (1781), 142, 143; *Julie, or the New Héloise* (1761), 142, 193; and general will, 143; distrust of dissent of, 143–44; on role of government, 144; Benjamin Constant on, 149; on link between Christianity and toleration, 184–85; on Islam, 185

Ruiz de Padrón, Antonio J.: on freedom of press and religious tolerance, 110

Rushdie, Salman, x, 171

Russia: censorship in, xx, 65–67, 72–73, 76, 192; establishment of private presses in, 64, 207; under Catherine the Great, 71–73

Sánchez Barbero, Francisco, 114, 119, 130n59, 210

Santa Clara, Abraham a: pulpit oratory of, 93

The Satanic Verses, x, 171

Schaeffer, Francis, 173

Scio de San Miguel, Felipe, 126n33

Scruton, Roger, 188

Sedition Act of 1798 (U.S.), 70

seditious speech, 29, 45, 46, 47, 71, 115, 119, 134, 146, 147, 192, 203, 204

Shipley, William: libel trial of, 36, 43n56

Skokie vs. U.S., ix, xxiiin6

slovo i delo Gosudarevo (Russia): as treasonable offense, 71, 207

Sonnenfels, Joseph von: attempts of, to reform Viennese stage, 88–91, 92, 93, 96, 206

Spain: slowness of scientific revolution in, xx; advent of public opinion in, xx, 106, 112, 114, 123n6, 123n7, 209, 210–12; character of empire, 103–4, 123n6; Enlightenment in, 104, 122n2, 123n9; and Habermasian model, 104; role of Catholicism in Enlightenment in, 104, 118, 122n1; debates over religious tolerance and freedom of expression in, 105–6; aims of censorship in, 107; growth of political press in, 108, 128n40; fear of heresy in, 110; effect of French Revolution on, 112, 113; radicalization of colonies of, 112, 127n37; beginnings of political liberalism in, 113, 116; changes in cultural consumption in, 115; and freedom of press during Napoleonic wars, 115; Cortes of Cádiz and protection of confessional nature of, 116, 117; association of liberalism and religious intolerance in, 118, 129n55; religious legitimacy of political power in, 118; religious intolerance as guarantor of cultural unity in, 118, 119, 129n56; development of religious tolerance in, 119, 120; growth of freedom of the press and publicity in, 120; concept of "opinion" in, 120, 131n63; good government arguments for freedom of expression in, 126n29; post-independence publishing in colonies of, 127n38, 131n62; exclusion of dogma from "opinion" in, 128n44; growth of concepts of "tolerance" and "toleration" in, 131n64

Spinoza, Benedict, xv, 4, 30, 39, 53, 54, 62, 173, 174, 201; effect of, on Enlightenment, xvi, 8, 173–74; controversies concerning, 4; on freedom of expression, 8, 10, 5; criticisms of, 8, 9–11, 14; influence of, on Struensee, 13, 46, 48, 53; and *libertas philosophandi*, 30, 53; influence of, on Radishchev, 62

Staël, Madame de: and distrust of journalism, 149, 153–54

Star Chamber, 22, 36, 177; effects of, on publication, 174, 203; effect of abolishment of, 174–75

Stowe, Harriet Beecher, 63

Stranitzky, Josef Anton, Viennese theater impresario, 82, 83–84, 86, 206

Struensee, Johann Friedrich: intellectual influences on, 11, 13–14, 49, 53–55; press reforms of, 10–12, 45, 52–53, 205; education of, 49; influence of cynic philosophy on, 50–53, 55–56; ruling style of, 52; downfall of, 53; reversal of press edicts of, 54–55, 205; influence of, on Virginia Declaration of Rights (1776), 55

Système de la nature (1770). *See* d'Holbach, Paul Henri Thiry

The Tenure of Kings and Magistrates (1650). *See* Milton, John

theater: as forum for political dissent, 84–85, 89, 91; reforms of, in Vienna, 86–95; in England, 179–80

Thomson, James: on the Theatrical Licensing Act, 23

Tindal, Matthew: *Reasons against restraining the press* (1742), 28, 201; *Christianity as Old as Creation* (1741), 54, 205

Tocqueville, Alexis de: on public opinion in America and Spain, 125n28

tolerance: link of, with economic growth, xix, xx, 111, 195; Enlightenment character of, 166, 174, 195

"Torzhok." *See Journey from St. Petersburg to Moscow* (1790)

Tractatus Theologico-Politicus. See Spinoza

Trenchard, John, *Cato's letters* (1720–1723), 31, 201

Tronchin, Jean-Robert, *Letters Written from the Country* (1763), 140

truth: in arguments for freedom of expression, xvi, 23, 24, 28, 68, 120, 137; Holbach on, 4, 15, 138; Frederick the Great on, 5–6; Condorcet on, 6; Voltaire on, 7, 136; and advance of society, 14; Helvétius on, 14; search for, justified by ancient texts, 22; religious, 23, 27; Milton on, 27; in cases of libel, 35; Constant on, 155

Uncle Tom's Cabin (1852): xviii, 63

Ursinus, Zacharias: on freedom of speech, 22

Van der Capellen tot den Pol, Joan Derk, *To the people of the Netherlands* (1781), 31, 201

Villava, Victorián de: on freedom of expression in Peru, 114

Virginia Declaration of Rights (1776), 46, 54, 67, 205

Voltaire, xi, 1, 13, 46, 54, 137; as moderate, xvi, 6–8, 136; disagreement of, with radical philosophes, 6; on the "people," 7; on censorship, 7, 135; praise for Struensee by, 12; influence of, on Radishchev, 62; *Lettres philosophiques* (1734), 135

the West: definition of, xxivn17

Wilkes, John, 38–39, 201

Wycliffe, John, 174